Photography & Culture

Volume 4   Issue 1   March 2011

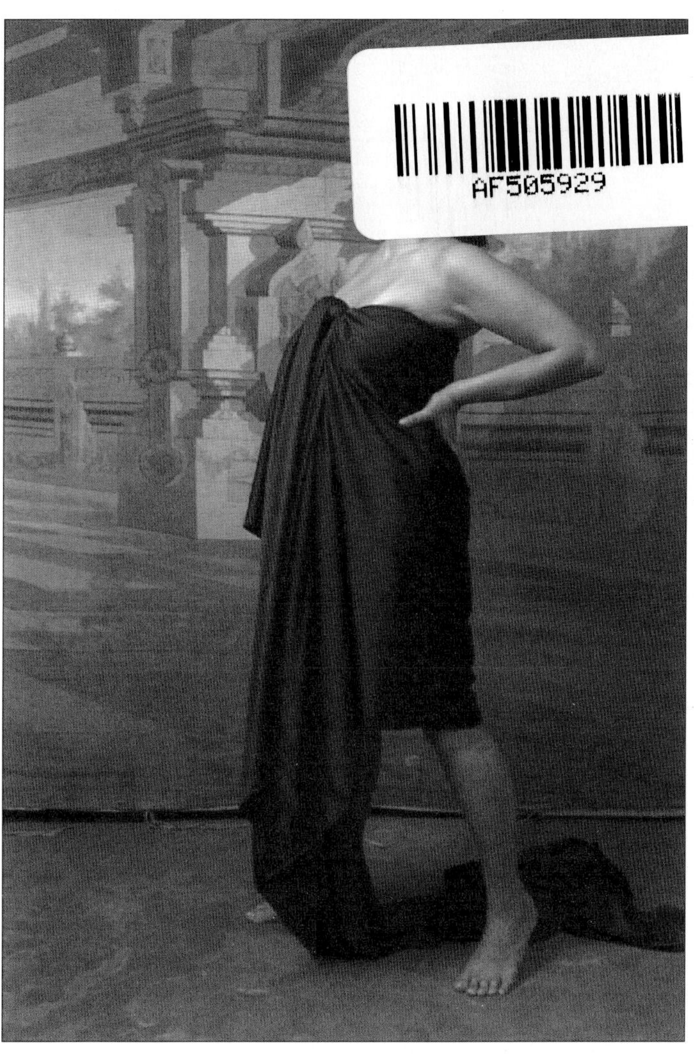

Editors
Kathy Kubicki
Thy Phu
Val Williams

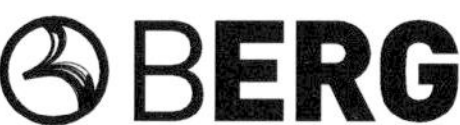

Aims and Scope
Photography & Culture is a new refereed journal that will be international in its scope and inter-disciplinary in its contributions. It aims to interrogate the contextual and historic breadth of photographic practice from a range of informed perspectives and to encourage new insights into the media through original and incisive writing.

Photography & Culture publishes research papers, discursive critiques and reviews. It appears at a key moment as photography evolves; once again, to embrace a technological change that is shifting both contemporary usage and historic understanding.

Photography & Culture will quickly establish itself as a leading platform for critical thinking on photography and as essential reading the world over for academics, curators and practitioners with a central and indeed tangential interest in the media.

Submissions
To submit an article for consideration please contact Monica Takvam at photographyandculture@bergpublishers.com

Subscription Information
Three issues per volume (only two issues in 2008). One volume per annum. 2011: volume 4

Online
www.bergpublishers.com

By Mail
Berg Publishers
C/o Customer Services
Turpin Distribution
Pegasus Drive
Stratton Business Park
Biggleswade
Bedfordshire SG18 8TQ
UK

By Fax
+44 (0)1767 601640

By Telephone
+44 (0)1767 604951

Subscription Rates
Institutional
Print and Online: 1 year: £167/US$326; 2 year: £268/US$522
Online only: 1 year: £142/US$277; 2 year £227/US$444 (VAT charged as applicable)

Individual
Print: 1 year: £38/US$70; 2 year: £60/US$112

Full color images available online
Access your electronic subscription through **www.ingentaconnect.com**

Reprints for Mailing
Copies of individual articles may be obtained from the publishers at the appropriate fees. For information, write to

Berg Publishers
1st Floor, Angel Court
81 St Clements Street
Oxford OX4 1AW
UK

Inquiries
Editorial:
Julia Hall, email: jhall@bergpublishers.com

Production:
Sophie Basilevitch, email: sbasilevitch@bergpublishers.com

Advertising:
Ellie Graves, email: egraves@bergpublishers.com

Berg Publishers is a member of CrossRef

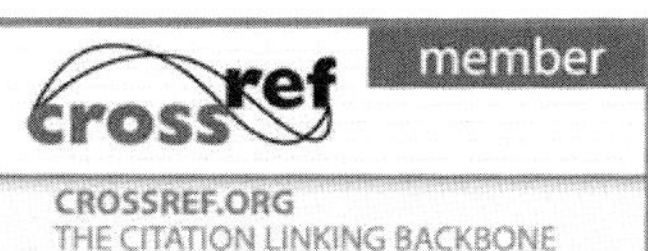

Photography & Culture
Volume 4   Issue 1   March 2011

Contents

**Photography
& Culture**

Volume 4—Issue 1
March 2011
pp. 5–6
DOI:
10.2752/175145211X12899905861276

Reprints available directly from
the publishers

Photocopying permitted by
licence only

From the Editors

Histories very much concern the writers in this issue of *Photography & Culture*. Carol Mavor explores the synergies of relationship, hers with her subjects and her subjects with each other, drawing us into those connections with a beguiling and authoritative magic.

Michael Berkowitz looks, through close reading of archives, at the narrative of historian Peter Pollack's role as sub Editor for the section "Jews in Photography" for the 1971 issue of *Encyclopaedia Judaica*. Pollack, whose *Picture History of Photography* was published in 1958 and is still used as reference today, was one of the first post-war historians of photography. Berkowitz's essay forms a part of his ongoing scholarship around the role of Jews in the history of photography, and presents us with a revealing narrative about inclusion and exclusion, while at the same time exploring the pioneering (and sometimes frustrated) efforts of post-Second World War photo historians to chart some of photography's many histories.

Gabrielle Moser's essay on local and global tensions in the circulation of Stan Douglas's *Every Building on 100 West Hastings* meticulously and thoughtfully documents the making and impact of Douglas' 2001 photo series in Downtown Vancouver, while Simon Watney is the first contributor to the new section "One Photograph". He writes about a photograph bought in the vintage gay erotica shop Gay Treasures and combines autobiography and cultural history, captured through the prism of a 1960s photograph of a young man.

One Photograph aims, like its sister sections Archive and Portfolio, to enable many and varied voices to speak about photography, proposing that the discourse around photography is not limited to the traditionally 'academic', and that photography itself, with its multiplicity of meanings and applications should be allowed to retain its unique, remarkable and sometimes slippery identity. *Photography & Culture* recognizes that research can emerge in many different ways, including (but not exclusively), through practice and theory.

In the Archive section, Martha Langford and John Langford present a series of photographs from Warren Langford's archive, in "A Cold War Tourist and His Camera". Martha Langford, in her writings on the family album has proved that she, more than most, appreciates and understands the eerie narrative of the familiar.

In 2010, *Photography & Culture* and the Photographers Gallery (London, UK), supported by the Photography and the Archive Research Centre (London, UK), held a series of seminars, introduced by Maggie Humm's talk on the photographs of Virginia Woolf. Once again, we are struck by the remarkable-ness of historians, bringing us information and insights born of intense archival study and discovery.

The seminar series will continue throughout 2011. For information and booking, visit the Photographers Gallery website at www.photonet.org.uk.

For news and events information, please join our Facebook group Journal of Photography & Culture.

Note on the Cover Image

Descendants of the Unfamiliar 2010, by Faye Claridge

Born in Birmingham, UK, Faye Claridge has had numerous shows, residencies and commissions. *Descendants of the Unfamiliar* is a striking series from Claridge, who is well-known for her crafted photographs that are beautiful, unsettling and controversial in content.

Claridge creates portraits similar to Renaissance paintings, as she locates the sitters in scenes with specially painted backdrops. In this series, a number of different Morris Dancers are photographed in their traditional costumes, including some with blackened faces for disguise.

By picturing this social group on the peripheries of mainstream culture, often associated with rural rather than urban communities, Claridge uses these photographs to question and take a closer look at the role of "tradition" in modern life, and asks how our current identity is shaped by our relationship to the past. Claridge has created photos that force the viewer to confront the ethics of identity and representation, explore the act of interpretation, and decipher aspects of contemporary and historical aesthetics.

Though primarily exploring notions of identity and social issues, this series also has a celebratory and humorous aspect to it, as the spirit of the dancers is evident in this work that presents Morris dancing as a strangely fascinating and enduring social phenomenon that deserves closer attention.

Claridge has stated (2010): "Morris dancing is often ridiculed but it's a rare tangible example of the social and political history we've all inherited. It informs our sense of *Englishness* and influences every personal and political decision of the present and the future. The dancing can seem daft on the surface, but it's actually really important."

Photography & Culture

Volume 4—Issue 1
March 2011
pp. 7–28
DOI:
10.2752/175145211X12899905861357

"Jews in Photography": Conceiving a Field in the Papers of Peter Pollack

Michael Berkowitz

Abstract

This article explores the initial attempt to write a comprehensive overview of the involvement of Jews in photography. To the editorial board of the *Encyclopaedia Judaica* in the late 1960s, it was self-evident that Jews were represented well out of proportion to their number in the field of photography, and therefore, their project demanded that this be dealt with in a general article and individual entries. Peter Pollack, a pioneering curator and historian of photography, was selected to edit this sub-section. Pollack immediately devised a broad and penetrating survey. But his efforts were severely constrained because the editors did not deem this area to be very significant, and because the basic research they promised Pollack about Jews in photography simply did not exist. They were not about to undertake such an original, complicated and far-flung effort. Pollack's intuition, that this comprised both an important element of modern Jewish history and the history of photography, only came to partial fruition in the *Judaica*. But his papers held at the Getty Research Institute (Los Angeles) will be tremendously helpful for scholars wishing to further investigate the question of Jews and photography.

Keywords: Jews, ethnicity, networks, Peter Pollack, *Encyclopaedia Judaica*

As a historian of photography Peter Pollack (1911–79) has garnered little posthumous acclaim. Critic A. D. Coleman, lauding Helmut Gernsheim (1913–95) and Beaumont Newhall (1908–93), ungenerously distorts Pollack's major work, *The Picture History of Photography* (1958, revised edition, 1970) as comprising "primarily rewritten press releases and exhibition wall labels and contains little original scholarship."[1] Newhall and Gernsheim are widely acknowledged for elevating photography into the realm of fine arts scholarship, and more generally, its appreciation as a pre-eminent form of human creativity.[2] Newhall, concomitant with his writing, was the first to take photography seriously at New York's Museum of Modern Art, and was the founding director of the International Museum of Film and Photography at the George Eastman House in Rochester, New York. Gernsheim, a refugee from Nazi Germany who lived most of his life in London, emerged as the leading historian of photography in post-Second World War Britain and Western Europe. He aspired to establish a national photographic museum in London based on his immense, assiduously cultivated collection—but this never came to fruition. Gernsheim eventually sold his library, papers, and the bulk of his photographs (containing most of the masterpieces from Britain and France) to the University of Texas, and later, another portion of his trove to the Reiss-Engelhorn-Museen in Mannheim, Germany, which included many photographers who worked in color.[3] In retrospect, all three men were at the forefront of transforming the history of photography from a concentration on optics, chemistry, and mechanics, to a complex phenomenon that belonged to greater social, economic, and intellectual currents—and history, writ large.[4]

Yet until quite recently, neither Gernsheim and Newhall, nor Pollack, have received scholarly treatments worthy of their pioneering contributions to the history of photography.[5] Pollack's papers, held mainly in the Getty Archives in Los Angeles, are a rich collection concerning key personalities and themes in photography,[6] especially the emergence of an "art market" for photographic books and prints and the integration of photography into "art publishing."[7] Pollack's records, moreover, are remarkable for illuminating a dimension of photography never addressed directly by Gernsheim and Newhall: the disproportionate over-representation of Jews in the field. Two bulging folders in the Pollack *Nachlass* directly enjoin this subject, which derive from his role as

the sub-editor for "Jews in Photography" in the *Encyclopaedia Judaica* (1971).[8]

In the late 1960s, the editorial board of the *Encyclopaedia Judaica* decided that "Jews in Photography" comprised an important enough topic to deserve a place in the project. The multi-volume work, a sort of Jewish answer to the *Britannica,* was envisioned as the most authoritative compendium on Jewish matters ever to appear.[9] Overall the Jerusalem-based endeavor was hugely successful. The instinct to tackle "Jews in Photography" was prescient, but terrible editing and a preconceived notion that it did not merit more than a tiny sliver of space marred its execution.[10] The *Judaica* board showed little appreciation for networks and collaborative efforts that facilitated the evolution of science, business, journalism, scholarship, collecting, and art relevant to photography—in which Jews did, in fact, play signal roles, and were frequently well out of proportion to their numbers. Historical context, in which Jews figured as neither heroes nor victims, or were not active in expressly Jewish interests, was dismissed out of hand. Nevertheless, details of the coverage of Jews and photography in the 1971 *Judaica,* in the Pollack papers[11] offer insight into a type of cultural history which had long been anathema to scholars of Jewish subjects, and moreover, *terra incognita* to historians of photography.[12] Even forty years later there is no reputable book-length study of "Jews in photography."[13]

Pollack, recruited as "Departmental Editor" for "Jews in Photography"—but having nothing to do with the *Judaica*'s photographs, generally— has left a remarkably transparent picture of the attempted conception of an academic field, nearly *ex nihilo.* Born in Wing, North Dakota, in 1911, Pollack served in the US armed forces in the Middle East during the Second World War as a Red Cross Field Director, where he dedicated himself to programing for Negro (African American) servicemen. He aspired to do similar work after his hitch, but never attained a position in "race relations" or civil rights advocacy. Instead he studied photography in Chicago, eventually turning to museum work. At the Art Institute of Chicago beginning in 1945, Pollack helped integrate photography into the museum's permanent collection and its exhibition program. In 1957 he left Chicago for New York, employed as a consultant to galleries, publishers, collectors, and museums, and was Director of the American Federation of the Arts from 1962–4.[14] Pollack's *Picture History of Photography*, published in 1958 and revised in 1970, was among the first histories of photography to be issued by an established art history press—that of Harry N. Abrams, with whom Pollack was long involved in several capacities.[15] Pollack also was a leader in creating what may be termed "an art market" for photography.[16] Indeed, it is difficult to think of someone better suited for the *Judaica* job than Pollack. He was oblivious, though, to the fact that he was part of the story he wished to tell.

Despite a number of truly exceptional and path-breaking scholars in the ranks of the *Judaica* editorial board, its handling of "Jews in Photography" was pedestrian. But Pollack's ideas, including basic questions about the task before him, are an unheeded guide for an area of inquiry that is only beginning to be rigorously explored. Gender and social class have been increasingly, fruitfully employed as interpretive frameworks within the history of photography. But thus far there has been little attention to the significance of secularized ethnic backgrounds and networks that often influenced or spurred photography's evolution.[17]

The main contours of the unfolding presentation of photography in the *Judaica* play out in correspondence between Pollack and Dr. Frederick R. Lachman (1902–98), the Executive Editor based in New York. Upon his death, the Breslau-born Lachman was extolled as a "noted Jewish scholar, author and historian." Although he clearly distinguished himself in Israeli public service, records of his publications are sparse.[18]

Exchanges between Pollack and others he consulted, as he undertook the project, also are enlightening.[19] The first letter from Lachman to Pollack asserts his gratitude for Pollack's positive response to the editorship offer, yet also hints that Pollack may not have been the first choice. Work on the *Judaica* began "in earnest" in 1967, but Lachman did not write to Pollack until May 23, 1968.[20] The next page, a list of sixty-two names (having originated with Pollack), is entitled "TENTATIVE PHOTOGRAPHY INDEX" which is typed, and includes additions in pencil, red and blue ink.[21] It reads:

> Aarons, Slim?
> Arbus, Diane
> Avedon, Richard
> Bacharach Studios—2 Brothers
> Bidermanas, Izis—(Paris)
> Blumenfeld, Erwin {in blue pen is written No}
> Bondi, Inga
> Brassai
> Capa, Robert (Friedman)
> Capa, Cornell (Friedman)
> Chim (David Seymour)
> Davidson, Bruce
> Deschin, Jack
> Eisenstadt, Alfred
> Elisofon, Eliot
> Erwitt, Elliot
> Feifer, George
> Feininger, Andreas
> Frank, Robert
> Gernsheim, Helmut
> Glinn, Bert
> Godowsky, Leopold
> Goro, Fritz
> ? Hine, Lewis
> Joel, Yale
> Kalischer, Clement
> Kertesz, Andre
> Kessel, Dmitri
> Lieberman, Alex

Lyon, Danny
Mannes, Leopold
Mayer, Grace
Newman, Arnold
Pollack, Peter
Rado, Charles
Ray, Man (Paris)
Rothstein, Arthur
Rosskam, Edwin
Rodkin, Charles
Salomon, Erich
Siegel, Arthur
Shahn, Ben
Siskind, Aaron
Steiner, Ralph
Stieglitz, Alfred
?Strand, Paul
Vishniac, Roman
Werner, Dan
Margaret Weiss
Get ASMP. LIST {in pencil}
Kline[22]

These names show that Pollack was beginning to think rather broadly and creatively. As mentioned in Lachman's initial letter, it seems that some of the first individuals who sprang to Pollack's mind were not photographers per se, but rather two scientists, Leopold Mannes and Leopold Godowsky, Jr., the classical musicians who invented Kodachrome. Another seminal figure was arguably the greatest practitioner and advocate of photography, Alfred Stieglitz.[23] Lachman was happy with this. But other suggestions of Pollack's were rejected. It seems that the two men had another conversation between the letter of May 23 and the next, in which Lachman sent Pollack the "official letter of appointment," again saying "how delighted" he was with Pollack's acceptance. Lachman assured him that "I have already written to Jerusalem, and every effort will be made to help you with reference to those countries you

mentioned to me and where we shall be looking for photographers." For his labor, Pollack would receive $50; "pro rata to the amount of work completed by contributors and approved by you. The honorarium for articles written by you will be based on four cents per word."[24]

Pollack responded with another list, including "more than photographer's names," as he strongly wished to consider those "who are professionally involved with photography." The tone suggests that Lachman might not have understood what he was after. "Would there be space in the index to list their names, dates, position, and perhaps most important accomplishments—e.g.—Grace Mayer's job at the Museum of Modern Art and her book—Once Upon a City, New York as photographed by Byron and his son [?]."[25] Here Pollack is trying to give credit to a woman who was responsible, in no small part, for promoting rigorous scholarship about photography. Mayer had begun her career "at the Museum of the City of New York in 1930, when it was a fledgling institution in Gracie Mansion." There she organized "more than 100 shows, including the first notable Berenice Abbott exhibition in the United States." Edward Steichen was the most visible figure in photography in the New York museum world, but it was Mayer—first working with Beaumont Newhall, and later, Steichen—who was instrumental in making the Museum of Modern Art into a bastion of photography. "[I]n 1962 she became curator of photography, organizing, among other things, the inaugural show in the Modern's first photography-collection galleries, which opened in 1964."[26] Pollack furthermore appreciated the quality of her work on the Byron family of photographers, whom he may have suspected had Jewish origins. Upon her death, Peter Galassi, head curator of photography at the Museum of Modern Art, said that Mayer "was well ahead of her time in recognizing the art of photography. And generations of photographers are indebted to her careful and sympathetic attention to their work."[27]

Pollack shared this sentiment, and he too was ahead of the curve in seeking to call attention to Mayer's achievements in the *Judaica*. By no means was he a feminist, but Pollack made an effort to include a number of women whom he perceived as integral to photography's evolution, such as Mayer and Inge Bondi of the Magnum agency,[28] who eventually opened her own photography gallery. He was, however, insensitive to the unusual number of women among professional, and even notable, Jewish photographers.[29] Yet along with curators, editors, and facilitators, Pollack believed that it was crucial to recognize historians and collectors, and for this reason also sought to include the previously mentioned Helmut Gernsheim, who was preeminent in both realms.

Beginning in 1942 Gernsheim became a leading figure in a massive photo-documentation project[30] aspiring to capture, during wartime, Britain's architectural and artistic treasures which were literally under attack.[31] He also, as noted earlier, was a prolific and immensely important historian of photography.[32] Occasionally described as a half-Jew, Gernsheim was uneasy with his origins. His widow, however, simply referred to her late husband as "Jewish,"[33] and Gernsheim included himself in a list of "Jewish photographers."[34] After the war, with the sage and generous advice of Beaumont Newhall, Gernsheim began amassing what was to become one of the world's largest and most important collections of early, and in particular, British, photography—now housed at the Ransom Center of the University of Texas.[35] In his personal relations Gernsheim often exhibited characteristics of what has been described as "Jewish self-hatred," a hyper-critical and stereotyped antipathy toward Jews—especially those of immediate East European origin.[36] He expressed revulsion toward what he regarded as the uncouth character of many Jewish photojournalists and agents. In a 1950 letter to Beaumont Newhall Gernsheim asserted that "photographers and photographic editors belong to the most uneducated class of people, and the less contact one has with them the better"—a sentiment not shared by Newhall.[37] But he also sought to assure his family's place in the pantheon of historically prestigious German Jews. Germsheim made a point of sending Beaumont Newhall an off-print of an article he wrote about his family's illustrious history, with its origins in medieval Worms—while leaving himself out. Furthermore, this was expressly written for the leading journal of German-Jewish history, the *Year Book of the Leo Baeck Institute*.[38]

From their correspondence concerning the use of images owned by Gernsheim, for the second edition of Pollack's *Picture History*, there is no doubt that Pollack came to distrust and even dislike Gernsheim, as he made abundantly clear in correspondence with Paul Strand.[39] Nevertheless, they were extremely helpful to each other for an extended period, and Pollack sincerely tried to assist Gernsheim in attempting to place his collection in the United States.[40] This antipathy, though, which never abated, stood in stark contrast to Pollack's distinctly warm, jocular exchanges with most Jewish colleagues— such as photographers Sanford Roth, Cornell Capa, and Philippe Halsman, and colleagues at the Arbrams publishing house.[41] Particularly because his career in Britain was both saved and launched under the auspices of the Warburg Institute, Gernsheim, whether he wanted to admit it or not, benefited from Jewish networks and a predisposition (on the part of gentiles, generally, and government bodies) to entrust Jews with important photographic assignments.[42] Pollack had no clue, however, that there were Jews in addition to Gernsheim with astounding photographic collections, cultivated over decades, such as Albert Kahn[43] and Raoul Korty, whose trove was recently exhibited at Austria's National Library. Korty, born into a banking family in Vienna in 1889, was murdered in Auschwitz in 1944.[44] In the published version of Pollack's "roof" article, Gernsheim is mentioned only as "a photography

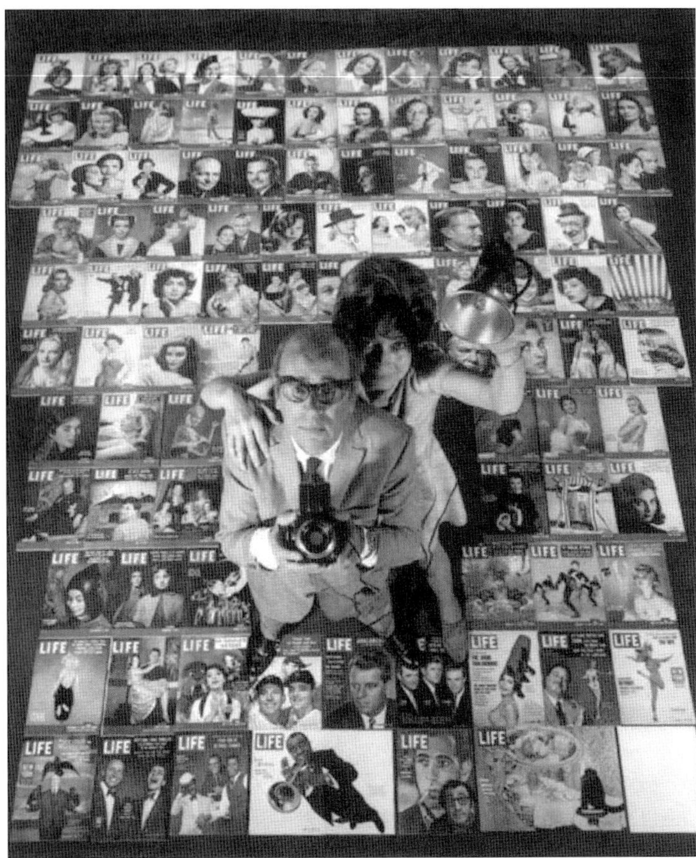

Fig 1 This self-portrait shows Philippe Halsman with his wife Yvonne among the 98 covers he produced for *Life* magazine. It was sent to Peter Pollack (and others) as a New Years greeting, accompanied with their wish that: MAY THE NEW YEAR BRING PEACE AND HAPPINESS TO YOU AND PEACE AND THE 100TH *LIFE* COVER TO US. Magnum Photos.

historian."[45] Collectors, photographic (or otherwise), apparently, did not strike a chord with Lachman or anyone else at the *Judaica*. Scholarly interest in the collection or art, antiquities, and historical artefacts (by Jews) would develop only decades later.[46]

Pollack identified three people in particular whom he believed deserved mention in the historical essay on "Jews in Photography," which was referred to in the *Judaica* lingo as the "roof" article, as well as meriting the maximum-length articles of 200 words: "Mannes, Godowsky, and Stieglitz." These names are repeated, almost like a mantra, throughout Pollack's correspondence with Lachman and others. Pollack perceived

Mannes, Godowsky, and Stieglitz as having the greatest impact on photography overall—which shows that he was concerned with photography's role in consumer culture, as well as commercial and "art" photography per se. Without saying precisely why, he saw all three as distinctly "Jewish." In addition to attempting to ensure that all of those he deemed significant would be given their due, Pollack also was keen to begin receiving the kind of assistance that Lachman said the *Judaica* was ready and able to offer. "To write a comprehensive essay," Pollack asserted, apparently repeating a point he had made in his initial conversation with Lachman, he needed to know about "Jewish photographers in the latter half of the 19th century and early 20th, working in the various countries of Europe [and] Latin America," and if "their work [is] available for reproduction in the historical article." He also asked "Who among the 19th century U.S.A. photographers were Jewish? Falk? Is the group that formed around Stieglitz, Camera Work, and the New York Camera Club—anyone besides the founder? I don't think so but how would I know? Could your researchers check the records please? Was William Notman in Canada? … Lewis Hine? … Riis was an Anti-Semite—was he hiding his hatred, perhaps? As little capital was required to open a photography studio in the 19th and early 20th centuries, it would not surprise me to learn that many well-known studios were run by 'landsmen.'"[47] "Landsmen," in a narrow sense, means "countrymen" in Yiddish. But it is also an in-group term signifying "Jews", or more colloquially, "members of the tribe."

Since his first conversations with Lachman we can assume that Pollack was giving a good deal of thought to the subject, and probably asking around. Although he himself was an accomplished photographer, a professional in the field as a curator, historian, editor, and informal agent for collectors—it seems that before being approached by Lachman he did not dwell on the ethnic composition of his own world. He now made connections between his own milieu—and attempted to grapple with the basic fact that it was—well, so "Jewish." Pollack's hypothesis, that a great number of studio photographers worldwide were Jewish, was never challenged. (He was, in fact, correct.) He also knew, for certain, that Jews comprised the lion's share of photojournalists. But he was troubled by the fact that he could not back up these observations with hard data. He wanted surveys, studies, and monographs—anything to lend some substance, to prove, or maybe even to disprove these claims. Neither Lachman nor anyone else connected with the *Judaica* was ever completely candid with Pollack. They

never told him that the background material was simply not there. Furthermore, the *Judaica* was not about to commence original research. After all, the project had begun early in 1967, it was now spring 1967, and they hoped to publish their massive work in the early 1970s. In the end, all they did was to provide Pollack with some additional tips. The failure, however, of the *Judaica* to furnish Pollack with the information he believed was necessary in order to do a credible job was a source of frustration, and part of the reason why he almost never discussed his work for the *Judaica* after it was completed.

A memo following the letter from Pollack to Lachman reveals how Pollack's thoughts on the subject were developing. The list, called the "Tentative Photography Index" is longer, and includes more explicit reference to those in various supporting roles for photography. Rather than following the general instructions to be extremely selective, and limit the number of words to 5,000, Pollack calls for no less than 4,500 words about individual figures— in addition to his "roof" article. He added photographers, agency directors, editors, critics, and curators—including those from the realm of sports and fashion[48]—and the next list would specify their affiliation to magazines such as *Life*, *Time*, and *Look*, and the Magnum agency.[49] Another list following the revised group of photographers is headed: "PRACTICING PHOTOGRAPHERS AND MEMBERS OF THE SOCIETY FOR PHOTOGRAPHIC EDUCATION … COLLEGES AND UNIVERSITIES … SEND INQUIRIES TO ASCERTAIN WHETHER OR NOT THEY ARE JEWISH … THESE ARE THEIR HOME ADDRESSES… REQUEST SCHOOL AFFILIATION AND ONE PAGE GENERAL BIOG." Some of the twenty-five were well-known, such as Albert Freed, Arthur Goldsmith, and Walter Rosenblum. Pollack wished to convey two messages in sharing this attachment with Lachman: that this was the kind of thing he was after, an institutional record, and second, that he wanted the staff of *Judaica* to pursue some research of its own.[50]

Between May 28 and June 4, Pollack drew up another list, which he apparently sent to Lachman.[51] Margaret Weiss's role was specified as "Photography Critic—Saturday Review." After Avedon, "fashion." The number 250, which seems to be a request for 250, as opposed to 200 words, follows several names, including Brassai,[52] Capa (only one, most likely Robert), Halsman, [Arnold] Newman, Man Ray, and [Erich] Salomon. For the first time, Joe Rosenthal appears, with the note "(Iwo Jima) Raising of Flag." Lewis Hine is crossed out. "Feininger, Andreas" is crossed out, and red ink warns: "doesn't want to be included." Other additions are "Solomon Carvalho 250"—a result of a suggestion from the editorial board. Paul Schutzer is noted as "killed Israel War Life Mag."[53]

Lachman was impressed, and possibly surprised by Pollack's immediate and substantial revisions. He also insisted that there must be an article on Pollack himself.[54] Although this last statement of Lachman's was a sign of friendliness and professional respect, it does reveal a good insight. Lachman knew that Pollack was a *Macher*, an important person, and perhaps he was curious to see how Pollack would present himself.

After a month, Pollack received word from the central office in Jerusalem, which gives a strong taste of the response to come. He was admonished that "It must be realized that this is primarily a Jewish Encyclopedia, and that persons are considered worthy of entry because they are Jews as well as because of their distinction. The person who uses the Encyclopedia will not expect a detailed analysis of the technical details of a man's work."[55] It is reasonable to assume that Pollack was not alone in having once been assigned his role, finding that there was a great deal to say: numerous individuals deserved mention, and many needed substantial treatment. Even more important: he found that it was nearly impossible to say something

intelligent about an individual and his (or her) role, relevant to photography, without placing the subject in context. Yet another vexing issue with this directive given to Pollack (and others) is that it was woefully inadequate in dealing with Jewishness as a form of secular identity. The board demanded that sub-editors devise a spectrum in judging the Jewishness of individuals using the nebulous concept of "involvement."[56] Herein lies a fundamental problem: there is little or no allowance for Jewishness as an ethnic, cultural identity. Therefore, the vast majority of those active and important in photography, for whom their Jewishness was lightly worn—but critical for their interwoven social and professional lives—would not have been perceived as significant in the eyes of the *Judaica* editorial board.

Upon his return from Jerusalem, Lachman contacted Pollack with anxiety—fearing, perhaps, that he might give up on the project upon being confronted with the Jerusalem missive.[57] However much Pollack's plan was out-of-step with the concerns of the board, it was now too late to replace him. The same day Lachman wrote to Pollack, Pollack sent a short note to Lachman.

> I met with Andreas Feininger over the week-end. Though he admits his mother is Jewish, I don't think that he wants to be included in an encyclopedia or any other publication which singles him out as a Jew. I feel that no person who does not want to be, should be listed. May I suggest that a letter be sent [to] all photographers saying that a biographical entry is being contemplated, and would he or she kindly cooperate by sending a one-page précis of their life and work, and then ask if permission is granted for inclusion.
>
> I would rather that this enquiry be sent over your signature with a mention in the last paragraph that I am the editor of the material dealing with photography.

Let's discuss ramifications of this point when you get back.[58]

Interestingly, Feininger is a notable photographer of New York's Lower East Side while it was drenched with *yiddishkeit*.[59] Similar to Alfred Eisenstaedt, the reestablishment of his career in the United States was certainly facilitated through heavily Jewish refugee networks.

In any event, there is no evidence that any action followed this request. It seems that Pollack's investigation of the Jewishness of his subjects was discreet and informal.[60] He caught on that Brassai may not have been Jewish, but Paul Strand— one of the most important members in the circle of Alfred Stieglitz, and a giant of American photography—certainly was. Pollack had no inkling that Jewishness was, indeed, something that mattered in the orbit of Stieglitz.[61]

The endeavor to satisfy the commission gave Pollack an opportunity to re-connect with Jewish photographers with whom he had dealt in the past, including "Izis" (Israel Biderman, or Bidermanas)[62] who, along with Roman Vishniac, was one of his few sources from Eastern Europe.[63] It also afforded a chance to make an initial acquaintance with some whom Pollack had not previously encountered, and admired, such as Edwin Land, the founder and president of Polaroid.[64] Given Pollack's expressed concern for highlighting the achievements of Mannes and Godowsky, it is not surprising that he sought to include Land—a striking omission on the earlier lists. Land was, in fact, happy to be included, and Polaroid's publicity department cheerfully obliged.[65]

While underway, Pollack was still struggling to figure out who was and who was not Jewish. Photographer Arnold Newman, a close friend of Pollack's, on at least one occasion had delivered a lecture on Jewish photographers. Newman apparently told Pollack that he was assisted by Jacob Kainen, the Curator of Prints

and Drawings at the National Collection of Fine Arts (later, the National Gallery) in Washington, D.C. Pollack, then, wrote to Kainen for "any information" on "photographers and inventors of the 19th and early 20th centuries … [in the United States] and abroad. … to ascertain whether they were Jewish." To his trinity of Stieglitz, Mannes, and Godowsky, Pollack added "Carvalho" as "definitely" Jewish. He implored Kainen for "perhaps a list" for those "of Jewish background."[66]

Kainen answered, "I don't know much about the subject," but preceded to relate some interesting material. "Max and Louis Edward Levy, brothers," Kainen wrote, "perfected the half-tone screen early in the 1890's and became [its] outstanding manufacturers … [it] has been the most widely used since 1895. They operated in Philadelphia, as did Elias Goldensky,[67] a photographer who worked with Frederick E. Ives[68] … Lew Sipley and Gene Ostroff know much more about [this] subject, but you have probably consulted them already."[69] Kainin's information no doubt derived from the work of Louis Walton Sipley.[70] Pollack, perhaps, had not even heard of Sipley and Ostroff.[71] Kainen was himself unaware that there were similar developments in Britain. Simultaneous with the efforts of the Levy brothers and Elias Goldensky in Philadelphia, Jews in London worked for the large Downey firm, with H. W. Barnett (1862–1934) as one of their leading photographers, who gained fame in Britain, France, America, and his native Australia.[72] Goldensky, according to Sipley's *Half-Century of Color* (1951), "was the most famous of American portrait photographers during the early part of the twentieth century," which was when the popularity of portrait photography "reached its peak."[73]

Pollack wrote to Sipley—but it was too late. Sipley died October 19.[74] Sipley, "an art and graphic arts historian,"[75] founded the American Museum of Photography in Philadelphia in 1940, which apparently was "the first [privately-owned] photographic museum in the United States." Trained in mechanical and electrical engineering, Sipley was involved in a 1939 publication "devoted to the first century of photography." As a consequence he "became concerned over how much irreplaceable historical material was being lost. He went to various museums urging them to start photographic collections. When he met with no favorable response, he decided to found a museum himself."[76] Gernsheim, in fact, attempted something similar in Britain and Europe.[77] After becoming aware of Sipley and the Philadelphia museum, Gernsheim and Sipley became close collaborators and even good friends.[78]

Sipley's collection, although less known than that of Gernsheim, was astounding, with "fifty to fifty-five thousand images … nearly five thousand books, pamphlets and periodicals (including a complete set of [Stiegltiz's] *Camera Work* and material found in no other library) and about three hundred pieces of photographic apparatus including a very rare eighteenth-century camera obscura. The motion picture archives contain unusual and unique titles, such as THE YELLOW GIRL, a 1916 experimental film."[79] In 1970 "the 3M Company acquired the collection," and in March 1977 it was donated to the International Museum of Photography at George Eastman House.[80] It is frustrating to think that Sipley might have provided Pollack with the kind of data he was seeking, at least for the United States. No one, apparently, had asked such questions.[81] Sipley, along with Kainen, and the assiduous bibliographer and publisher Albert Boni, are mentioned in the conclusion of Pollack's "roof" article, a fascinating thread that remains to be appreciated in the history of photography.

Eugene Ostroff responded courteously to Pollack's inquiry, but he also qualified that he was "not familiar with any list naming photographers and inventors by religion…"[82] Some years later, however, Ostroff edited a volume, *Pioneers of Photography: Their Achievements in Science and Technology* (1987) including an article by Peter

Krause with the innocuous title, "Pioneering Photographic Color Systems." Krause's piece mainly concerned Arthur Traube (1878–1948). Foremost among the author's "reasons for focusing on Traube's work" was the fact that Traube's "contributions have not always been fully acknowledged: in fact, they were deliberately ignored by some photographic historians." Traube's ill treatment was due, Krause shows, largely to anti-semitism.[83] This is one of few articles to reveal how ethnic origins may impinge, and distort, the historiography of a supposedly scientific field and detached analysis. The only other scholar of photography who commented on how anti-semitism had influenced the historiography was Sipley.[84]

The first batch of inquiries Pollack sent in September 1968 also included a letter to Roman Vishniac, who Pollack had met the year before at the Museum of Modern Art. Pollack had a straight-forward request: "To be sure the facts are all correct, would you kindly send me biographical data and any information about your work as a photographer that you would like to see included. I look forward to showing [you] the entry before it goes to press."[85] Four days later Pollack received a hand-written response, the first in a barrage of self-promotion:

> My dear Mr Pollack, Thanks for our interest. Did you see my program on NBC T.V. in May-June? I am working now on another full hour color program for NBC. How long can be your writing about each individual? I enclose the text that seems to be rather long. Cordially yours Roman V.
>
> R.V. is one of the European pioneers who introduced together with Erich Salomon, Brassai, and Henry Cartier Bresson photojournalism in the thirties. His photographs became a one-man effort to save from destruction by Hitler and Soviet Russia the memories and images, the faces of individuals and pictures of life of the

Jewish communities in Central Europe. In 1930–1940 he photographed in stills and movies with hidden cameras from the big cities with large Jewish populations—Warsaw, Lublin, Lodz, Prague, Munkatch, to the communities in the Carpathian Mountains. His films, the first ones taken with hidden cameras, were acclaimed as the strongest documentary of Jewish life. R.V. succeeded in saving the films and escaped Nazi agents. He was many times in prisons and concentration camps and even behind cage bars. But the films were later destroyed by a welfare organization expecting damage by true presentation for their campaign. From the thousand of pictures around two hundred will be incorporated into Vishniac's book on Jewish life in Central Europe appearing at Holt Rinehart and Winston.[86]

Pollack's response was kind and tactful. But Vishniac resisted simple answers to Pollack's direct questions. Given that Pollack hardly ever referred to him in his publications or courses, it seems that he did not take seriously Vishniac's claims about his centrality to the history of photojournalism, with the likes of Salomon, Brassai, and Cartier-Bresson. A questionnaire followed, asking very specific questions[87] to which Vishniac responded with a four-page letter, again, not quite answering the questions—but providing insight into how he wanted his legend portrayed.[88]

Vishniac's bombast and vagueness tried Pollack's patience. Pollack was a perfectionist and also wanted to get the job done. But he was charmed by Vishniac's old-world aura, gregariousness, and bravado. Still, Pollack persisted in trying to extract specifics that could be used for the *Judaica*. He surmised that it would take a face-to-face meeting to satisfy his many remaining questions. He added, this time, "with warm regards from my wife and myself to you and yours."[89] Most likely, they both had been with

their wives when they first met at the Museum. Vishniac's response was much more to the point, which concluded with a personal invitation for Pollack and his wife to visit him in his Upper West Side apartment—but he warned it would be an alcohol-free evening.[90] Along with accepting Vishniac's social invitation—"though I do like my 'shnapps'—good conversation I've always found to be more than a preferable substitute"—Pollack enclosed a draft of his article on Vishniac.[91]

Recognizing Vishniac's role as a Jewish photographer of European Jewry—apparently what the *Judaica* was after—he sought to give him pride of place in the roof article, and for the most part allow him the benefit of the doubt.[92] Pollack presented Vishniac as heroic in his photography of East European Jewry "before and during the Holocaust," but was generally restrained in comparison with Vishniac's potted autobiography. Pollack's main concession to Vishniac's boast of being "pioneering" was "in the field of cytoplasmic circulation in microscopic algae as connected with photosynthesis, and photographing the formation of thrombosis in blood vessels," complementing the fact that he had "won widespread recognition in the field of scientific cinematography." The editors of the *Judaica*, though, did not believe that Vishniac warranted more than a single photograph and 150 words.[93]

At the end of October, Lachman knew that Pollack would be displeased, if not indignant, with what had been done with his work. "You will find," Lachman wrote, "a copy of your Photography article which has been edited somewhat. I am sure you will want to do further editing but I want to give you here a few explanations before you start reading it." In short: they demanded more about Jews, and less about photography. Pollack felt that the all-important context was crudely excised. The editors did, however, make some specific requests for additions, which were indeed useful. Cecil Roth, the general editor and a leading scholar on Jewish art and Anglo-Jewry, himself recommended that Pollack include:

RAPHAEL MENDOLA, an Englishman of the 19th century, was an authority on photochemistry (if that has anything to do with the subject); GARBRIEL LIPPMANN discovered color photography (he was French and got the Nobel prize 1908); HEINRICH HERTZ is said to have discovered photo electricity; STIEGLITZ was so important that he might deserve mention at greater length and earlier in the article, even if there is a separate article on him.

We come now to the serious problem, which you understood from the beginning yourself, of photographers outside the U.S. Obviously the article will have to have something on photographers in Israel but that part can be provided by somebody in Jerusalem. There must, however, be internationally famous photographers in other countries. Professor Roth mentions BENOLIEL in Portugal[94] who once stopped a Eucharaistic procession for a snapshot.[95]

This was, in fact, all good advice, however much it reflected the 'great man' approach to history favored by the *Judaica*, which Pollack perceived as inappropriate to a scholarly treatment of the significance of Jews in photography overall. And predictably, Pollack was irritated. Above all, he wanted Lachman to bear in mind that there were huge gaps in basic research—which he was promised the *Judaica* would provide—while at the same time, all signs indicated that there was a compelling story to be told. "I must remind you," Pollack pleaded:

> of our first conversations, in which I reiterated that I (a) did not know which photographers of the 19th century were Jewish, and (b) research was needed to ascertain who were Jewish photographers or inventors in the medium during the 19th century not only in Western Europe but in Eastern Europe as well, Poland and Russia

particularly. And Latin America research should include Spain and Portugal. *I also said that I did not have the time to do the necessary research and you assured me that the staff of the Encyclopedia Judaica would come up with the answers.* So far, I have your note of a book on Brazil with a list of photographers who bear German or Russian names who may be Jewish. *Please—please— either have your staff do the necessary work or get me a substantial grant so I can take a year or two out to ascertain who they were and whether or not they accomplished work worth considering for inclusion in the Encyclopedia.* The time I mentioned above is for the research time needed to do both Europe and South America, but, your international group of researchers and writers should be able to come up in much shorter time with some of the answers—plus pictures— and then I shall decide whether to include [these] in [the] essay or write a complete biographical entry…Thanks for sending the edited copy of the essay. *I'll complete it when I hear from you re the research needed to fill in the references to 19th and early 20th century Jewish photographers of the world.*[96] [emphases added]

Pollack was beginning to suspect that the research he had requested would never be forthcoming. He also got a taste of the editorial style that would cause him deep distress, and severely compromise the quality of his work.

In the process of gathering data, Pollack's correspondence with "Izis" is especially moving. The specificity and self-deprecation in the autobiographic statement Izis submitted to Pollack could barely have been more different from that related by Vishniac. Izis was born in Mariampole in 1911 and was apprenticed to a (Jewish) photographer in 1924, working "in different places in Lithuania as a photographer, my sideline being painting … In 1930 at the age of 19 I went to Paris." In Paris he continued working as a photographer, retouching negatives and copying prints, and eventually established his own studio.[97] Pollack had, in fact, seized on Izis as an exceptional photojournalist some fifteen years earlier, presenting his work at the Art Institute of Chicago (January 15 to March 1, 1955).[98] Yet as much as Pollack wrote brilliantly about Izis,[99] he was blind to something Izis took for granted: that photography, in general, was a Jewish business in his native Lithuania. The life and work of the leading photographer based in Telsiai, Chaimas (Chaim) Kaplaskis, is the recent subject of a modest but highly informative catalogue from the museum of Samogitia, a region of western Lithuania.[100] Although it would have been difficult to get the kind of firm data Pollack longed for, he might have used his relationship with Izis with better effect had he asked him not only about his own life and career but more generally about Jews and studio photography. At the very least, this would have given Pollack a partial answer to one of his most important unanswered questions.[101]

Although there certainly were some exceptions, photography—as Pollack had surmised—was disproportionately in Jewish hands throughout Eastern, Western, and Central Europe until the 1930s. Regarding Germany and Austria, this has been substantiated through investigation of the "aryanization" (state robbery) of Jewish property under the Nazis.[102] According to Lucjan Dobroszycki, famed historian of Lodz, "if you had your portrait taken in Central or Eastern Europe any time before the Second World War it would probably have been taken by a Jew—even if you were the Tsar."[103] We also can take, for example, members of the Jasvoin (also Yasvoin, Iasvoin, Yasvoyn) family, which originated in *shtetls* such as Paususys and Saukotas, near Kaunas, Lithuania, and established photographic studios in St Petersburg and its suburbs, as well as in Kaunas, Kibartai, and Vornezh. The most eminent member of the

family was Wulf Jasvoin,[104] who photographed the Romanovs. His work, and that of his descendants, exists in the holdings of the Smithsonian, the Hermitage, the Moscow House of Photography, the University of Istanbul, the Lithuanian Museum of Photography in Siauliai, and the St Petersburg Museum of Photography.[105] Wulf Jasvoin also was one of the photographers on an imperial ethnographic expedition to Bukhara in 1890 and most likely participated in other missions around 1900.[106] Until 1939 his descendants were proprietors of portrait studios and the "Photo-bazaar" in central Kaunas, one of several Jewish-owned photography equipment stores in the Lithuanian capital.[107] Israel Jasvoin apparently began as photographer to the local magnate in Baisogala; he had the second largest postal bank account in his community, 200 rubles, in 1902.[108] After the Second World War, there was only a single survivor or refugee with a connection to the earlier business, Boris Muzykant in Buenos Aires, who retained the name "Jasvoin" (from his mother's family) for his studio.[109] Beyond a sound suspicion, Pollack had no inkling that family enterprises like those of the Jasvoins were typical, and typically Jewish.

In June, drawing near the date of 1970 that the board of the *Judaica* set as a target, Lachman pressed Pollack to finish his assignment—"the remaining articles on photographers as well as your roof article." Without any apology for disregarding the long lists and accompanying discussions that had passed between them, Lachman reduced the individual entries to what he described as "seven 'musts': Land, Pollack, [Man] Ray, Salomon, Siskind, Stieglitz, and Vishniac." His next comment surely caused Pollack's eyes to roll: "There may however be others whom you think worthwhile." Had Lachman and the editors absorbed anything from Pollack's efforts? Again, there was a request to include "Gabriel Lippmann (Nobel Prize Winner) … [who] seems to be the precursor of color photography."[110] This was, indeed, a good catch. Most likely the material on Lippmann was available mainly in French and German. Only in 1987 did a historian of science comment that Lippmann's work and reputation had been appropriated or ignored "for chauvinistic reasons"—related to both his French and Jewish identity.[111] It is remarkable how the original lists had been changed—not only pared down in number but limited in scope from Pollack's earlier, more thoughtful suggestions.[112]

Pollack's rejoinder was a masterpiece of tact. He said he was "glad I was able to get the assignment done—enclosed herewith profiles on Man Ray, Dr. Erich Salomon, Aaron Siskind, and Alfred Stieglitz." Then he confronted Lachman with the fact that the number was well beyond seven: "You already have my pieces on Roman Vishniac, Dr. Edwin H. Land and the cover or 'roof' piece as you term it. If these have gone astray, I have carbon copies which you may have. As to complete the record I sent you entries on: Carvalho—Capa—Chim—Eisensta[e]dt—Godowsky—Mannes— Halsman—Newman—and Izis Bidermanas."[113] Concerning coverage of himself, Pollack was self-effacing to a fault—an entry would never appear.[114] Despite severe cuts to his "roof" article, which left it disjointed, Pollack was content to let it stand with only a few "suggestions"—above all, that the first two paragraphs of historical context be retained.[115]

Pollack was not, however, complacent about the edited versions of the articles he received over the next months. The letter of September 13 to Lachman makes clear that Pollack was furious. "This letter is just because I want to go on record about my feelings re. the editing that [is] being done on the articles I wrote for you. … Why didn't you just ask for a fact sheet? That is just about what your Mrs. Chaikin of the Central Office has made of it. So far I've seen her hand on the pieces I wrote on Capa, Chim, and Eisenstadt (sic). Perhaps there is still time to have these entries and others brought somewhat into line with the intention of the author."[116] The next item in the file is a copy of a memo from

G[eoffrey] Wigoder to Lachman, a month later. Wigedor, an English Jew who settled in Israel in 1949, was named chief editor upon the death of Cecil Roth. The woman editing Pollack's work was Hanna (Chaikin) Ben David, one of twelve people listed as "Supervisors." One of them, Yishai Geva, has a "B.A." after his name. Although the list of "Supervisors" is distinct from that of "Secretarial and Technical Staff" which follows, the boundaries between "secretaries" and "administrators," and the editorial board generally, was very confused.[117] Most likely the higher-level editors were so awash in a sea of contributions, many of them running over word limits, that they believed they had no choice but to let low-level staff cut contributions to shreds. Moreover, those subeditors entrusted with themes that were deemed integral to the objectives of the *Judaica*, such as those centered on Zionism and the Hebrew language, might have been given free rein.[118] "I noted the ire of some of the contributors on receiving the proofs," Wigedor wrote. "In some instances these may be expected, in others it is surprising. Please tell them [section blacked out] that all their comments are being seriously considered and in some cases we have gone back to their original text as requested. I am sure we are going to have many more problems in this matter in the future."[119] In response, the editing process seems to have undergone a change. In contrast to the first batch of edited pieces, Pollack was informed, directly by Mrs. Chaikin—when she returned his article on Philippe Halsman—that he would have an opportunity to make comments on the edited version and to return it within a given period.[120] There is no evidence, however, that this shift in policy made any difference. It is little wonder that Pollack seems to have hardly ever spoken or written of his experience with the *Judaica,* as he was not anxious to be associated with the truncated pieces that appeared.

The gulf between Pollack's submissions, versus what appeared in the *Judaica*, is striking. The original of his "roof" article remains the best writing ever on Jews and photography—especially considering the slender and fragmented body of information with which he was working. One of the early paragraphs that was deleted—and never restored, despite Pollack's explicit protest—is among the most important general observations Pollack had to offer:

> Throughout the 19th century inventors and photographers made impressive contributions to the art and craft of photography but few persons of Jewish ancestry can be specifically identified. Historians have not recorded their names and research into this area of the art has not been attempted to date. It is hard to believe that photography which required so little capital and so little artistic skill from an enterprising young man to open his studio, or be an itinerant portraitist with a camera, did not have more than its proportionate share of youngsters from Jewish homes.[121]

It also may be said that the roles of Jews in photography accorded with notions of respectability. It seems that Jews were able to enter photography not only because of its novelty and availability, but because of its marginal status in terms of what was considered "respectable."

It will suffice to illustrate only a few examples of how Pollack's work was savaged. The cuts to his entry on Edwin H. Land were atrocious.[122] In sacrificing detail and context, Pollack's references to Jews and non-Jews who collaborated with Land, such as Joseph Mahler were removed. Mahler, a refugee from Czechoslovakia and relative of Gustav Mahler, worked with Land on the "vectograph." This led to the development of diagnostic tools for assessing vision with both eyes and stereoscopic projection techniques.[123] As much as it is important that Land is included at all, Pollack's incisive treatment would have enabled students and scholars from a number of

disciplines to draw further connections. Likewise, a hatchet-job was perpetrated on the article for Alfred Eisenstaedt.[124] Pollack wrote incisively about the informal Jewish networks that helped Eisenstaedt launch his career in Germany, ease his transition from Germany to the United States, and facilitated the tremendous impact he and other European Jews had on the conception of *Life* magazine.[125] Thankfully, though, the Pollack papers serve as a sort of cutting-room floor.

Frederick Lachman was right that Pollack deserved the separate entry in the *Encyclopaedia Judaica* he never received.[126] Pollack's *Nachlass* in the Getty archives, besides documenting his fascinating career, reveals the extent to which he mapped out a potential field of "Jews in Photography" in a matter of days—which was truly remarkable. Yet it also suggests that these thoughts might have been germinating, in Pollack's mind and in private conversations, for some time. Certainly there were blinders and limitations in Pollack's approach—such as exclusion of the Soviet Union (totally missing El Lissitzky as a photographer), and, as mentioned previously, failure to recognize that there were several women among the renowned European photojournalists and studio photographers, such as Eve Arnold and Lotte Jacobi.[127] Yet these shortcomings of Pollack, if such a term is even fitting, were exacerbated by the *Judaica* editorial board, who never made a good-faith effort to supply him with the information he requested at the outset. This would have given Pollack's work the kind of social-historical base he deemed, correctly, to be essential. Pollack's eloquent and interdisciplinary essays were reduced to distillations and fragments, which have deprived students and scholars the benefit of his expertise, wisdom, good sense, and even humor. Yet Pollack's papers at the Getty, especially if consulted to complement the vast archives of Beaumont and Nancy Newhall (also at the Getty), the Gernsheim collection (Harry Ransom Center, University of Texas), and the rich oral testimony of Helmut Gernsheim (from the British Library), comprise a treasure trove for scholars interested in numerous aspects of the evolution of photography. It also is a superlative source for probing the complex Jewish engagement with photography, which was in many respects decisive.

Notes

Most of the work for this article was made possible by a Library Research Grant from the Getty Research Institute, Los Angeles, and further research was supported by Schusterman and Dorot Postdoctoral Fellowship from the Harry Ransom Center, University of Texas at Austin. For assistance and helpful suggestions I would like to thank Bernard Friedman, Dorothy Bohm, Jack Jacobs, Lars Fischer, John Efron, Gail Levin, Val Williams, Lisa Silverman, Maya Benton, Gail Feigenbaum, David Coleman, Linda Briscoe Meyers, David Leviatin, Joe Struble, Leslie Morris, William Meyers, Claudia Wedepohl, Grant Romer, and the referees of *Photography and Culture*.

1   A. D. Coleman, "Bringing Up Baby: Helmut Gernsheim, Beaumont Newhall, and the Childhood of Photo History," in *Helmut Gernsheim. Pionier der Fotogeschichte/Pioneer of Photo History*, eds. Alfried Wieczorek and Claude Sui (Ostfilern-Ruit: Hatje Catz Verlag, 2003), p. 63.

2   Roy Flukinger, with Foreword by Alison Nordström and Afterword by Mark Haworth-Booth, *The Gernsheim Collection* (Austin: University of Texas Press, 2010). This excellent volume accompanies a major exhibition at the Ransom Center, "Discovering the Language of Photography: The Gernsheim Collection," September 7, 2010–January 2, 2011 [hereafter the Gernsheim Collection at the Harry Ransom Center, University of Texas at Austin, will be cited as GC, HRC]; see also Van Deren Coke, ed., *One Hundred Years of Photographic History: Essays in Honor of Beaumont Newhall* (Albuquerque: University of New Mexico Press, 1975); Peter Walch and Thomas F. Barrow, eds., *Perspectives in Photography: Essays in Honor of Beaumont Newhall* (Albuquerque: University of New Mexico Press, 1986); Beaumont Newhall, *Focus: Memoirs of a Life in Photography* (Boston: Little, Brown, 1993).

3   A huge collection of Gernsheim's own photographs, taken under the auspices of the Warburg Institute and the National Building Record project during World War II, are in the photographic collection of the Warburg Institute, London, and a few of his letters, which are not duplicated, are in the Warburg Institute archives..

4   Certainly there were others who contributed to this; see Robert Taft, *Photography and the American Scene: A Social History, 1839-1889* (New York: Dover, 1942); Reese Jenkins, *Images and Enterprise: Technology and the American Photographic Industry, 1839-1925* (Baltimore: Johns Hopkins University Press, 1975).

5   Beaumont Newhall and Helmut Gernsheim worked in partnership with their (first) wives, Nancy Newhall and Alison Gernsheim, who contributed significantly to their husband's efforts. Both men outlived their partner/wives and remarried.

6   Peter Pollack papers, 900283 [hereafter cited as PP], Getty Research Institute archives [hereafter cited as GRI].

7   See Pollack to Ken Poli, Editor, *Photography*, November 25, 1974, file 39, box 5, PP, GRI. The correspondence between Pollack and Gernsheim held at the Ransom Center deals in large part with photography publishing. Interestingly, both Pollack and Gernsheim did not choose to keep all of their correspondence.

8   Files 1 and 2, box 6, PP, GRI. Although the *Encyclopaedia Judaica* is spelled with an "ae" (Encyclopaedia), the correspondence usually uses "Encyclopedia" with only an "e." Throughout this article all references to *Encyclopaedia* or *Judaica*, unless otherwise specified, refer to the *Encyclopaedia Judaica* which appeared in the early 1970s, published by Keter Press in Jerusalem. Hereafter, in its published form, it will be referred to as *EJ*. The most recent version of *Encyclopaedia Judaica*, which has republished Peter Pollack's article with a small addition, and a new section about the photography of "Jewish subjects" instead of the previous one on photography in Israel, will not be considered here. There are, however, several additional entries, particularly of Jewish woman photographers. See Peter Pollack and Yeshayahu Nir, "Photography," in *Encyclopaedia Judaica*, ed. Michael Berenbaum and Fred Skolnik, Vol. 16, 2nd ed. (Detroit: Macmillan Reference USA, 2007), pp. 125–31.

9   *EJ*, Volume 1: Introduction [and] Index, pp. 1–3.

10 Editing varied tremendously, depending on the subject and subeditor. Raphael Loewe, for instance, recalls no particular problems or tensions as Departmental Editor for the section on Christian Hebraists. He was allowed some twenty-four pages, including extensive tables and figures, for his "roof" article—that is, the general discussion of the field, and there were no cuts to his numerous individual entries; see below, note 118.

11 The letters are in file 1, box 6, PP, GRI.

12 The collection in the Getty is complemented by correspondence held at the Ransom Center between Helmut Gernsheim and Peter Pollack; Gernsheim, H/Letters/Gernsheim, H/22 TccL to Pollack, Peter/1956–62, and Gernsheim H/Recip/Pollack, Peter/9 ALS, 26 TLS to Gernsheim, 1956–63, GC, HRC.

13 The only book-length treatment, a labor of love which is more an antiquarian compendium, is George Gilbert, *The Illustrated Worldwide Who's Who of Jews in Photography* (Riverdale, NY: privately published, 1996). The single most informative article, after Pollack's essay, is Nahum (Tim) Gidal, "Jews in Photography," in *Leo Baeck Institute Year Book* 32 (1987): 432–53; see also Lisa Silverman, "Reconsidering the Margins: Jewishness as an Analytical Framework," in *Journal of Modern Jewish Studies* 8, 1 (2009): 103–20. Regarding Eastern Europe, the best overview is David Shneer, "Photography," in *YIVO Encyclopedia of Jews in Eastern Europe*, vol. 2, pp. 1350–53. Most of the work concerning Jews and photography has dealt with the photographing of Jews "as Jews" and explorations of the portrayals of Jews as victims of the Holocaust. An exemplary treatment on Jewish ethnography and photography is Eugene Avrutin, Valerii Dymshits, Alexander Ivanov, Alexander Lvov, Harriet Murav, and Alla Sokovla, eds., *Photographing the Jewish Nation: Pictures from S. An-sky's Ethnographic Expeditions* (Hanover, NH: Brandeis University Press of the University Press of New England, 2009). For a foundational view of Roman Vishniac see Carol Zemel, "Imagining the Shtetl: Diaspora Culture, Photography, and Eastern European Jews," in *Diaspora and Visual Culture: Representing Africans and Jews*, ed. Nicholas Mirzoeff (London: Routledge, 2000), pp. 193–206. A reappraisal and inventory of Vishniac's vast

work is underway at the International Center of Photography (ICP), New York, directed by Maya Benton; see Alana Newhouse, "A Closer Reading of Roman Vishniac," in the *New York Times Sunday Magazine*, April 4, 2010, MM36. In 1992, William Meyers "organized a colloquy at the National Foundation for Jewish Culture titled *The Light from the Dark: Jews and Photography*, with Naomi Rosenblum, Roberta Newman (photoarchivist, YIVO), Michael Wyschogrod (philosopher, Baruch College, CUNY), Evelyn Cohen (art historian, Stern College), Richard Siegel (executive director, NFJC)"; e-mail to the author, September 27, 2009.

14 *EJ*, Volume 1, p. 35; modified with information from the GRI CataloguePLUS website summary of "Peter Pollack papers." There is some question about his date of birth; the New York Public Library catalogue lists it as 1909.

15 Pollack also was author of *Understanding Primitive Art* (New York: Lion Press, 1969), a book for children.

16 See Pollack to Ken Poli, Editor, *Photography*, November 25, 1974, file 39, box 5, PP, GRI.

17 For an example of the potential of this approach, see David Shneer, *Through Soviet Jewish Eyes* (New Brunswick, NJ: Rutgers University Press, 2010), on Jewish photographers of the USSR during the Second World War. Not surprisingly, the GRI archive is useful for the subject of Jews and photography, generally, as well; see Nancy Newhalls' notes from an interview with Paul Strand, "interview with Paul Strand, May 29, 1942," in file 9 (labeled "Strand, Paul—material misfiled), box 115, Beaumont and Nancy Newhall papers [hereafter cited as BN-NN], GRI, and the early drafts of Dorothy Norman's biography of Alfred Stieglitz; see "Stiegliz, Alfred—D. Norman transcripts of his stories," file 8, box 13, BN-NN, GRI. Regarding the United States, a 2002 exhibition held at the Jewish Museum in New York focused on the overwhelming number of Jews in New York who photographed the city in the 20th century. Both the *New York Times* review of the exhibition, as well as at least one essay in the catalog—that of Max Kosloff, "Jewish Sensibility and the Photography of New York," in *New York: Capital of Photography*, ed. Max Kosloff, with contributions by Karen Levitov and Johanna Goldfeld (New York: Jewish Museum, under

the auspices of the Jewish Theological Seminary, and New Haven: Yale University Press, 2002), discusses the extent to which Jewishness may have been important to their photographs and careers. In agreement with the review in the *Times*, however, I do not find Kosloff's argument about a specific Jewish perspective on the city to be convincing, and in both this piece and the volume overall, salient connections between the United States and Europe are left unexplored.

18 Paid Notice: Deaths LACHMAN, DR. FREDERICK R., December 17, 1998, *New York Times*, section B, p. 15; Introduction-Index, *EJ*, Volume 1, p. 32: "LACHMAN, FREDERICK RICHARD, born in Bresau, 1902. He settled in Eretz Israel in 1933 and was entrusted with academic and organizational missions abroad. From 1952 he served as the personal U.S. representative of the Minister of Education. He was director of the American Friends of the Hebrew University and of the American Israeli Cultural Foundation. He wrote *Die Studentes des Christophorus Stymmelius and ihre Buehne* (1926) and *La salud y la enfermedad en la conciencia del pueblo judio* (1943)."

19 As it was the late 1960s, there were important matters discussed on the phone—of which we have reference but no record.

20 Lachman to Pollack, May 24, 1968, PP, GRI.

21 The list follows the letter from Lachman to Peter Pollack, May 24, 1968, PP, GRI.

22 Ibid.

23 Michael Berkowitz, "'Man and God' in Rochester, New York: Mannes and Godowsky at the Eastman Kodak Research Laboratory; or 'What are Two Nice Jewish Boys Like These Doing in a Place Like This?'" Johns Hopkins University Fifth Laboratory History conference, Baltimore, June 5, 2009, unpublished paper; and Michael Berkowitz, "Classically-minded Jazzy Jews and the Invention of Color Film," ETHNOISE: Ethnomusicology colloquium, University of Chicago, April 23, 2009, unpublished paper.

24 Lachman to Pollack, May 28, 1968, file 1, box 6; list follows page 2, PP, GRI.

25 Pollack to Lachman, June 4, 1968; list follows letter, file 1, box 6, PP, GRI.

26 Michael Kimmelman, "Grace Mayer, Photography Curator, Dies at 95," in *New York Times*, December 24, 1996, section D, p. 17.

27 Ibid.

28 Byron Dobell, "Magnum," in *Popular Photography* (September 1957), p. 136; circular letter from Inge Bondi, identified as "Editor for Special Projects" at Magnum, February 15, 1960, file 15, box 72, BN-NN, GRI; http://blog.magnumphotos.com/inge_bondi.html.

29 Helmut Gernsheim's list of fifty-eight Jewish photographers includes thirteen women; GC, HRC.

30 Val Williams conducted extensive interviews with Helmut Gernsheim for the British Library's Oral History of British Photography; (listen to) C459/66, especially tapes 1 and 2, British Library, London.

31 Historian of art and architecture Christy Anderson is currently working on the collaboration between Gernsheim and Rudolf Wittkower of the Warburg Institute. Pollack to Lachman, June 4, 1968; list follows letter, file 1, box 6, PP, GRI.

32 Peter Ride, "Helmut Gernsheim" [obituary], in *The Independent* (London), August 5, 1995.

33 Gernsheim first wife, Alison (Eames), was his long-time collaborator. The author of this recollection is his second wife, Irene; see "The Fascination of Photography" in *Helmut Gernsheim: Pioneer of Photo History*, p. 11.

34 I am indebted to Roy Flukinger for mentioning this to me, and tracking down the list in the Gernsheim Collection. I also wish to thank David Coleman and Linda Briscoe Meyers for informing me of relevant material in the collection, which will contribute substantially to the next phases of this project.

35 See Roy Flukinger, *The Gernsheim Collection*.

36 See Steven E. Aschheim, *Brothers and Strangers: The East European Jew in German and German Jewish Consciousness*, 2nd ed. (Madison: University of Wisconsin Press, 1999); Sander Gilman, *Jewish Self-Hatred: Anti-semitism and the Hidden Language of the Jews* (Baltimore: Johns Hopkins University Press, 1986).

37 Helmut Gernsheim to Beaumont Newhall, 14 April 1950, file 9, box 53, BN-NN, GRI; see also Michael Berkowitz, "Beaumont Newhall and Helmut

Gernsheim: Collaboration, Friendship, and Tension amidst the 'Jewishness' of Photography," in *Woolf Institute Perspectives: Studying Relations between Jews, Christians, and Muslims* (Spring 2010): 17–21.

38 Helmut Gernsheim, "The Gernsheims of Worms."

39 See Pollack to Paul Strand, March 2, 1967, file 38, box 5, PP, GRI.

40 See note 11.

41 See for example, Newton Pincus [Senior Vice President, Harry N. Abrams] to Pollack, September 25, 1974, file 32, box 6, PP, GRI.

42 Warburg Institute Archive, General Correspondence, Helmut Gernsheim to Fritz Saxl, 30 December 1941.

43 David Okuefuna, *The Dawn of the Color Photograph: Albert Kahn's Archives of the Planet* (Princeton: Princeton University Press, 2008); this appeared originally with BBC Books, in association with Musée Albert-Kahn, France, to accompany the BBC television series "Edwardians in Colour: The Wonderful World of Albert Kahn", first broadcast in 2007.

44 See Michaela Pfundner and Margot Werner, eds., *Zur Erinnerung an schönere Zeiten: Bilder aus der versunkenen Welt des jüdischen Sammlers Raoul Korty* (Wien: Österreichischen Nationalbibliothek, 2008). Helen Bartos kindly acquired this important book for me.

45 "PHOTOGRAPHY" in *Encyclopaedia Judaica*, Vol. 13, P-Rec, (Jerusalem: Keter, 1972), p. 486. This is the published version of the "roof" article.

46 See Richard I. Cohen, *Jewish Icons: Art and Society* (Berkeley: University of California Press, 1998); Veronica Grodzinski, "The Art Dealer and Collector as Visionary: Discovering Vincent van Gogh in Wilhelmine Germany, 1900–1914, *Journal of the History of Collections*, 21, 2 (2009): 221–28.

47 Pollack to Lachman, June 4, 1968, PP, GRI.

48 List follows letter of Pollack to Lachman, June 4, 1968, file 1, box 6, GRI.

49 Undated list, following letter and lists of Pollack to Lachman, June 4, 1968, file 1, box 6, PP, GRI.

50 Ibid.

51 Ibid.

52 Brassai was eventually removed, as Pollack learned he was most likely not Jewish.

53 Undated list, following letter and lists of Pollack to Lachman, June 4, 1968, file 1, box 6, PP, GRI.

54 Lachman to Pollack, June 5, 1968, file 1, box 6, PP, GRI.

55 Circular letter from Jerusalem editorial office to Pollack, July 4, 1968, file 1, box 6, PP, GRI.

56 Ibid.

57 Lachman to Pollack, July 11, 1968, file 1, box 6, PP, GRI.

58 Pollack to Lachman, July 11, 1968.

59 Among the photographs of Feininger on the George Eastman House archives website are some of the last to capture the Lower East Side as a Yiddish-speaking enclave, such as: the "New York 1940—Ghetto, Orchard Street, Lower East Side," 76:0606:0118; see a poultry shop at http://www.geh.org/fm/feininger/htmiscrc/m197806060118_ful.html#topofimage and a shop selling religious books and articles, called "Jewish shop on Lower East Side, Manhattan," 76:0606:0029, at http://www.geh.org/fm/feininger/htmiscrc/m197806060029_ful.html#topofimage

60 See Y. Rischin, Deputy Managing Director to SECTION COORDINATORS AND ALL EDITORS OF SECTION 6. BIOGRAPHICAL ENTRIES FOR SECION 6, August 5, 1968, file 1, box 6, PP, GRI. There is no indication if Pollack followed through or simply ignored these directions. He nevertheless went ahead with his assignment.

61 See, for example, Waldo Frank on the significance of Steiglitz's Jewishness, in *Our America* (New York: Boni and Liverright Publishers, 1919, repr. 1920), p. 186. Although he did not perceive Jewishness as significant in his own historical work, Beaumont Newhall writes that his initial contact with Stieglitz was prompted the encouragement of Paul Sachs, his teacher and mentor at Harvard; see "Meeting Stieglitz," Memoirs, III [drafts], file 5, box 203, BN-NN, GRI.

62 Pollack to Izis (Bidermanas), September 11, 1968, file 1, box 6, PP, GRI.

63 "EXHIBITIONS OF PHOTOGRAPHY-THE ART INSTITUTE OF CHICAGO" [typescript], folder 14, box 5, PP, GRI.

64 Pollack to Edwin H. Land, September 11, 1968, file 1, box 6, PP, GRI.

65 Richard O. Berube, Acting Publicity Manager, Polaroid Corporation, to Pollack, September 23, 1968, file 1, box 6, PP, GRI.

66 Pollack to Jacob Kainen, September 11, 1968, file 1, box 6, PP, GRI.

67 A collection of Elias Goldensky is in the International Museum of Film and Photography at the George Eastman House archives, Rochester, New York.

68 Grace Mayer would have been the best person to ask for assistance on this, given her expertise with Ives.

69 Jacob Kainen to Pollack, October 1, 1968, file 1, box 6, PP, GRI. Kainen's letterhead identifies his institutional affiliation as Smithsonian Institution, National Collection of Fine Arts, Eighth and G Street, NW, Washington, D.C.

70 Louis Walton Sipley, *A Half Century of Color* (New York: Macmillan, 1951), pp. vii, 11; Sipley, *The Photomechanical Halftone* (Philadelphia: American Museum of Photography, 1958), pp. 22–4.

71 On the letter, in red handwriting, "Curator of Photography, Smithsonian Institution, Wash 25 DC" appears next to Ostroff's name, and next to Lew Sipley: "Dr. Louis Walton Sipley[,] Dir.[,] Amer. M???[,]" and Phil[adelphia]; Pollack's notes on Kainen's letter, possibly from a follow-up phone call, ibid.

72 Barnett's parents were London-born Jews; see Roger Neill, "Barnett, Henry Walter (1862–1934)", *Oxford Dictionary of National Biography*, online edn, first published October 2006 ://dx.doi.org/10.1093/ref:odnb/66742.

73 Sipley, *A Half Century of Color*, p. viii.

74 "DR. LOUIS SIPLEY OF PHOTO MUSEUM. Head of Private Institution in Philadelphia is Dead," *New York Times*, October 19, 1968, p. 37.

75 "The Sipley/3M Collection," in *Image: Journal of Photography and Motion Pictures of the International Museum of Photography at George Eastman House*, Vol. 21, No. 3 (September, 1978), p. 1. Sipley's work also includes *Frederic E. Ives, photo-graphic-arts inventor* (Philadelphia: American Museum of Photography, 1956); *Photography's Great Inventors* (Philadelphia: American Museum of Photography, 1965).

76 "DR. LOUIS SIPLEY," *New York Times* obituary.

77 See typescript of Newhall, "The Gernsheim Collection" for *Image* 8 no. 3 (Sep. 1959), pp. 114–17, file 9, box 53, BN-NN, GRI.

78 Ms/Gernsheim/Letters/Gernsheim H/11 TccL to the American Museum of Photography/1953–63; Ms/Gernsheim/Recip/American Museum of Photography, Philadelphia, 15 TLS/FSL to Gernsheim/1955–62, GC, HRC.

79 "The Sipley/3M Collection," in *Image: Journal of Photography and Motion Pictures of the International Museum of Photography at George Eastman House*, Vol. 21, No. 3 (September, 1978), p. 1.

80 Ibid.

81 See Roger Neill, "Barnett, Henry Walter (1862–1934)," *Oxford Dictionary of National Biography*.

82 Ostroff to Pollack, October 14, 1968, file 1, box 6, PP, GRI.

83 See Peter Krause, "Pioneering Color Systems," in *Pioneers of Photography: Their Achievements in Science and Technology*, ed. Eugene Ostroff (Springfield, VA: Society for Imaging Science and Technology, 1987), p. 208.

84 Sipley, *A Half Century of Color*, pp. 34–8.

85 Pollack to Roman Vishniac, September 11, 1968, file 1, box 6, PP, GRI.

86 Vishniac to Pollack, September 14, 1968, file 1, box 6, PP, GRI.

87 Pollack to Vishniac, September 17, 1968, file 1, box 6, PP, GRI.

88 Vishniac to Pollack, September 20, 1968, file 1, box 6, PP, GRI.

89 Pollack to Vishniac, September 24, 1968, file 1, box 6, PP, GRI.

90 Vishniac to Pollack, undated [between September 24 and October 1, 1968], file 1, box 6, PP, GRI.

91 Pollack to Vishniac, October 7, 1968, file 1, box 6, PP, GRI. A brief note from Vishniac, with a few corrections, closed the correspondence, and there is no indication, in Pollack's papers, that he had any further dealings with Vishniac; Vishniac to Pollack, October 18, 1968, file 1, box 6, PP, GRI.

92 Pollack to Vishniac, September 17, 1968, file 1, box 6, PP, GRI.

93 Entry for VISHNIAC, ROMAN (1897–), in *EJ*, Volume 16, column 166.

94 *Joshua Benoliel, 1873–1932. Reporter Fotografico. Photojournalist* (Lisboa: Lisboa Photo, 2005).

95 Lachman to Pollack, October 29, 1968, file 1, box 6, PP, GRI.

96 Pollack to Lachman, November 10, 1968, file 1, box 6, PP, GRI.

97 Undated letter from Izis to Pollack, mid-November to December 1968, file 1, box 6, PP, GRI.

98 EXHIBITIONS OF PHOTOGRAPHY-THE ART INSTITUTE OF CHICAGO, file 14, box 5, PP, GRI.

99 Again, his efforts were hacked to shreds in the *Judaica*. His original piece on Izis was over 500 words; Pollack to Izis, December 16, 1968. An undated copy of the original is in file 2, box 6, PP, GRI.

100 *Photographer Chaimas Kaplanskis. Western Lithuania, 19ᵗʰ–20ᵗʰ c.*, edited by Marina Petrasukiene (Telsiai-Vilnius: Vilniaus dailes akademijos leidykla, 2007); see Michael Berkowitz, "Photography as a Jewish Business: From High Theory, to Studio, to Snapshot," in *East European Jewish Affairs*, Vol. 39, No. 3 (December 2009): 389–400.

101 The treatment of photography in the recent YIVO encyclopedia is more sophisticated than the updated edition of the *Encyclopedia Judaica*. See David Shneer, "Photography," in *YIVO Encyclopedia of Jews in Eastern Europe*, vol. 2, 1350–3.

102 Rolf Sachsse, "'Dieses Atelier ist sofort zu vermieten': Von der 'Entjudung' eines Befursstandes," in *"Arieserung" im Nationalsozialismus: Volksgemeinschaft, Raub und Gedächtnis: Jahrbuch 2000 zur Geschichte und Wirkung des Holocaust*, Fritz Bauer Institut (Hg.) von Irmtrud Wojak and Peter Hayes (Frankfut/New York: Campus, 2000), pp. 269–86. Sachsse highlights, for example, the enterprises of the Jacobi family, Mario von Bucovich, and Imre von Santho of Berlin, Emil Bieber of Hamburg, Hans Holt of Cologne, and Nini and Carry Hess, Frankfurt.

103 I am extremely grateful to William Meyers for sharing this with me.

104 Great-great-great grandfather of the author, for whom the author's father, William Berkowitz, was apparently named.

105 Dmitri Shneerson; Hermitage website: www.hermitagemuseum.org/html_En/05/hm5_7_10_1_1_0.html.

106 Andrei G. Nedvetsky, ed., introduction by D.Y. Arapov, series editor, Vitaly Naumkin, *Caught in Time: Great Photographic Archives: Bukhara* (Reading, UK: Garnet, 1993), pp. 31, 33.

107 See the photographic collection of Boris Feldblyum, which includes unusually detailed information: www.bfcollection.net/indphoto/bfc01956.html.

108 Tax and voter information from JewishGen (Jewish genealogical website): data.jewishgen.org/wconnect/wc.dll?jg~jgsearch~model2~[TAXVOTERS]TAXVOTERS10.

109 Personal communication with Lily Titova.

110 Lachman to Pollack, June 5, 1969, file 1, box 6, PP, GRI; see P. Connes, "Silver Salts and Standing Waves: The History of Interference in Colour Photography," in *Journal of Optics* (Paris) 1987, vol. 18, no. 4, pp. 147.

111 Connes, "Silver Salts."

112 The majority appear, in the end, as fleeting references in Pollack's "roof" article, whereas Pollack would likely have seized the opportunity for separate entries for nearly all of the individuals he listed, had he the chance.

113 Pollack to Lachman, June 9, 1969, file 1, box 6, PP, GRI.

114 Ibid.

115 Pollack to Lachman, June 10, 1969, file 1, box 6, GRI.

116 Pollack to Lachman, September 13, 1969, file 1, box 6, GRI. Carbon copies of Pollack's original

articles mainly are in file 2, box 6, except for the original of his "roof" article, PP, GRI.

117 See Volume 1: Introduction [and] Index, *EJ*, pp. 1–3.

118 Personal (telephone) communication of the author with Raphael Loewe, subeditor for HEBRAISTS, CHRISTIAN, *EJ*, October 15, 2009. I appreciate my colleague, Emeritus Professor Loewe of University College London, for sharing with me his extremely positive experience with the *Judaica*. He was well acquainted with the project's original chief editor, Cecil Roth. Loewe does not recall any interference in his work, and he was encouraged to use several pages of tables and a number of illustrations, in addition to several thousand words of text, for his "roof" article.

119 Photostat of memo from G. Wigoder to Dr Lachman, October 18, 1969, file 1, box 6, PP, GRI.

120 See Letter from Mrs. Chaikin to Peter Pollack, Jerusalem, December 25, 1969, file 1, box 6, PP, GRI.

121 Undated manuscript of photography "roof" article, before letter of Lachman to Pollack, October 29, 1968, file 1, box 6, PP, GRI.

122 See entry for "LAND, EDWIN H. (1909–)" in Volume 10, Jes-Lei, *EJ*, col. 1384. The original text of Pollack's article follows the letter from Richard Berube to Pollack, September 23, 1968, file 1, box 6, PP, GRI.

123 See Grover A. Swartzlander, Jr, Arvind Marathay, Jennifer M. Harwell, Joshua Gordon, and Jason Figueiredo, "Optical vortex vectorgraphs," in *Optics Letters*, Vol. 34, No. 8, April 15, 2009, pp. 1216–8.

124 EISENSTADT, ALFRED (1898–), in *EJ*, Vol. 6, Di-Fo, column 552; the original is in file 2, box 6, PP, GRI.

125 See C. Zoe Smith, "Germany's Kurt Korff: An Émigré's Influence on Early Life," in *Journalism Quarterly*, Vol. 65, Issue 2/3 (summer 1988): 412–24.

126 Lachman to Pollack, June 5, 1969, file 1, box 6, PP, GRI.

127 A partial beginning also includes Gerda Taro, Dorothy Boehm, Eva Besnyö, Gisele Freund, Alice Schalek, Grete Stern, Ellen Auerbach, Aenne Biermann, Doris May Ulmann, Ilse Bing, Mariana Yamplosky, Nini Hess, Lotte Errell, Trude Fleischman, and Marianne Breslauer.

Michael Berkowitz is Professor of Modern Jewish History at University College London. His most recent book is *The Crime of My Very Existence: Nazism and the Myth of Jewish Criminality* (2007).

Photography & Culture

Volume 4—Issue 1
March 2011
pp. 29–54

DOI:
10.2752/175145211X12899905861915

Reprints available directly from
the publishers

Love-Love. Ni-Ni: Roland Barthes and Bernard Faucon, A Butterfly Effect

Carol Mavor

This essay knits together the philosophy of Roland Barthes (1915–1980) and the photographs of Bernard Faucon (b.1950), the latter famous for gathering manikin-boys, dressing them with care, then staging their birthdays, snowman building, first communions, picnics and more, often with a dash of boyish pyromania, at times coupling the *unreal* boys with *real* boys. (The word "manikin" is from the Dutch *mannekijn*, meaning little man.) Together, Roland Barthes and Bernard Faucon are lit with ephebophilia (ephebe=early manhood+philia=love): an adolescent love for the "little man", who is neither child, nor adult. In a 1978 essay on Faucon, Barthes claims the ruse of the photograph as matched by the trick of the manikin: both *are* apparently real and not real; both are infinitely reproducible; both are immobile. Such doubling is tidy for Faucon (whose manikins savour post-war hygiene) and for Barthes (whose texts often bank on the cleanliness of structuralism). In a handwritten note scrawled out to Faucon, Barthes said it best: "Your photos are marvellous; for me, it's ontological, if you'll allow this loaded word. The photo [in your work] is in the limits of its own being: that is the fascination."

Keywords: adolescence; animation; binarism; boys; butterfly; department store window; doll; fairy tale; homosexuality; movie theatre; pupa; reduplication; third language; toy

I then realized that there was a sort of link (or knot) between Photography, madness, and something whose name I did not know. I began by calling it: the pangs of love. Was I not, in fact, in love with the Fellini automaton? Is one not in love with certain photographs? (Figures 1–4) Roland Barthes, *Camera Lucida*

"Ni-ni adolescence" *knots* and *knits* together Roland Barthes (1915–80) and the photographer Bernard Faucon (b.1950), the latter famous for gathering manikin-boys, dressing them with care,

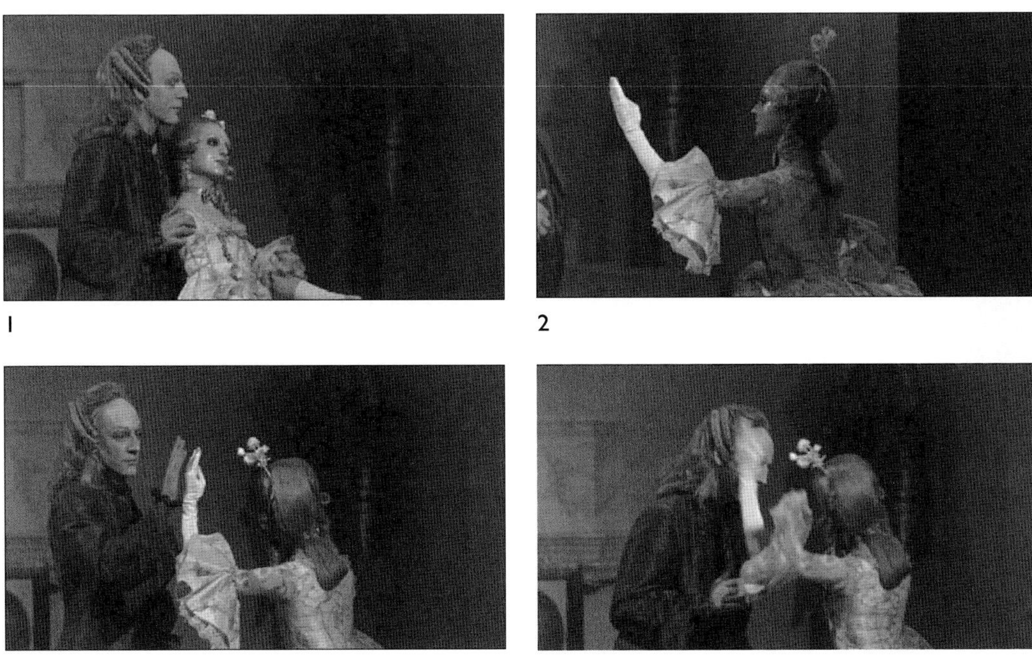

Figs 1–4 Federico Fellini, *Casanova* (1976)

then staging their birthdays, snowman building, first communions, picnics and more, often with a dash of boyish pyromania, at times coupling the *unreal* boys with *real* boys as in his *Diabolo menthe,* 1980 (Figure 5). Faucon's manikin photographs, under the series title of *Les Grandes vacances* (1975–81), are a big family of Pinocchios, without the strings. Made not of pieces of wood, but of plaster (or plaster-like substances) found in the already-formed bodies of the commercially produced manikin, Faucon's Pinocchio story is modern French, not old world Italian.

It's a little Eugène Atget. It's a little Raoul Ubac (as in his photograph of André Masson's construction of a caged manikin head with a big pansy in her mouth as "prey"[1]).

Faucon's grandmother offered him his first camera in 1967, a Semflex (France's post-war challenge to the Rolleiflex). He was seventeen.[2]

Faucon's career as an artist-photographer began in the mid 1970s and was stopped voluntarily in 1995.[3] Furthermore, he has not let anyone photograph him for over ten years.

Faucon's final photograph was part of a series entitled *La Fin de l'image* (1993–95). These small format colour photographs feature fragments of poetic text, written in thick white "ink," like sugar icing, on the skin of boyish youth, offering itself to be licked off. The culinary script could almost be from Barthes' own bits of journal writing, which we have been made privy to after his death (*Incidents* and *Mourning Diary*[4]). Nevertheless, and although infused with the philosophy that he studied at the Sorbonne, Faucon's snippets of tender text are lighter, more youthful, more

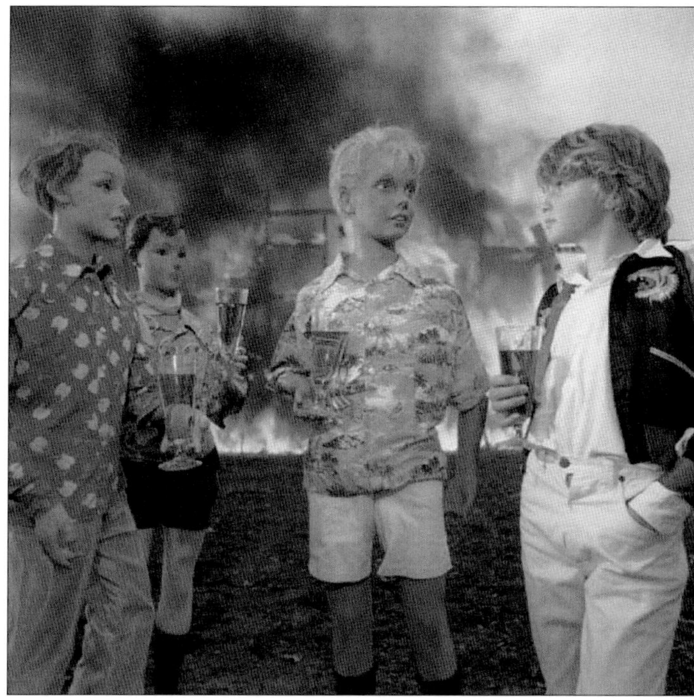

Fig 5 Bernard Faucon, *Diabolo Menthe* (1980)

hopeful than those of Barthes'. On the skin of the boys, as flesh made word, Faucon writes Hansel and Gretel fairy tale lines, like: *"Tu es l'alphabet en pain d'épices qui cache les mots"*; *"Comme une effraction dans une construction de sucre d'orge"*; *"Tendre cannibalisme"*; and *"Ni ange ni ogre mais le malheur veut…"* (Figure 6).

As Faucon has remarked: "The skins and bodies are no longer the skin and body of any particular child, they are the skins and bodies of our lost childhoods. A big, unique body unfolding infinitely. The very childhood of life, the source of all nostalgia."[5]

With the end of his photography, with the *La Fin de l'image* (one bit of flesh from the latter, simply reads 'fin'), Faucon's sweet adolescence, preternaturally harboured for such a long time through the bodies of boys that infused his work and his own boyish looks, must have departed, like a butterfly escaping its chrysalis-skin (Figure

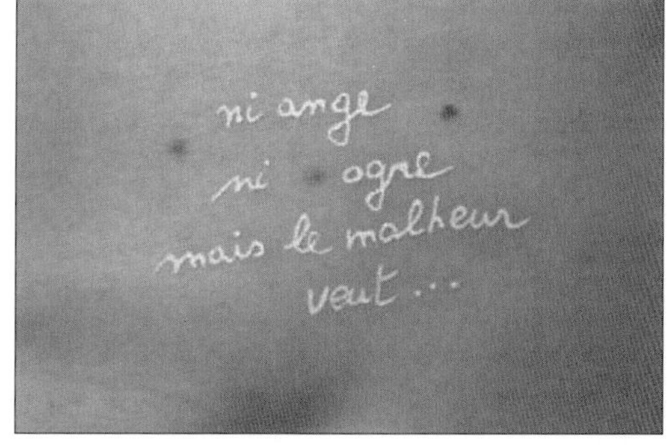

Fig 6 Bernard Faucon, *Ni ange ni ogre*, from *La Fin de l'image* (1993–1995)

7). The situation is not unlike Faucon's *Le Départ* (1978): here the manikins are caught as they are leaving for their summer vacation (a time when butterflies will emerge from their cocoons). A

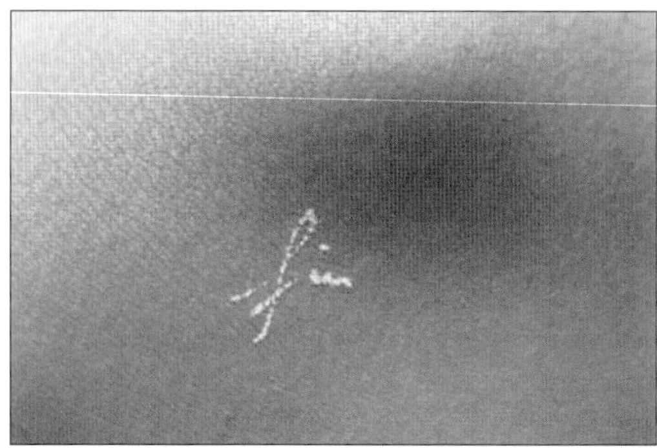

Fig 7 Bernard Faucon, *Fin*, from *La Fin de 'l'image* (1993–1995)

The fluttery theme of *Le Départ* is repeated in *La Chasse aux papillons* (1978). In both, images of butterfly nets hail the metamorphosis of all children, who move from caterpillar to pupa to butterfly. Flight (though of a birdly, not butterfly nature) is even in the photographer's own name, which in French means falcon. All of these winged metaphors merge with the recurrent images of soaring to be found in Faucon's work: as in *L'Avion* (1977) which pictures a boyish fascination with flight; or *L'Enfant qui vole* (1979), which turns on the magical childish wish to transgress, to fly like Peter Pan.

******

few of the 'little men" onboard the train cast butterfly nets out the windows. Cerulean blue, buttercup yellow and turquoise blue: these butterfly catchers are party flags in anticipation of monarch and swallowtail days (Figure 8).

Both Barthes and Faucon have sartorial egos of woolly caterpillar ephebophilia (ephebe=early manhood + philia=love, hence love for the adolescent). What follows is one ill-fitting, awkward pupa suit, made with neither-nor knitting

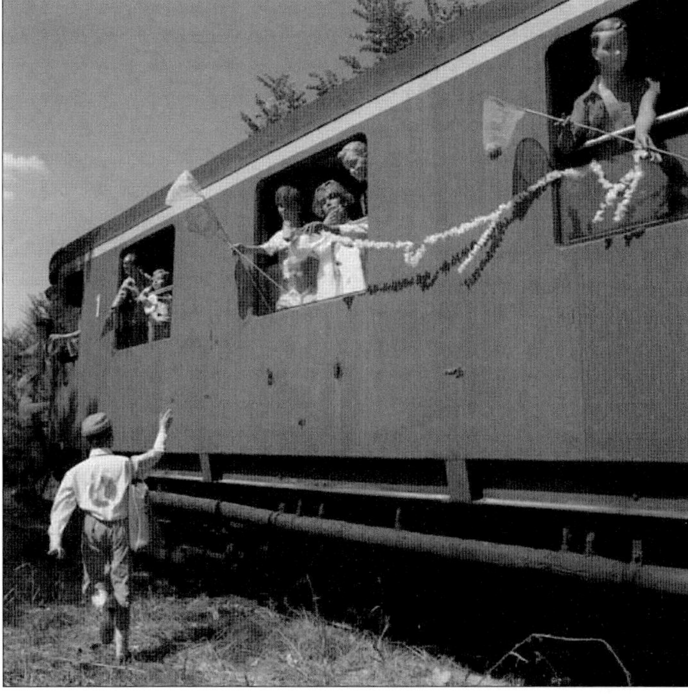

Fig 8 Bernard Faucon, *Le Départ* (1978)

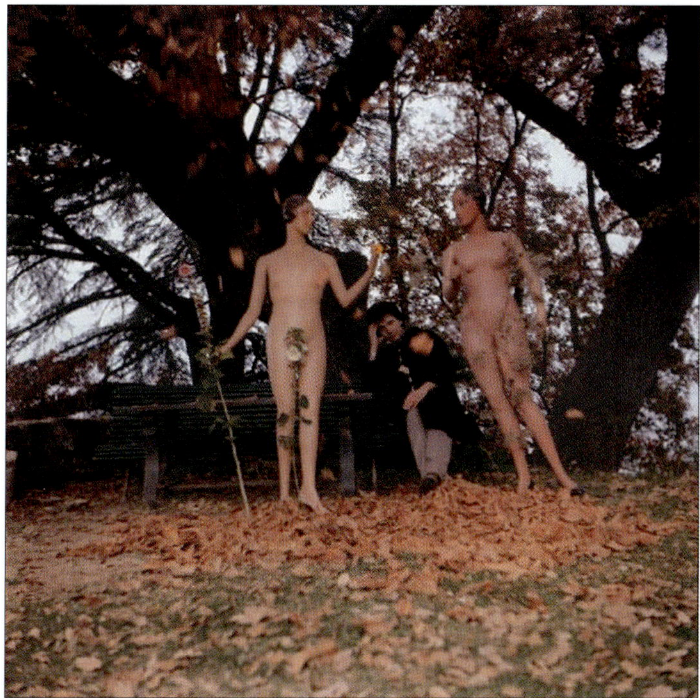

Fig 9 Bernard Faucon *Les Mannequines* (1975)

needles for these two ancient adolescents; these two aged boys, these little men, these manikins. The word 'manikin' is from the Dutch *mannekijn*, meaning little man.

Faucon gives himself up as *mannekijn*, when he seats himself between two parental, if naked, manikins in *Les mannequins* (1975, Figure 9). In *Roland Barthes par Roland Barthes* (also of 1975), Barthes gives himself up as a gentle *mannekijn* in a photograph from his *lycée* days, where he steps out with two other schoolboy adolescents in their ill-fitting suits made for grown men. Below the picture, Barthes writes: *"In those days, lycée students were little gentlemen"* (Figure 10).

Love

As Tzvetan Todorov, who wrote his post-graduate thesis under Barthes, has remarked, the boyish philosopher of semiology was an eternal adolescent, even when he was playing the role of professor. In his own words:

> There was always something adolescent, even childish, in him. He had no truth to impose upon others, nor even upon himself; perhaps this is why he was so vulnerable to the attacks which he was periodically subjected and protected himself so badly against them (a poor warrior decidedly). He always seemed to be the age of the students in his latest seminar (whereas the earlier "promotions" were growing older), and he had no difficulty in keeping up with the latest innovations. *A Lover's Discourse* is also rooted in adolescent language: *Werther's…* In his universe of sensations, the negative pole is represented by the sticky, as it is for children, and his fantasy of the family was

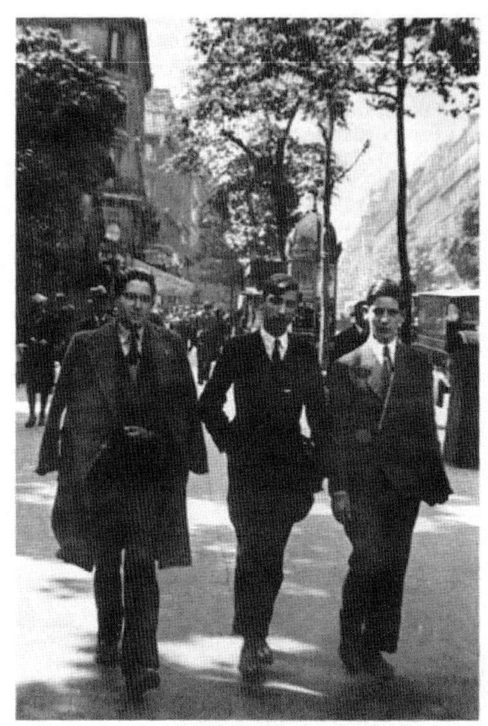

Fig 10 From *Roland Barthes par Roland Barthes*

still that of children…And is his death not a
child's death—crossing the street?[6]

This, too, is a story of love. Knitting love.

As Shakespeare writes in his fairyish *A
Midsummer Night's Dream:*

Love takes the meaning in love's conference.
I mean that my heart unto yours is knit.
So that but one heart we can make of it.

Romeo-and-Juliet (Roland-and-Bernard)
adolescent love.

It is a *mise en scène* of adolescent games
of "prisoner's base" in fields of sweet-smelling

lavender, with captives of love running in all
directions. Crushing the velvet, crushing the
lavender, as in Faucon's 1980, *Le Champ de
lavande* (Figure 11).

To have a streak of lavender is not only to be
the colour of pale blue with a trace of red, it is to
be queer, to be a boy who is crushed by boys.

And the language play, the punning continues:
"*lavande, lavanderie,* lavender and laundry."[7]

Furthermore, fields of lavender are ubiquitous
to Faucon's work. In *Les Etendoirs* (1982), bright,
clean, just-washed, postwar clothes are hanging
out to dry on a seemingly endless thread of
laundry line over a field of fresh, sweet lavender
(Figure 12). In *Jeu d'approche* (1980), the
photograph is taken from down low, as if Jacques
Henri Lartigue was among the manikins tramping
through the field of lavender: a big white flag
flies high in the blue sky, calling all little men to
surrender to the game (Figure 13).

Mine is a story of crushes: Barthes' crush on
Faucon; my crush on Barthes; Faucon's crush on
Barthes. It is all rather crushing.

Faucon not only saved the letter in which
Barthes praises his photography, he also saved
a cigar butt given to him as a gift by RB and
tucked it away in a special envelope, dated and
inscribed with this: *mégot d'un cigare offert per
Roland Barthes*—"*offert*" refers to the sentimental
attachment (Figures 14 and 15). That's a crush.

On the covers of the American edition of
Barthes's *Incidents* and (its companion volume)
D.A. Miller's *Bringing Out Roland Barthes* are two
images from Bernard Faucon's manikinless series
entitled *Les Chambres d'amour* (1984). Although
the books were published, and the photographs
were made, after the death of Barthes, these two
rooms of love are an apt meeting of Faucon and
the "professor of desire". Indeed, these covers
were my first exposure to the work of Faucon.

La Première chambre d'amour (Figure 16),
which appears on *Bringing Out Roland Barthes*,
features a bedroom with two boys sleeping on
the floor: between them sits a twinkling form

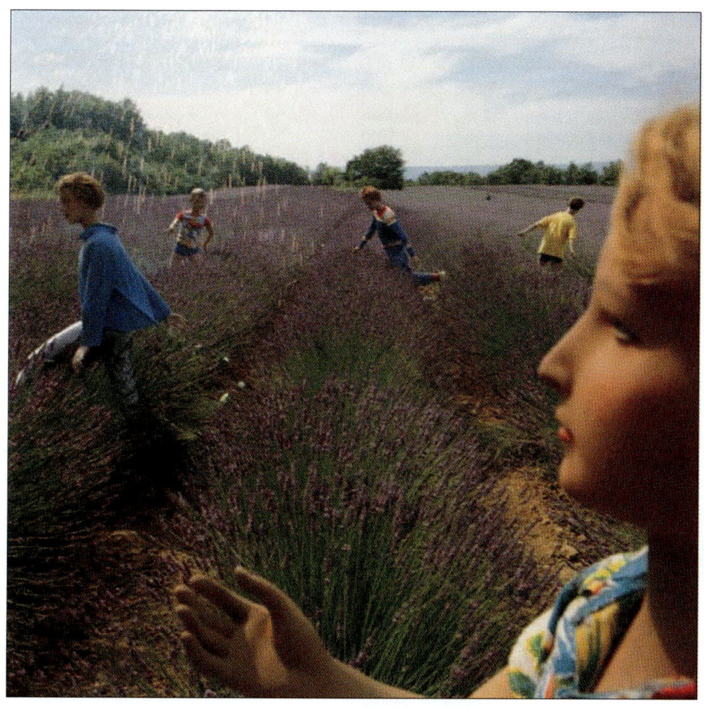

Fig 11 Bernard Faucon *Le Champ de lavande* (1980)

Fig 12 Bernard Faucon, *Les Entendoirs* (1982)

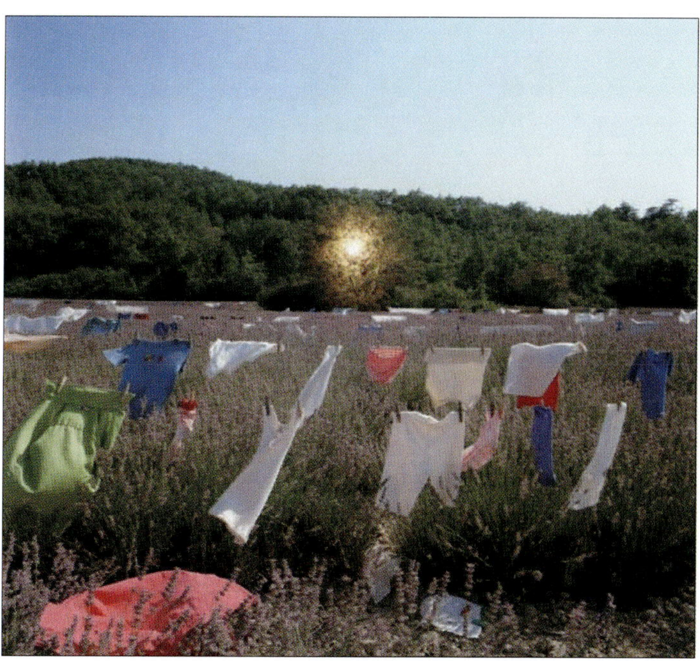

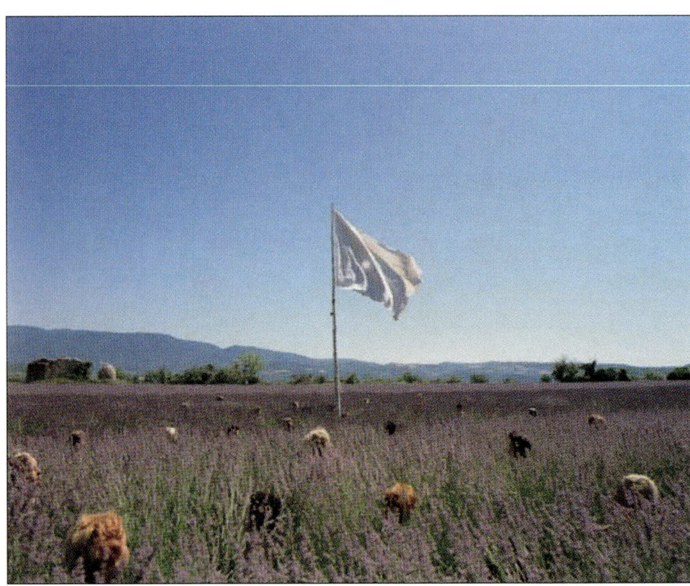

Fig 13 Bernard Faucon, *Jeu d'appoche* (1980)

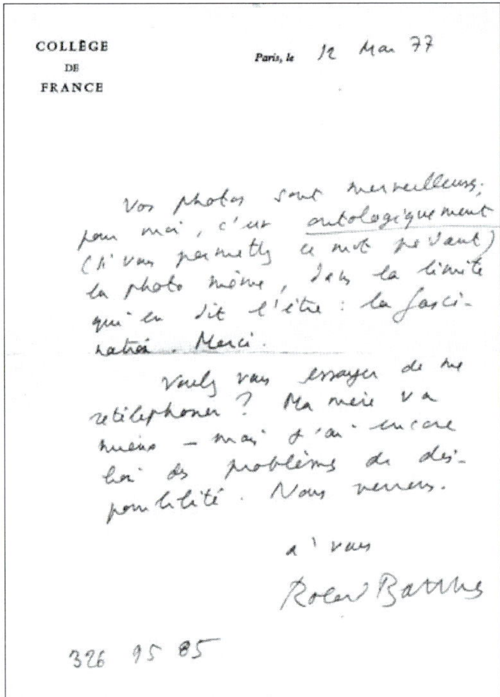

Fig 14 Note to Faucon from Roland Barthes

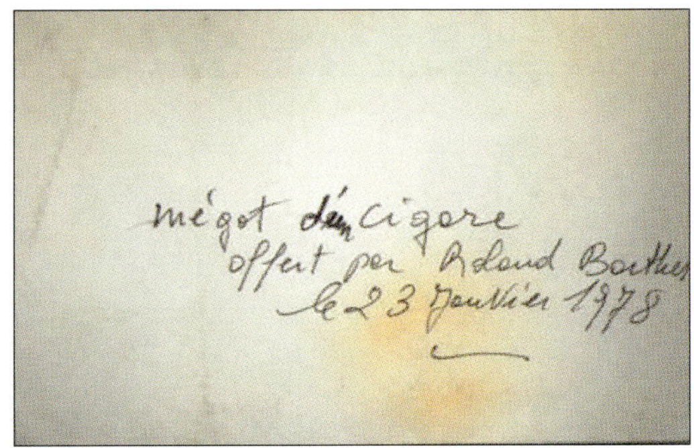

Fig 15 Roland Barthes' cigar butt as saved by Bernard Faucon

of silver foil; perched on one boy's hip is a torch flashlight (turned on). Cast aside on the white padded floor is a spoon and an empty yogurt pot. The curtains are pulled open. The room is painted pale yellow and the picture has an overall golden feel.

La Trezième chambre d'amour: le vitrail (Figure 17), which appears on the cover of *Incidents*, features a bedroom with an empty bed (no

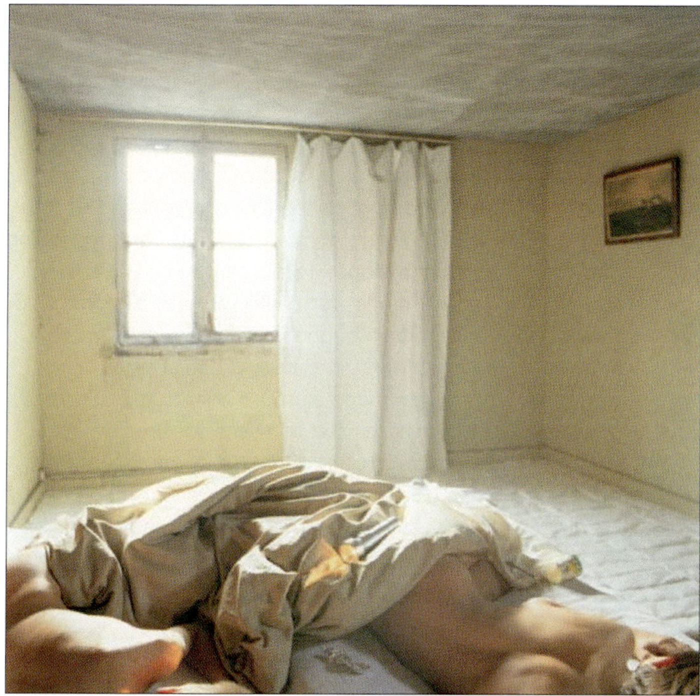

Fig 16 Bernard Faucon, *La Première chambre d'amour* (1984)`

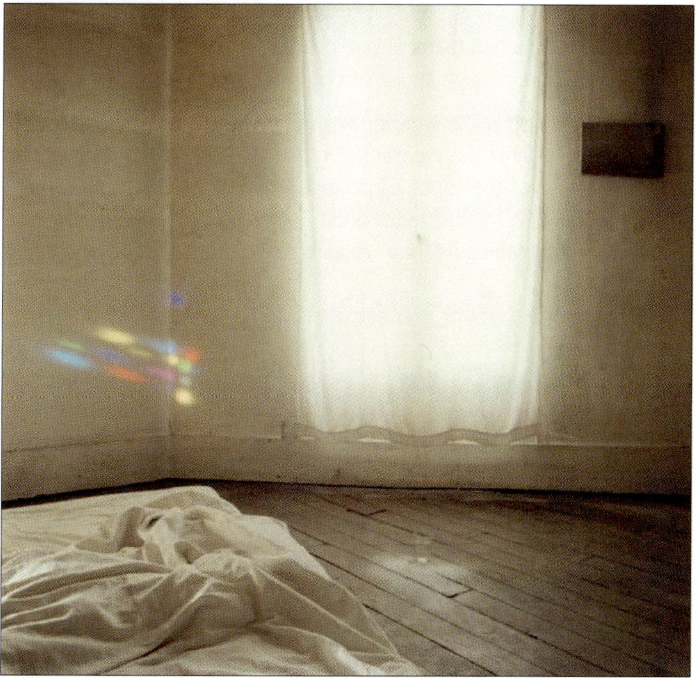

Fig 17 Bernard Faucon, *La Trezième chambre d'amour: le vitrail* (1984)

boys of plaster, no boys of flesh). Next to the boyless bed on the floor, and in the centre of the photograph, is a clear glass of clean water: it twinkles a rainbow of coloured dots (violet-blue, sky-blue, pale blue, orange-red, pale-yellow, lime-green, fuchsia-pink) on the dirty-cream coloured wall of this empty room. A white sheet covers the window, but light shines through.

Both rooms, the one with the boys in bed and the curtains open, the other with no boys in bed and the curtain closed, play with light and the possibilities of love that flicker with Daniel Boudinet's 1979 *Polaroid,* which famously begins *Camera Lucida.*

All three are pictures of the textures of light, of little gentleman (if at times invisible) through a homoerotic lens. It is all about what Renu Bora calls "outing texture."[8]

As Elizabeth Freeman has written:

> For me, having a "crush" is about texture, like crushed velvet or crushed foil. My surface gets all uneven, my underneath shows through, things shine up suddenly. It's like "being" crushed material, but also like wearing it, alternately slithery and itchy.[9]

Having a crush is like wearing velvet: scratchy on the inside against the wearer's skin; and, soft on the outside for the touch of others. Velvet is neither soft, nor itchy. It is neither-nor. Likewise, brushing or smoothing its "nap" reveals its neither-nor colours.

In French, neither-nor is constructed as ni-ni.

Ninisme

The adolescent is neither adult, nor child. Often androgynous, the adolescent is neither masculine, nor feminine, is what Barthes would label as *le neutre.* (In French, *neutre* holds all of the variants that interest Barthes, including the "third term between genders", "the domain of international law", and even a "contempt" for the way in which journalists perform a neutral position, which is anything but.[10]) Likewise the photograph, like

the manikin, is neither real, nor not real. The adolescent, the manikin, the photograph: they are all ni-nis, especially in the neither-nor hands of Barthes and Faucon.

Furthermore, ni-ni is a replay sound to make a phoneme. It is an echo of Freud's Grandson Ernst who whirled the sound of fort and da into a wooden spool thrown back and forth, gone and there, on a string. He played fort-da with ma-ma.

Ernst made wood into sense, into a Pinocchio-induced yo-yo phoneme, a further development of his likely first utterance of "ma-ma."[11]

Faucon made plaster manikins into sense, in all of its senses: the non-*sense* of the fairy tale, the *sensual* erotics of their play, the *senses* of touch (real knitted sweaters on smooth cold bodies), taste (so much sugar), sound (silent, yet explosive with pyromaniac antics) and sight (blind plastic-eyed, yet exquisitely colourful, and highly detailed).

Baudelaire's 1853 essay, "La Morale du joujou" (Philosophy of Toys), chooses "not *jouet,* the unusual words for toy, but rather an almost pet name with a nursery ring…its repetition hints at baby talk and hence at playing."[12]

First words, like the rhythmic maternal ma-ma and the rhythmic paternal da-da and the rhythmic grandparental na-na and pa-pa, grow out of reduplicating sounds. They are doubles: like a mother and child, like the referent and its photograph. As Craig Owens has argued: a photograph is an endless mirroring, is like a child's first babbles, is "en abyme."[13] (Photographs were once referred to as Daguerre's Mirror.)

Photographs and first words reproduce "in miniature the structure of the text [or its sound] in its entirety."[14]

There is something childish about ni-ni.

For Barthes (whom Thomas Clerc refers to as "the artist-professor"[15]), this fantasy of neither-norism (*ninisme*) took on other names and forms, including the zero degree, satori, third language, the neutral (*neutre*) and even twinklings (*scintillations*).

As Denis Hollier and Rosalind Krauss have thoughtfully pointed out, "the fantasy on which Barthes's penultimate course [at the *Collège de France*], 'Le Neutre' is based… held steady…over the trajectory that took him from *Writing Degree Zero*, with the zero degree an early version of 'le neutre,' through all the rest of his books."[16]

As Barthes "ni-ni"'s about himself as neither object nor subject in *Roland Barthes by Roland Barthes* (1975), a text that is neither novel, nor non-fiction, neither biography nor autobiography, but rather a neither-nor gesture in the spirit of his beloved Proust's long philosophical musings on childhood, memory and time sold as a novel: "For a certain time, he went into raptures over binarism: binarism became for him a kind of erotic object. This idea seemed to him inexhaustible, he could never exploit it enough. That one might say everything *with only one difference* produced a kind of joy in him, a continuous astonishment… intellectual things [it turns out] resemble erotic ones…"[17]

I cherish Barthes' double ways, his raptures over binarism, his delight in tearing "himself in two" Rumpelstilzchen-style, as written and lectured through his ni-ni, velvety voice: "resonant and what the French call *chantante*."[18] If it were a fabric, Barthes tells us with his haptic aurality, the neutral would be "velvet."[19]

As a child, Barthes transgressed all the rules of prisoner's base and turned it into a ni-ni pastime: where, you guessed it, there were neither losers nor winners. It was a boyish gesture towards the critic he would become:

> When I used to play prisoner's base in the Luxembourg, what I liked best was not provoking the other team and boldly exposing myself to their right to take me prisoner; what I liked best was to free the prisoners—the effect of which was to put both teams back into circulation: the game started over again at zero. In the great game of the powers of speech, we also play prisoner's base: one language has only temporary rights over another; all it takes is for the third language to appear from the ranks for the assailant to be forced to retreat; in the conflicts of rhetorics, the victory never goes to any but the *Third Language*. The task of this language is to release the prisoners: to scatter the signified, the catechisms.

Is not Faucon's *Jeu d'approche* (Figure 12) a photograph of this *Third Language*, a re-play of Barthes's memory of playing "prisoner's base" as re-imagined in a swishy field of lavender?

In *Première communion* (1979, Figure 18), Faucon, who grew up on postwar structuralism, scatters his own catechisms, by focusing on two boys in very, very clean sailor suits: one is a manikin-boy and the other a real boy. Their white shirts, with crisp blue ties, reflects the fashion of Faucon's family of boys, who in the words of Guy Davenport, have a taste for "leisure toggery suitable for summer and play" with that "just-ironed, worn-for-the first-time look."[20] As Davenport notes:

> Faucon grew up in a postwar France that embraced new ideas of hygiene, an "Americanization" of washing machines, modernized bathrooms, shampoo—a wave of consumerism boosted by fashion magazines such as *Marie-Claire* and *Elle*… On the lavender field clothesline [in *Les Etendoirs*, Figure 12] we can see, between a blouse and a dishtowel, a pair of boy's underpants, the *slip à poché* introduced in 1945 according to *Marie-Claire*…[21]

Faucon's models' clothes carry the history of the development of department stores, iconic holders of shopping history, like La Samaritaine and their big glass windows of dressed manikins; but what they actually wear hails the presentness of "Prisunic."[22]

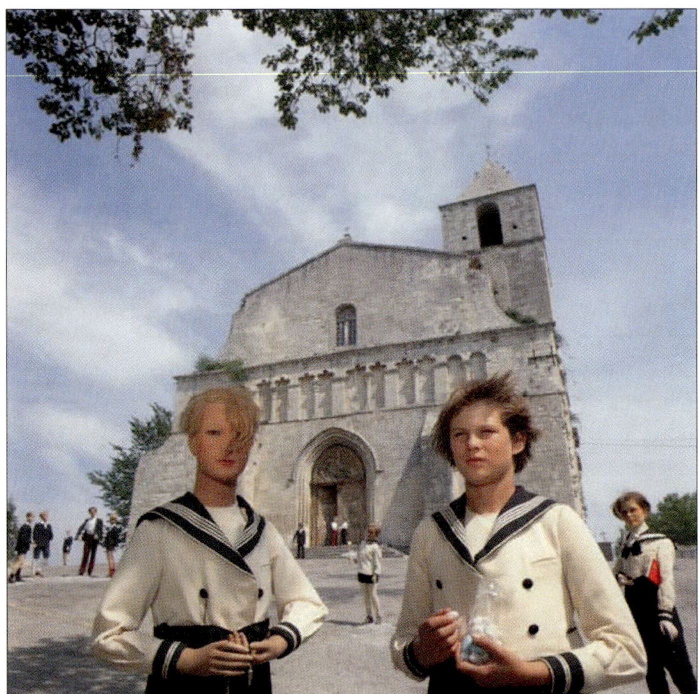

Fig 18 Bernard Faucon, *Première communion* (1979)

And just as they dress Prisunic (though there is a strong heft of the thrift shop and the sparkle of a good retro-find), they are printed with a secret technology known as the "Fresson process," which gives the photographs an incredibly rich and intense colour, served up in a texture of "matte porcelain."[23] The Fresson process, coupled with the dreams of Faucon, makes the images appear more like postwar "ornamental cookery" than real life (real food). "A print takes days to develop: each color has it its own template, and is oil pigment infused into *gelatine*."[24]

The look and taste of Faucon's Fresson photographs are a recollection of Barthes' essay entitled "Ornamental Cookery" (*Mythologies*, 1957). There, Barthes describes the visually appealing artifice of glazes and colours of the weekly prepared dishes in *Elle*, well-orchestrated cuisine "meant for the eye alone."[25] Barthes' language could be describing Faucon's

photographs. *Elle*'s "ornamental cookery" appears to have a (photographic) "smooth coating." And, all that matte-porcelain smoothness (through "sauces, creams, icing and jellies"[26]) is there to support "ornamentation": "chiselled mushrooms, punctuation of cherries, motifs of carved lemon, shavings of truffle, silver pastilles, arabesques of glacé fruit…a whole rococo cookery (there is a partiality for a pinkish colour)."[27] Like Faucon's worlds, it is a "fairy-land reality", a "dream-like cookery". It comes as no surprise that Faucon has published his own cookbook (more on that later).

Returning to *Première communion*, one notes that the boy made of flesh eats not the body and blood of Christ, but blue and white sugar almonds, which also have the texture and colour of matte porcelain. They look like coloured Easter eggs. This detail holds me, with adolescent madeleine memories of not only the disappointment of my first communion wafer (at age fifteen), but also the pleasure of eating sugar almonds in the darkness of the movie theatre. (As Barthes writes with his own swishy flavour: "I look for *what is going to move me* [when we were children we used to look in the undergrowth for chocolate eggs which had been hidden there]…I wait for the…fragment which will concern me and establish *the meaning for me*."[28]) In the background of this springtime picture, the viewer is blessed with hordes of manikin boys. I spot one overly grown, adolescent manikin-man. But the traditional nuclear family is absent.

Barthes, who has written little on individual photographers, did publish a very short piece on Faucon (*Zoom*, 1978). Barthes' little essay reveals how the ruse of the photograph is akin to the ruse of the manikin: *both* apparently real and not real; *both* infinitely reproducibility; *both* immobile, so as to throw back a series of twice, neither-nor "double fruits."[29] As Barthes writes: Faucon "does not photograph a tableau vivant: he produces a redoubled photograph in tableau vivant: he accumulates two mutually informing immobilities."[30] Spick and span for Faucon (who savours postwar hygiene) and tidily for Barthes (who is excited by the cleanliness of structuralism), when the manikin meets the photograph (as caught in a butterfly net of boyish sensibility) form is content *and* content is form. Maybe Barthes said it best in the aforementioned handwritten note scrawled out to Faucon, so cherished by its receiver: "Your photos are marvellous; for me, it's ontological, if you'll allow this loaded word. The photo is in the limits of its own being: that is the fascination."

Like Pinocchio, Faucon's life-size dolls with unblinking eyes ("even though their gestures could be 'alive', their eyes remain fixed"[31]) are neither dead nor alive, neither awake nor asleep, neither adult nor child. Like Pinocchio, they "excite our imagination because we know they're impossible, requiring us to simulate belief, to play at make-believe."[32] Faucon's teenage dolls (disturbing for their real size, like real adolescents) make a festival

out of the concept of "ni-ni," so as to restore life back into our own static adulthood. The after-life of looking at Faucon's picnics, vacations, snowball fights and other everyday activities, enables us to transgress our own lifelessness. The "vocation" of Faucon's manikins, Barthes notes, "is having had resuscitated:"[33] as is implied by *Les Amis* (Fig. 19, 1978), a *tableau vivant* which suggests that the breathing "real boy" may have once been a manikin himself. Instrumental to Barthes's notion of resuscitation, however, is that Faucon's "little men" appear to hold the magic dust for animating new life into the body of the viewer as well. Faucon's manikins enchant us with childhood, pleasure and erotics, and bring us as viewers back to life. They resuscitate us as if we were Briar Rose being awoken from our 100-year sleep by the just-right kiss of the Prince Faucon. So that we, too, are released from the shop window, the glass box, the snow-white coffin by an adolescent kiss bestowed upon us as viewers by our princely artist. Smack! We too, are delightfully "*dévitrine*"[34] (de-windowed).

As Faucon writes:

> I would hurriedly set up the dummies, and after the shot, pack up and set off again. As they invested those places that bore the mark of my childhood I imagined that those little men freed from their shop-windows, released unknown forces, brought to light sublime, masterful evidence.[35]

The adolescent is a *transgression*, is neither child nor adult, just as the department store window is neither inside nor outside. The etymology of transgress is to "step across" (de-window).

"Curiouser and curiouser," as Alice might say, for the new concept of adolescence rose hand in hand at the end of nineteenth century with the development of the French Department store. In the second half of the nineteenth century, new "iron and glass technology allowed the increases in window size that became essential to modern

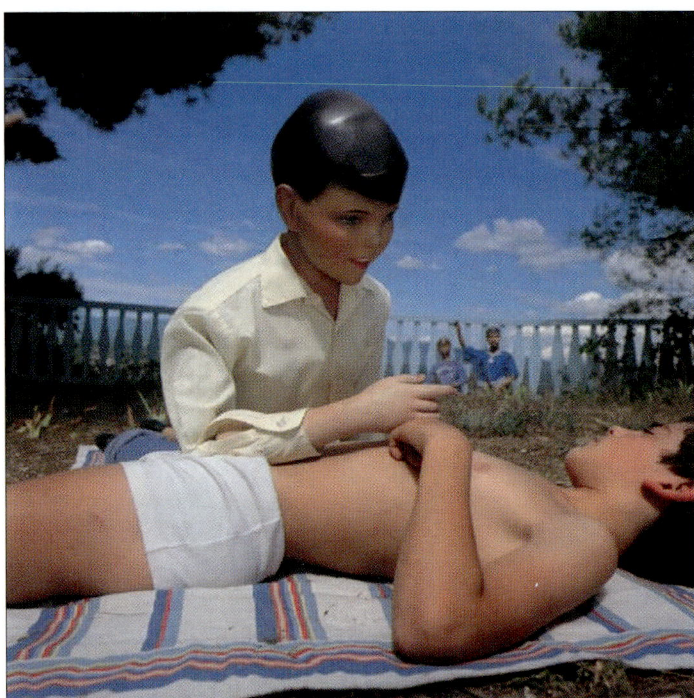

Fig 19 Bernard Faucon, *Les Amis* (1978)

display of merchandise, while improvements in artificial lighting enhanced the theatricality of that display."[36] The *mise en scène* is desirously described by Émile Zola in his *The Ladies' Paradise* (1883). By the end of the twentieth century, we find that the adolescent is most at home cruising the mall, manikins everywhere whetting their desire.

Faucon's manikins manage, in the double stillness of themselves, of photography, of childhood lost, to make a double negative, a fragment of magical time: twice killed, twice treasured. As I learned in high school Algebra I: a double negative makes a positive.

Family Without Famialism

Barthes longed for "*Family without familialism:*" as he wrote above a charming photograph taken of himself as an adolescent alongside his mother and his brother in *Roland Barthes by Roland Barthes*. Faucon made his own family without familialism and took them on vacation as is documented by over 100 photographs in the series entitled *Les Grands vacances*. In these photographs of adolescent boys, seemingly without parents, the few adult-like figures seem to be the same age as the kids around them (not unlike Barthes who always seemed to be "the age of the students in his latest seminar"). They are transgressive families of mostly boys, boys, boys. We can only guess that the one in charge is a happy camp counsellor (as suggested in *Le Dortoir,* 1976) or a delightful androgynous aunt (as suggested in *Collation,* 1978). Some of us were lucky enough to have such an aunt whose devotion and laissez-faire, untroubled, open-mindedness stemmed partly from the lucky fact, at least for the nephews and nieces, that she had no children of her own, making her, perhaps, perpetually adolescent.

Another Alice: Aunt Alice

Barthes was at times mockingly referred to by the students of the Collège de France as being a *tante* (which in French is not only aunt, but is slang for nancy-boy and queer). Yet the androgynous auntie is perhaps the role he most envisioned in his utopian world of family without familialism. Barthes identified himself with his own beloved Aunt Alice, who never married, who gave him the gift of the piano, whose golden necklace is the shimmering, sparkling, twinkling power of *punctum* in *Camera Lucida*.

Alice and Gulliver

In *Roland Barthes by Roland Barthes,* we discover a photograph of his queer little, alone Aunt Alice. She is young and a little boyish. She is suffering as a pre-adolescent: it is all in her hands. Her fingers are twisted, knitted. Perhaps she fears the adolescent growth yet to come, a lot of shrinking and stretching, growing thinner in some places, bigger in others. Aunt Alice is not unlike Lewis Carroll's own Victorian heroine who had good reason to fear all of her shrinking and growing, who at one point becomes as awkward and tall as Ron Mueck's *Ghost* (1998). Mueck's eight-foot tall adolescent, polyester girl is just one foot short of Alice after she ate the cake that spelled out EAT ME in currants and grew to nine feet. Alice never grew as big as Mueck's giant *Boy* (1999). Bigger than a Macy's Thanksgiving Day parade balloon, one would have to measure his giant toenail in handbreadths. Before being unveiled in London's Millennium Dome, *Boy* travelled on a boat along the Thames in his own Christo-like chrysalis.

Likewise, when Alice ate the little-pebbles-turned-cakes, she got much smaller than Mueck's medium-small, thirty-three inch *Pinocchio* (1996), fitted out in his *slip à poché* undies: clean and white as if just pulled off of Faucon's clothesline in a field of lavender.

An interesting aside is the fact that Mueck's parents were toy makers and that he started out as a window dresser. Mueck's kids, like Faucon's, also embody the *de-windowed,* but because of the shifts in scale, they are not *neutral,* not *ni-ni.*

Interesting, also, is the fact that Frank Baum's animated straw Scarecrow, velvety Cowardly Lion and clanking Tin Woodman who inhabit the world Oz seem to have come directly out of the store window.

By 1900, "when…[Baum] sat down to write *The Wizard of Oz,*" he was *also* writing "a treatise entitled 'The Art of Decorating Dry Good Windows', a …[handbook] for would-be window dressers that culminated Baum's brief career as the editor of *The Shop Window.*"[37] Fascinated with the power of manikins in a shop window, one can find among Baum's *de-windowing* American Fairy Tales, "How the Dummy in Mr. Floman's Department Store Window Came to Life."[38]

Likewise I smile like a postwar manikin (before the war they were solemn-faced) at the fact that the famous window-decorator Gene Moore came up with the idea of giving manikins a belly button, bringing them that much closer to being alive, to being de-windowed.[39] According to Moore, who was famously photographed dancing with a manikin: "People recognized the manikins in my windows. Some of the manikins even acquired fans…I admit I once kissed one of my manikins, but I won't tell which. I just wanted to see what it would be like. It was like kissing a desk."[40]

Pupa/Doll

A manikin is a doll and a doll is a pupa. Pupa means not only the stage of life between caterpillar and adult butterfly, but is also Latin for doll.

> 'Who are *YOU?*' said the Caterpillar.

> This was not an encouraging opening for a conversation. Alice replied, rather shyly, 'I—I hardly know, sir, just at present—at

least I know who I *WAS* when I got up this morning, but I think I must have been changed several times since then.'

'What do you mean by that?' said the Caterpillar sternly. 'Explain yourself!'

'I can't explain *MYSELF*, I'm afraid, sir', said Alice, 'because I'm not myself, you see.'

'I don't see,' said the Caterpillar.

'I'm afraid I can't put it more clearly,' Alice replied very politely, 'for I can't understand it myself to begin with; and being so many different sizes in a day is very confusing.

'It isn't,' said the Caterpillar.

'Well, perhaps you haven't found it so yet,' said Alice; 'but when you have to turn into a chrysalis–you will some day, you know–and then after that into a butterfly, I should think you'll feel it a little queer, won't you?'

'Not a bit,' said the Caterpillar.

'Well, perhaps your feelings may be different,' said Alice; 'all I know is, it would feel very queer to *ME*.'

Faucon's *Gulliver* (1979, Figure 20) is an isolated manikin-boy, a doll of sorts, an adolescent content-looking pupa wearing shorts, mauve socks, schoolboy shoes and a creamy, velvety jumper, whose "normal" height is rather joyfully queered and diminished by the red-roofed Tudor-inspired plastic dollhouse behind him and the Los Angeles pool between his legs.

Faucon, as a small child, in search of his own Alicious bottle tagged "DRINK ME", asked if there

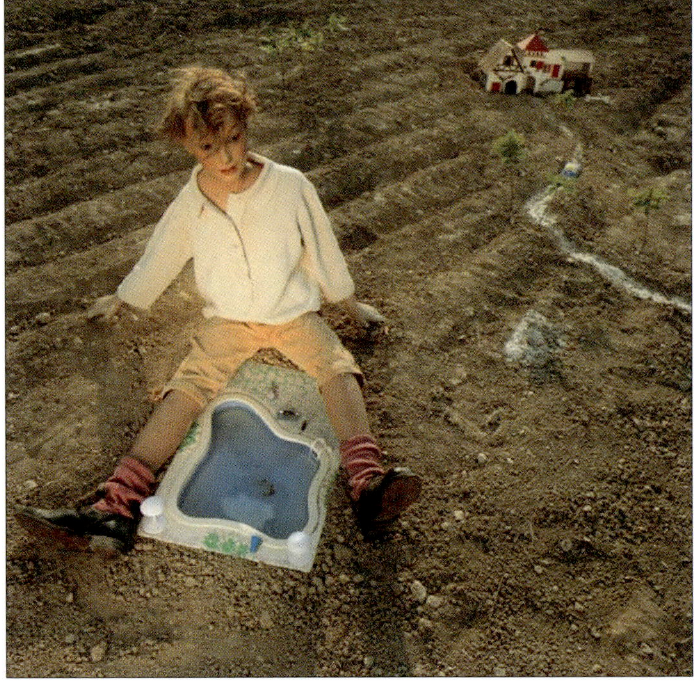

Fig 20 Bernard Faucon, *Gulliver* (1979)

were a medicine that could prevent his growing up. Perhaps that is the explanation behind the strange green drinks that the manikins and the real boy drink in *Diabolo menthe*. The green drink just might have a "sort of mixed flavour of cherry-tart, custard, pine-apple, roast turkey, toffee, and hot buttered toast."

Fils

I think of the work of the reclusive Morton Bartlett, who made his own realistic half-size family for almost three decades from 1936–63. Bartlett lived his entire life alone. His perfectly proportioned fifteen children (ages 8–16), with all the right clothes, mostly girls, were a long time in the making. About one year for each child. Striving for perfection "we know that his source material included anatomy and costume books as well as popular magazine growth charts…he

knitted hats, cardigans and sweaters, embroidered jackets and bags, and meticulously sewed skirts."[41] After dressing them in their handmade clothes and setting them up with props, he photographed them for his own family album. (See, for example, *Sitting Boy*, ca. 1943–63.) It was his secret family, not unlike D.W. Winnicott's, queer, "string boy," who made his own closeted family of bears: carefully sewing trousers for them and treating them like, if not a mother, a wonderful aunt.

In *Les Fils de laine* (1979, Figure 21), Faucon features an elaborate cat's cradle of strings in trees and on the ground, built by little-men (here the *manikins* are 'real'). In an exquisite play on the French word *fils*, which translates as threads or son/male child, Faucon here and through his whole body of photographs has knitted his own boys-only, close-knit family.[42] As a boy, Faucon "tied such a geometry of strings in a tree, with

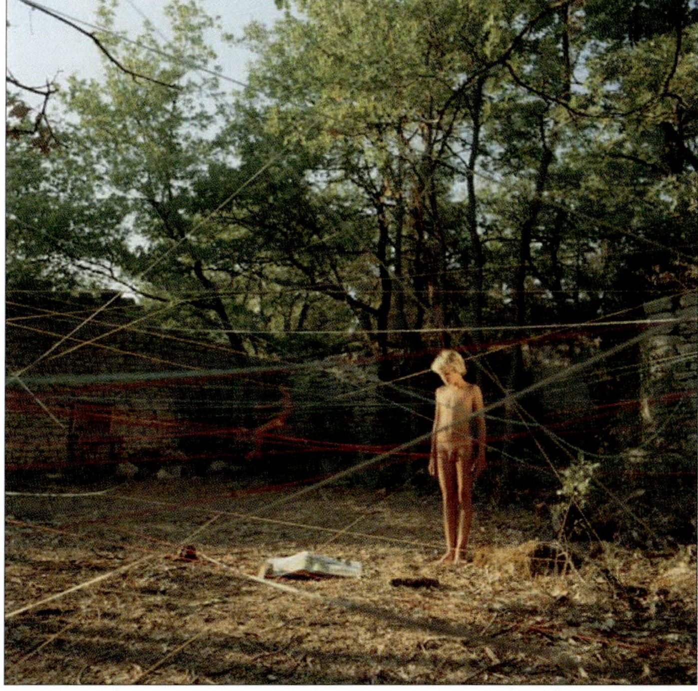

Fig 21 Bernard Faucon, *Les Fils de laine* (1979)

some hope that he might be able to walk among them."[43] Faucon's boyish gesture was a way of knitting writ large, a way of making trees into home, into family: a neither-inside-nor-outside place for *manikins* to be resuscitated.

Bartlett's family "without familialism" was found in 1992, after the artist's death: each "child" wrapped carefully in newspaper and stored in boxes. Bartlett's family stayed in the closet; they never went on holiday like Faucon's manikins.

Faucon often took his manikins to Japan for exhibitions. Today, since Faucon devotes himself entirely to writing and has stopped photographing, the manikins are retired (on permanent holiday) in Kyoto, Japan.

Japan

Faucon's ni-ni approach is a fierce emptiness, which is akin to the same empty-full gastronomy that feeds Barthes's *Empire of Signs* (1970). In the latter, Barthes feeds his ni-ni fantasy of a country that he calls "Japan:" a place neither fictional nor real, neither empty nor full ("which might be more properly called *The Empire of Empty Signs*"[44]). As Edmund White has written:

> If Japan did not exist, Barthes would have had to invent it—not that Japan does exist in *The Empire of Signs*, for Barthes is careful to point out that he is not analyzing the real Japan but rather one of his own devising. In this fictive Japan, there is no terrible innerness as in the West, no soul, no God, no father, no ego, no grandeur, no metaphysics, no "pro-motional fever", and finally no meaning…In Barthes's Japan, Zen is all-important, especially for "that loss of meaning Zen calls satori."[45]

Empty but full is the light of photography in *Camera Lucida* and the light of Japan in *Empire of Signs*. Likewise, Barthes finds *satori* in Faucon's empty, but full, manikins, made doubly full and doubly empty by photography itself. ("Un mot

oriental (japonais) conviendrait mieux: le *satori*.")[46]

As a gay man who did not speak Japanese, Barthes felt protected by the emptiness of signs he experienced in Japan, where there was "nothing to grasp." Barthes's love of his empty (but full) Japan, then, is a mirroring of Faucon's empty (but full) manikins, both of which mirror Barthes' love of the empty (but full) sign of the androgyne. Japan, manikin, androgyne. Barthes' neuter nesting-doll sign play. As Barthes said in his June 3, 1978 lecture from his course on *The Neutral*:

> The androgyne thus is the Neuter, but a Neuter conceived as the complex degree: a mixture, a does, a dialectic, *not* of man and woman (genitality) but of masculine and feminine. Or better yet: the man in *whom* there is feminine, the woman in whom there is masculine.[47]

In the spirit of Stendhal Syndrome (a love-sick swooning for Italy), Barthes Syndrome is a love-sick swooning for Japan: a kind of ephebophilia for a country that he dips in adolescent androgyny.

I can only smile at the fact that Faucon, with his empty but full manikins, is a star in Japan. I smile again at the fact that the Japanese television comedy program, *The Fuccons*, about a stereotyped Kennedy-era American family who comes to live in Japan, was inspired by Bernard Faucon. The television program features still photographs of manikins, who have been de-windowed.

Sugar Babies

As Barthes has written, the photograph and sugar over-fill. Like sugar, the photograph force-feeds sight, fills up space. As Barthes writes in *Camera Lucida*:

> The Photograph is violent: not because it shows violent things, but because on each occasion *it fills the sight by force*, and because in it nothing can be refused or transformed

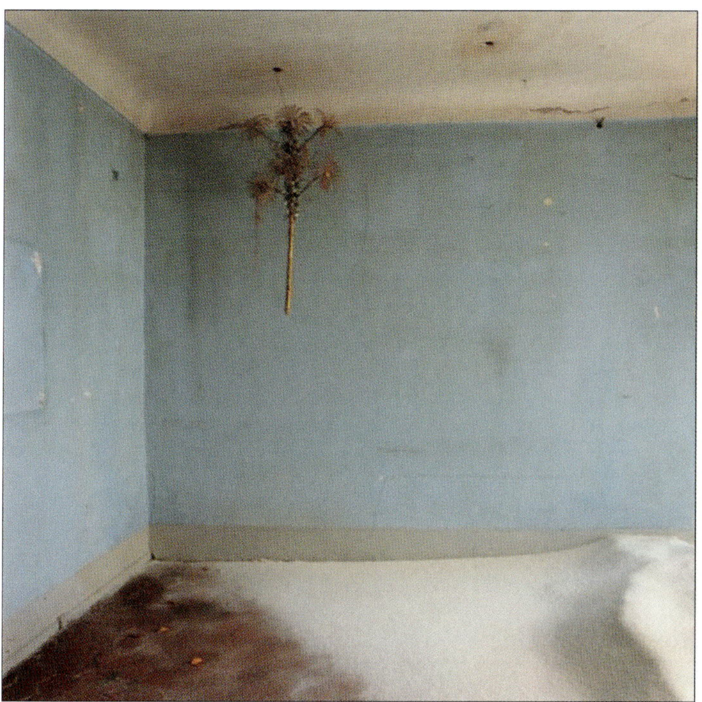

Fig 22 Bernard Faucon, *La Quatorzième chambre d'amour: la tempête de neige* (1984)

(that we can sometimes call it mild does not contradict its violence: many say that sugar is mild, but to me sugar is violent, and I call it so).[48]

Sugar is sweet, but it is the stuff of rotting decay. Sugar, you don't need it, but you desire it. Sugar is neither food, nor not food. Sugar is adolescent.

Faucon has been known to make use of plenty of sugar in his works. Returning to *Gulliver*, our boyish manikin with infinitely sad and sweet velvet eyes, even if made of plastic, we discover that the winding driveway that leads to his Tudor house is made of sugar. In other works by Faucon, the sugar comes in the form of snow, as in his 1985 *La Quatorzième chambre d'amour: la tempête de neige* (Figure 22), a room with its own windswept sugar drift. In the 1978 *Batailles de boules de neige* (Figure 23), we sense the

whiteness as sugar. Here, snow never melts and the manikin-boys, who are wearing shorts, never get cold. Nevertheless, they remain frozen. (Just as Faucon's manikins seem to be always wearing shorts, when I skim through *Roland Barthes by Roland Barthes,* I find that he, too, is most often wearing shorts, shorts, shorts: whether he is a child, an adolescent or the adult writer on holiday.)

In 1996, Faucon made a delicious tree festooned with gooey caramel cocoons, tinselled in translucent sugary filament and called his candyland, crystalline growth *La Naissance du caramel* (Figure 24). In his own cookbook, *Tables d'amis: Vingt-et-un menus de Bernard Faucon* (Figure 25), Faucon tells the reader that as an adolescent he used to thread grapes, which were soaked in caramel, on wooden skewers; he christened his creation as Viennese Brochettes and would sell them on the street.[49] (On the front of the

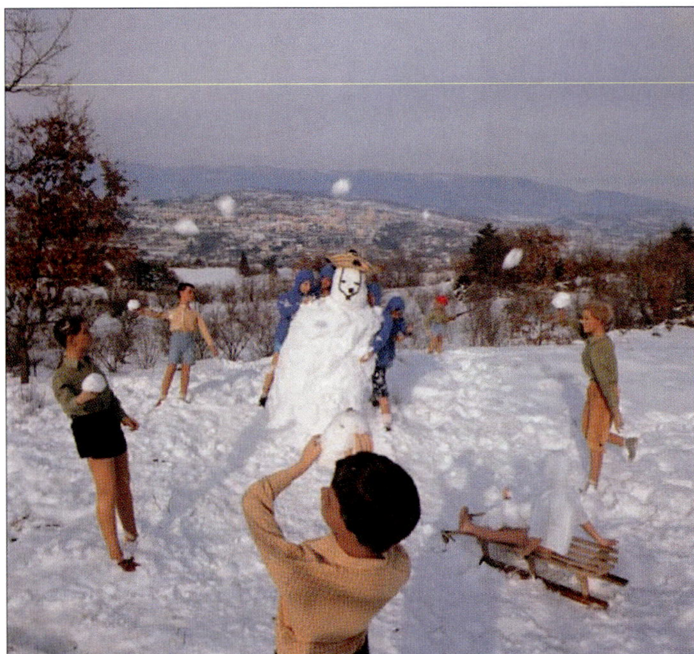

Fig 23 Bernard Faucon, *Batailles de boules de neige* (1978)

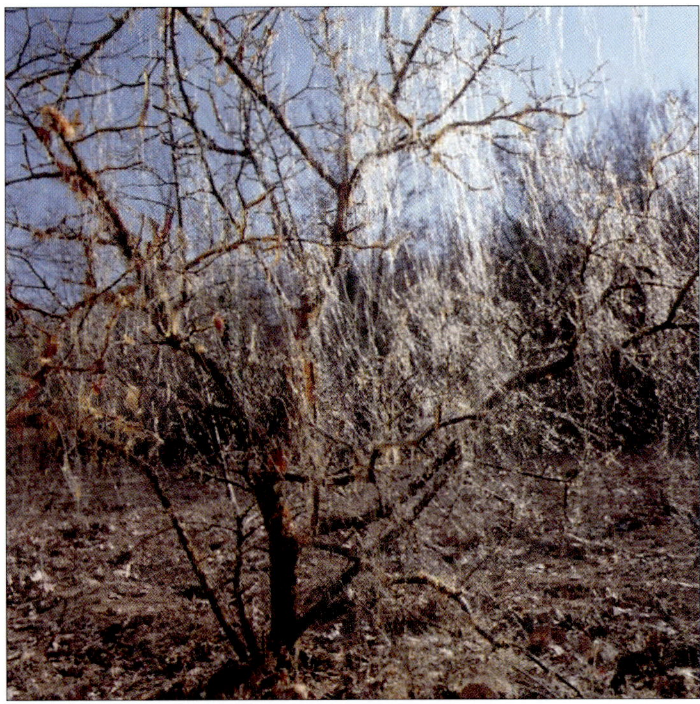

Fig 24 Bernard Faucon,
La Naissance du caramel (1996)

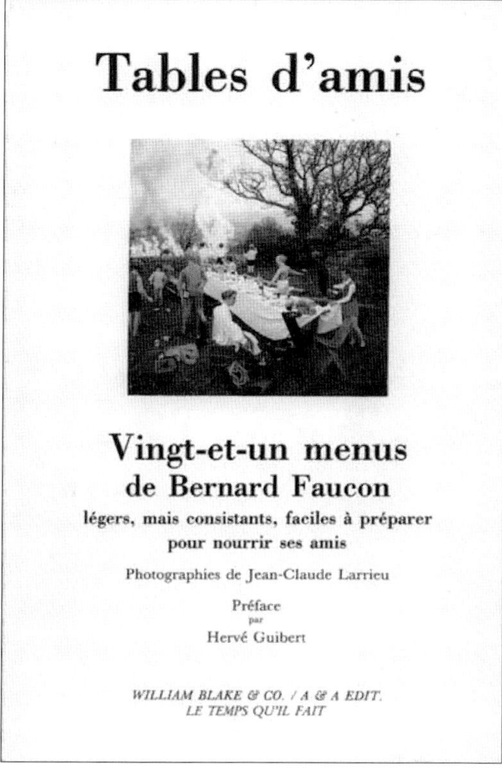

Fig 25 Bernard Faucon's cookbook *Tables d'amis*

cookbook is one of Faucon's most reproduced photographs, *Le Banquet,* 1978, Figure 26.)

Like Barthes, though, Faucon sees sugar as not so innocent. In the photographer's own words:

> Eating candy and cakes is surely above all
> to devour with one's eyes…However, as
> time goes by I am increasingly worried
> about something. Why is it that sugar makes
> dogs go blind? Could there be a mysterious
> relationship between sugar and sight? Could
> the punishment be designed to fit the sin?[50]

It turns out that sugar-as-snow is a perfect ni-ni. For while snow suggests the chilling metaphors of frozen youth and pure white innocence, even cold asceticism, sugar is also the food of

hedonism. By the way, "every day at exactly noon, even if in mid-sentence Morton Bartlett would interrupt whatever he was doing, forge a channel through the often knee-high accumulation of old newspapers, wrappings and every-day debris to make himself a malted milk-shake."[51]

Neutral as Scandal

A student in my seminar has written touchingly about Nabokov's Humbert Humbert, as not so much a pervert as a man wanting to escape the arithmetic of time. (The fact that Nabokov translated *Alice* into Russian is certainly something else that I can smile about.) In the words of Jihye Yang: "The obsession about a pubescent girl is not simply a perverted sexual desire which pursues the radical difference the middle-aged man can never achieve—the youth. Rather it is a fragile, neither-innocent-nor-perverted desire, which our social structure, its ideology and its absurd drama of morality, silently renders as taboo."

For Barthes, scandal moves from great subjects to small ones, with the perverse desire afforded by the neutral. In a passage from his published interview, "Dare to be Lazy," knitting, specifically knitting by a male, not unlike Bartlett's own knitting for his secret family, appears as a public, obscene act of open homosexuality. As you listen keep in mind that "laziness" is perhaps the trope of boyish adolescence:

> Perhaps the most unconventional and thus
> the most literally scandalous thing I ever
> saw in my life—scandalous for the people
> watching, not for me—was a young man
> seated in a subway car in Paris who pulled
> some knitting out of his bag and openly
> began to knit. Everyone felt scandalized, but
> no one said anything.
>
> Now, knitting is the perfect example of
> a manual activity that is minimal, gratuitous,
> without finality, but that still represents a
> beautiful and successful idleness.[52]

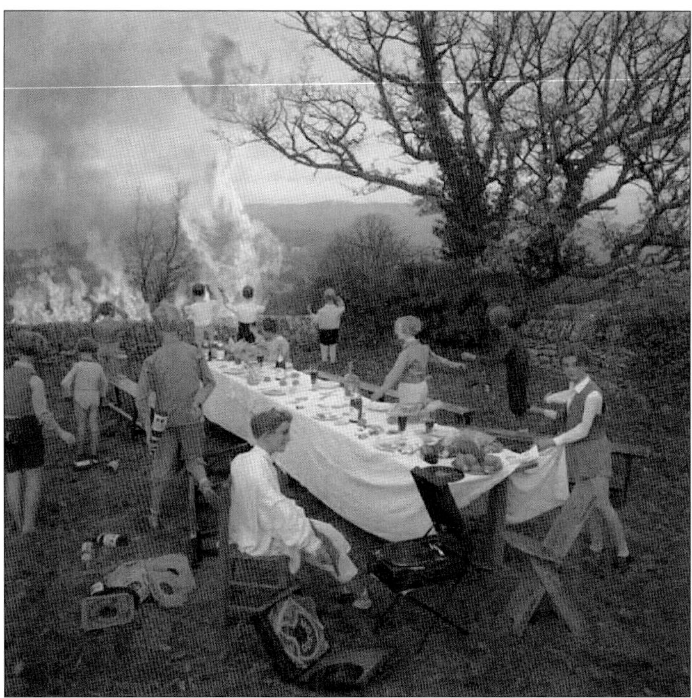

Fig 26 Bernard Faucon *La Banquet* (1978)

For Barthes, both the adolescent and knitting are examples of successful idleness, are performances of the neutral.

Adolescent knitting needles come to the fore in Oz as well.

In the second Oz book, *The Marvellous Land of Oz* (1904), Tip, who has already constructed his own manikin (Jack Pumpkinhead), meets an adolescent girl named Jinjur who is tired of her life of scrubbing floors and churning butter and milking cows. She has assembled a group of like-minded girls, armed with knitting needles. This adolescent "Army of Revolt" has its eyes on consumerism. As if raiding store windows, they take over Oz, turning the gems of the Emerald City wall into rings, bracelets and necklaces. Even the royal treasury is robbed to buy every knitting-needle-carrying girl twelve new gowns.[53]

Pupa

Like in a fairy tale, Faucon's manikins find themselves in sugar snow, wearing shorts, eating cake, drinking sweet green concoctions, sailing away, making movies, building a giant cat's cradle, having a picnic, playing (perhaps prisoner's base) in fields of lavender, escaping the landscape of middle-life, de-windowing the shop window. The view is neither intimate, nor distanced. It is neither inside nor outside. It is the space of being in love as described by Barthes in *A Lover's Discourse*: "The world plays at living behind a glass partition; the world is an aquarium; I see everything close up and yet cut off, made of some other substance."[54] Like Pinocchio, we expect enchantment. We wait for the little manikin-men to come to life. We wait for ourselves to come to life. We adolescently wait for love. "Waiting is an enchantment,"[55] writes Barthes, also in *A*

Lover's Discourse. Likewise, and still immersed in *A Lover's Discourse*, Barthes asks of himself and answers himself: "Am I in love? —Yes, since I am waiting."[56]

As if an adolescent pupa, as if nestled inside, I wait for the moving, the Faucon movie, to take place. "Invisible work of possible affects emerges from a veritable cinematographic cocoon…I appropriate the silkworm's motto *Inclusum labor illustrat;* it is because I am enclosed that I work and glow with all my desire" (Barthes, "On Leaving the Movie Theatre").[57]

The silkworm's cocoon is queer knitted velvet.

Nabokov, author and lepidopterist (he discovered his own blue butterfly), tells of his own adolescent waiting: "I remember as a boy keeping a hawk-moth's pupa in a box for something like seven years, so that I actually finished high school while the thing was asleep—and then finally it hatched…during a journey on a train."[58]

(I see the young Nabokov in Faucon's *Le Départ.*)

******

L'EFFET PAPILLON
Jeu: cherchez le papillon chez Faucon.
Cherchez qui manque dans les chambres.
J'ai compté.
THE BUTTERFLY EFFECT
Play: seek the butterfly at Faucon's place.
Seek who is missing in the bedrooms.
I counted.

Marie Darrieussecq[59]

Notes

1 Rosalind Krauss, "Corpus Delicti," *October,* Volume 33 (Summer, 1985), p. 50.

2 Jean-Luc Monterosso, "Bernard Faucon," in Lynne Warren (ed.), *Encyclopedia of Twentieth Century Photography* (New York and London: Routledge, 2006), p. 491.

3 After stopping photography, Faucon turned to writing.

4 Roland Barthes, *Incidents,* translated by Richard Howard (Berkeley: University of California Press, 1992). The four texts in *Incidents* were controversially published after the death of Barthes in France by *Éditions du Seuil* also under the title of *Incidents* in 1987. Two of the four short texts in *Incidents* had been published before: "The Light of the Sud-Ouest" (*La Lumière de Sud-Ouest*) and "At Le Palace Tonight…" (*Au Palace ce soir…*). The two texts that were written as journal entries, and perhaps were never intended to be published, are: one, a journal that he kept in Morocco from 1969, entitled "Incidents;" and two, an intimate journal form 1979, kept right before his death entitled "Soirées de Paris." The second book publication of journal (or diary) entries by Barthes (also published after his death) is *Journal de deuil, 26 octobre 1977–15 septembre 1979,* texte établi et annoté par Nathalie Léger (Paris: Seuil/Imec, 2009). This collection of over 300 bits of mourning writing was written after his mother's death and the entries were inscribed on slips of quartered pages of typing-paper that Barthes kept in full supply on his desk. At the time of writing this essay, the English translation is due out: Roland Barthes, *Mourning Diary,* translated by Richard Howard (New York: Hill and Wang, 2010).

5 This story of skin is on Bernard Faucon's official and very beautiful website: http://www.bernardfaucon.net/v2/index.php

6 Tzvetan Todorov, "The Last Barthes," translated by Richard Howard, *Critical Inquiry,* 7, No. 3 (Spring, 1981), p. 452.

7 Guy Davenport, "The Illuminations of Bernard Faucon and Anthony Goicolea," *The Georgia Review,* 56, no. 4 (Winter 2002), pp. 972–73.

8 Renu Bora, "Outing Texture," in Eve Kosofsky Sedgwick (ed.), *Novel Gazing: Queer Reading in Fiction* (Durham and London: Duke University Press, 1997), pp. 94–127.

9 Elizabeth Freeman, from the epigraph that begins Bora's "Outing Texture," p. 94.

10 Denis Hollier and Krauss, "Preface," to Roland Barthes, *The Neutral: Lecture Course at the Collège de France (1977–78),* translated by Krauss and Hollier, text established, annotated and presented by Thomas Clerc under the direction of Eric Marty (New York: Columbia University Press, 2005), pp. xiv-xv.

11   See Rosalind E. Krauss, "Yo-yo," in Yve-Alain Bois and Rosalind E. Krauss, *Formless: A User's Guide* (New York: Zone Books, 1999), pp. 219–23.

12   Marina Warner, "Out of an Old Toy Chest," *The Journal of Aesthetic Education,* 43, no. 2, Summer 2009, p. 3.

13   Craig Owens, "Photography *en abyme, October,*" 5 (Summer 1978), p. 75.

14   Owens, p. 75.

15   Thomas Clerc, "Preface", to Roland Barthes's *The Neutral,* p. xxv.

16   Hollier and Krauss, p. xiii.

17   Roland Barthes, *Roland Barthes by Roland Barthes,* translated by Richard Howard (New York: Farrar, Straus and Giroux, 1989), pp. 51-52.

18   Richard Howard, "Remembering Roland Barthes," in *Signs and Culture: Roland Barthes Today,* edited by Steven Ungar and Betty R, McGraw (Iowa City: University of Iowa Press, 1989), p. 35.

19   Barthes, *The Neutral,* p. 86.

20   Davenport, p. 973.

21   Davenport, p. 973. Of interest is the fact that Davenport notes that his perspective is supported by Kristen Ross's study of the new clean postwar, structuralist France. See her fine book: *Fast Cars, Clean Bodies: Decolonization and the Reordering of French Culture* (Cambridge, Massachusetts: MIT, 1996).

22   Davenport, p. 973.

23   Davenport, p. 961.

24   Davenport, p. 961. Emphasis is mine.

25   Roland Barthes, "Ornamental Cookery" in *Mythologies,* selected and Annette Lavers (New York: Hill and Wang, 1972), p. 78. In *Mythologies,* Barthes, of course, has a field day with 1950s postwar culture. His book feature essays that sport 1950s consumerist myths, with titles like "Soap-powders and Detergents," "Operation Margarine," "The Jet-Man," "Toys," "Plastic," "The New Citroën," and the aforementioned "Ornamental Cookery."

26   Barthes, "Ornamental Cookery," p. 78.

27   Barthes, *Mythologies,* p. 78.

28   Roland Barthes, *Sollers Writer,* translated and introduced by Philip Thody (London: The Athlone Press, 1987), p. 77.

29   Roland Barthes, "Bernard Faucon," in *Oeuvres complètes,* Tome V, *1977–1980,* edited by Éric Marty (Paris: Éditions du Seuil, 2002), p. 474. All translations of this text are the author's.

30   Barthes, "Bernard Faucon," pp. 472–74.

31   Barthes, "Bernard Faucon," p. 472.

32   Davenport, p. 963.

33   Barthes, "Bernard Faucon," p. 474.

34   Barthes, "Bernard Faucon," p. 472.

35   The story is told on Faucon's website: http://www.bernardfaucon.net/v2/index.php

36   Kristen Ross, "Introduction: Shopping," Émile Zola's *The Ladies Paradise,* pp. vi-vii.

37   Stuart Culver, "What Mankins Want: *The Wonderful Wizard of Oz* and *The Art of Decorating Dry Goods Windows,*" *Representations* 21 (Winter 1988), p. 97.

38   Culver, "What Manikins Want," p. 108

39   As Moore writes: "I longed for nipples, but I am not responsible for them. Someone else came up with nipples on the breasts of mannequins. The belly button is mine." Gene More and Jay Hyams, *My Time at Tiffany's* (New York: St. Martin's Press, 1990), p. 38.

40   More, p. 40.

41   Lee Kogan, "Folk Art Viewpoint," in Marion Harris (ed.), *Family Found: The Lifetime Obsession of Morton Bartlett* (New York: Gerngross & Company, 2002), p. 34.

42   Davenport, p. 971.

43   Davenport, p. 971.

44   Edmund White, "From Albert Camus to Roland Barthes," *The New York Times,* September 12, 1982, Book Review, sec. 7, p. 1.

45   White, "From Albert Camus to Roland Barthes," p. 1.

46   Barthes, "Bernard Faucon," p. 471.

47   Barthes, *The Neutral,* p. 193.

48   Barthes, *Camera Lucida,* p. 91.

49 Bernard Faucon, *Table d'amis, Vingt-et-un menus de Bernard Faucon*, p. 62,

50 As quoted by Adam D. Weinberg, in his essay "Bernard Faucon," as found in *Cross-References: Sculpture into Photography* (Minneapolis: Walker Art Center, 1987), p. 18.

51 Marion Harris, "Commentary and Acknowledgement: From Prinzhorn to Picasso," in *Family Found*, pp. 17–18.

52 Roland Barthes, "Dare to Be Lazy," in *The Grain of the Voice: Interviews 1962–1980,* translated by Linda Coverdale (Berkeley and Los Angeles: University of California Press, 1991), pp. 340–41

53 Frank Baum, *The Land of Oz* (New York: Ballantine, 1979). See also Stuart Culver, "Growing Up in Oz," *American Literary History,* Vol. 4, no. 4 (Winter 1992), p. 609.

54 Barthes, *A Lover's Discourse, Fragments,* translated by Richard Howard (New York: Hill and Wang, 1978), p. 88.

55 Barthes, *A Lover's Discourse,* p. 38.

56 Barthes, *A Lover's Discourse,* p. 39.

57 Barthes, "On Leaving the Movie Theatre," in *The Rustle of Language,* translated by Richard Howard (New York: Hill and Wang, 1987), p. 346.

58 Vladmir Nabokov, 'From Nabokov's Cornell Lectures, March 1951', in *Nabokov's Butterflies,* new translations from the Russian by Dmitri Nabokov, edited and annotated by Brian Boyd and Robert Michael Pyle (Boston: Beacon Press, 2000), p. 473.

59 From the untitled and very poetic series of fragments that begins Bernard Faucon's *Bernard Faucon* (Paris: Actes Sud, 2005), p. 23. Translation is the author's.

Carol Mavor is Professor of Art History and Visual Studies at the University of Manchester. She has published three books: *Pleasures Taken: Performances of Sexuality and Loss in Victorian Photographs* (Duke UP, 1995); *Becoming: The Photographs of Clementina, Viscountess Hawarden* (Duke UP, 1999); and *Reading Boyishly: J.M. Barrie, Roland Barthes, Jacques Henri Lartigue, Marcel Proust and D.W. Winnicott* (Duke UP, 2007). Her latest book, *Black and Blue: The Bruising Passion of Camera Lucida, La Jetée, Sans Soleil and Hiroshima mon amour* is forthcoming (Duke UP, 2011). Currently, she is completing a series of short essays on the colour blue to be published under the title *Blue Mythologies* (Reaktion, 2011).

A History of Visual Culture

WESTERN CIVILIZATION FROM THE 18TH CENTURY TO TODAY

Edited by
Jane Kromm and Susan Benforado-Bakewell

" The only treatment of visual culture with a broad temporal reach across a range of Western art practices that emphasizes the historical specificity of the visual experience. Very effective."

Kathleen Stewart Howe, Pomona College

A History of Visual Culture is a history of ideas. The recent explosion of interest in visual culture suggests the phenomenon is very recent. But visual culture has a history. Knowledge began to be systematically grounded in observation and display from the Enlightenment. Since then, from the age of industrialisation and colonialism to today's globalised world, visual culture has continued to shape our ways of thinking and of interpreting the world.

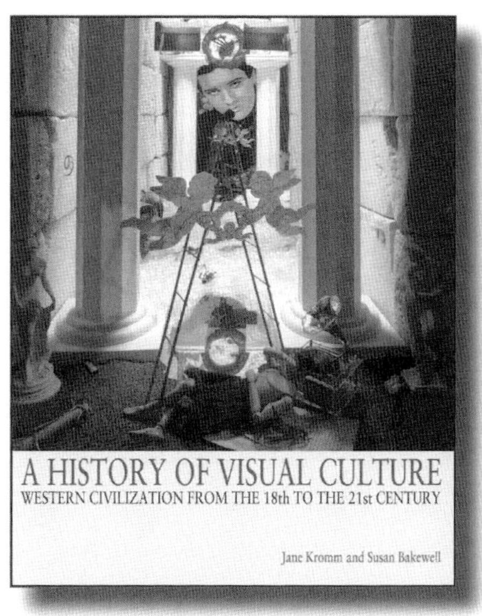

Carefully structured to cover a wide history and geography, *A History of Visual Culture* is divided into themed sections: Revolt and Revolution; Science and Empiricism; Gaze and Spectacle; Acquisition, Display, and Desire; Conquest, Colonialism, and Globalization; Image and Reality; Media and Visual Technologies. Each section presents a carefully selected range of case studies from across the last 250 years, designed to illustrate how all kinds of visual media have shaped our technology, aesthetics, politics and culture.

Photography & Culture

Volume 4—Issue 1
March 2011
pp. 55–72

DOI:
10.2752/175145211X12899905861393

Reprints available directly from the publishers

Photocopying permitted by licence only

Phantasmagoric Places: Local and Global Tensions in the Circulation of Stan Douglas's *Every Building on 100 West Hastings*

Gabrielle Moser

Abstract

Stan Douglas's *Every Building on 100 West Hastings* (2001) represents a seamless panorama of one block of the Downtown Eastside in Vancouver, a neighborhood known as "the poorest postal code in Canada." By documenting the block in detail, *100 West Hastings* functions as critique in its local viewing context by focusing on a discrepancy in the triumphalist narrative of global capitalism; while the rest of Vancouver has recovered from deindustrialization to participate in the global economy, Douglas's image demonstrates that the Downtown Eastside has declined, becoming an anxiety-inducing foil for the city. Despite these local significances, the political impact of the image changes when viewed in other contexts, including London's Serpentine Gallery and the lobby of Toronto's McCarthy-Tétrault law firm. This article charts these divergent readings of the photograph, attending to the ways locale is understood and questioning the limitations of fine art photography as a form of social critique.

Keywords: Stan Douglas, photography, *Every Building on 100 West Hastings*, Downtown Eastside, circulation

Introduction

Stan Douglas's monumental, sixteen-foot long photograph, *Every Building on 100 West Hastings* (2001, Figure 1), represents a seamless panorama of a block of the Downtown Eastside in Vancouver. The neighborhood it depicts is colloquially known as "the poorest postal code in Canada" and is synonymous with the dozens of missing and murdered women from the area, some of whose remains were

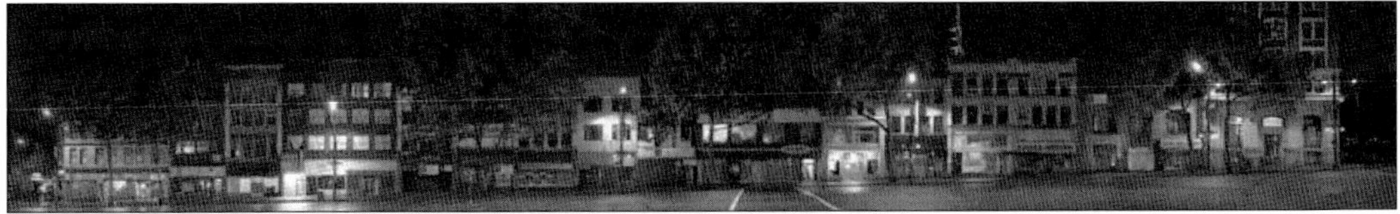

Fig I Stan Douglas, *Every Building on 100 West Hastings*, 2001. Courtesy the artist and David Zwirner, New York.

found on convicted serial killer Robert Pickton's farm.[1] A street that had its heyday during North America's industrial and resource booms of the late nineteenth and early twentieth centuries, West Hastings street has experienced a period of significant economic decline in the past few decades due to a complicated nexus of local and global forces. While the rest of Vancouver has recovered from deindustrialization to participate in the global, service-based economy—its prosperity driven in large part by the booming tech, film and tourism industries along North America's West Coast and by the city's proximity to the Pacific Rim and East Asia trade markets— the Downtown Eastside has, instead, declined, becoming an anxiety-inducing foil for the rest of the city.

On the surface, the decline of the area appears to have occurred in isolation and in contradistinction to the rest of the city's economic success. News and media outlets have therefore linked the Downtown Eastside's current state to causes as divergent as: the globalization of trade and a growing international drug market; the waning of a national welfare state; a shift in the provincial government's priorities from a resource economy to a post-industrial economy; and ongoing civic issues of city planning, law enforcement and the real estate market (O'Brian 2007). While Vancouver's affluent areas continue to succeed in the globalized economy in a process that has seemed to accelerate, the Downtown Eastside has proven resistant to these same forces, resisting gentrification and

redevelopment to pay testament to the unseemly (and therefore largely unrepresented) results of global capitalism: that, while those who have social and cultural capital continue to participate in and benefit from an international economy, those who are unable to participate now constitute a new Third World within the First World (Trinh 1987: 138). Geographers Jeff Sommers and Nick Blomley have gone so far as to argue that the Downtown Eastside operates as a point of contrast for the rest of the city, developing (or devolving) in direct relation to the city's economic prosperity and involvement in globalized trade. They write:

> That which now characterizes the neighbourhood—the open drug market, the deepening poverty and desperation, the run-down streetscape—are products of the same forces which induced the proliferation of condo towers, art galleries, restaurants, cafés, nightclubs, townhouses, heritage neighbourhoods, and inner city middle class consumers. (2002: 53)

Though the Downtown Eastside carries with it a particular set of references for Vancouverites accustomed to seeing it represented in local news media, it is not intelligible in the same way for national and international visitors. In many ways, it looks like some of the "before" images of the world's other downtrodden-neighborhoods-turned-chic, such as London's Soho neighborhood, or the Bowery area of

New York City famously documented by Martha Rosler. But unlike these other cosmopolitan areas, the Downtown Eastside has not reached an "after" stage of gentrification. Indeed, it seems to mark the impossibility of urban gentrification's promises for social amelioration. Much like Douglas's previous series of photographs of Detroit (1998) and subsequent suite of images of Cuba (2005), the *100 West Hastings* photograph depicts a specific locale where the promise of global capitalism and modern progress has gone awry. However, while Detroit and Cuba are sites of generalized poverty and decline caused by large-scale forces such as the collapse of the auto-industry, white flight and communism, the Downtown Eastside is an anomalous, localized version of this underdevelopment. When the city hosted the 2010 Olympic Games, for instance, the discrepancy between the Downtown Eastside and the prosperity of the rest of Vancouver became unmistakable. In particular, the rhetorical construction of the neighborhood as an off-limits "ghetto" for international visitors intensified despite its central location in the city's most affluent and commercially successful neighbourhoods. The Downtown Eastside cannot be obliterated from the urban landscape or the city's mapping system: it is located three blocks east of the downtown core and some of the most expensive housing in the city, two blocks south of the historic Gastown neighbourhood replete with tourist shops and trendy restaurants, and just north of False Creek's rapidly expanding condominium developments. As Sommers and Blomley succinctly argue, "if this place is an isolated ghetto, it must be the most accessible and well-known one in history" (2002: 29). The Downtown Eastside therefore operates locally as a rhetorical and visual discrepancy in the city's larger narrative of the triumph of global capitalism, serving as a persistent reminder of the local flipside of Vancouver's globalized prosperity.

Through its detailed exploration of the streetscape of the Downtown Eastside, Douglas's

100 West Hastings photograph provides evidence of the city's transformation through Vancouver's own particular engagement with the globalization of the economy. In its local viewing context, Douglas's photograph functions as critique by focusing on this discrepancy in the triumphalist narrative of global capitalism. I argue that to recognize *100 West Hastings'* relationship to the discourse on globalization, one must engage these broader issues through Vancouver's particular experience. This means that *100 West Hastings* constructs a paradoxical understanding of place where the material locale is haunted by immaterial and intangible global forces. *100 West Hastings'* street scene pictures a specific place—a "somewhere"—while mimicking processes that occur around the world, simultaneously representing "everywhere" and a kind of existential "nowhere." In the case of *100 West Hastings*, the image's role as a critique of globalization relies on the viewer's ability to identify the urban landscape it pictures, to call up what this space typically looks like in mass media depictions, and to recognize that it might constitute a critical alternative to progressive narratives of global capitalism.[2]

100 West Hastings' critical engagement with discourses of globalization is complicated, however, by the photograph's status as a physical art object that circulates, and is implicated in, the same economic systems it critiques. The photograph's participation in this global art market, as well as the conditions of its production, which borrow the aesthetic strategies and facture of high-end commercial photography and filmmaking, raise questions about the implications of borrowing techniques from dominant forms of representation in order to critique globalization. Does the photograph maintain its critical potential when viewed outside Vancouver? Or is its critical function displaced and negated by a viewing experience constructed through the glossy, aesthetic conventions of commercial film production? This article attempts to answer some of these questions by analyzing how the locale of Douglas's photograph is understood and misunderstood by viewers. As method, this paper follows Douglas's interest in connecting the individual circumstances of local sites to international discourses. By examining the circulation of Douglas's photograph in particular local and international contexts, I draw broader connections between the divergent and conflicting interpretive strategies brought to the image. Paying particular attention to three case studies—the photograph's first public exhibition in London at the Serpentine Gallery, its debut in Vancouver at the Contemporary Art Gallery, and its ongoing presentation in the lobby of Toronto's McCarthy-Tétrault law firm—I argue that the critical dimensions of Douglas's image are subject to the discursive setting in which the photograph is exhibited. Importantly, this susceptibility of the photograph's meaning indicates that the image can elicit readings that reproduce the very mechanisms of globalization—in particular, the homogenization of difference and the elision of specificity—which *100 West Hastings* aims to critique.[3]

"The Worst Block in Vancouver"

Every Building on 100 West Hastings, as its title suggests, depicts every lot on a block of Vancouver's Downtown Eastside. Taken at night and theatrically over-lit, it captures the buildings that occupy the south side of the block of 100 West Hastings in remarkable detail. Completely depopulated, the image calls up documentation of Hollywood film sets and studio constructions of city facades, referencing Vancouver's history as "Hollywood North," an affordable stand-in for American cities in movies and television series. The reference to film production also implies that the site is merely a set: that the "real" action and actors that will lend the scene its specificity and significance have yet to arrive. Hotels, pawnshops and convenience stores are the most common surviving businesses, while six lots are either

for sale or lease by realtor Fred Yuen, hinting at the economic downturn the neighborhood has experienced. Handmade signs in shop windows advertise closing sales, pawnshops offer to "buy, sell, or trade" goods, convenience stores announce ATMs and cheap cigarettes, and two closed circuit cameras surveil the left-hand street corner outside Jaysons Food Market.

Stitched together from twenty-one separate photographs, *100 West Hastings*'s formal composition and impressive scale create an uncomfortable perspectival position for the viewer. Its panoramic format, the only one of its kind in Douglas's photographic oeuvre, references a long history of landscape and geographical survey photography, which was meant to provide an authoritative, all-encompassing viewpoint over the land being depicted. But rather than providing an aesthetically pleasing organizational structure for Douglas's picturing of the Downtown Eastside, the massive scale of the panoramic image forces the viewer's eye to repeatedly skip across the length of the street in search of a resting place. A crosswalk and traffic light, slightly to the right of the centre of the image, offer a possible focal point, but they lead to an unseen destination behind the viewer. This view of the block, which would be impossible to replicate with unaided, natural vision, emphasizes movement across the surface of the photographed streetscape, mimicking Douglas's assertion that the Downtown Eastside is delineated by the "borders in the city which are caused by the movement of economics or people" (in Mackie 2002).

While these visual details provide clues about the block's relationship to its host city, it is actually that which Douglas *does not* picture—the block's residents, the other buildings in the community and the area's social history—that makes *100 West Hastings* a remarkable representation. Douglas's decision to remove the actors and props that might lend the street a specific reading is striking, especially in contrast to its historical precedents. Ed Ruscha's artist book, *Every Building on the Sunset Strip* (1966), in particular, served as the inspiration for both the title and form of Douglas's photograph. *Every Building on 100 West Hastings* was meant to be a direct "knock-off" of Ruscha's photograph, which Douglas created for a "Knock Off"—themed fundraiser for a Vancouver artist-run centre that was formerly housed in the same block (Mackie 2002). Replicating Ruscha's snapshot, "non-art" aesthetic, Douglas used a digital camera to take photographs of the block during daylight hours and roughly assembled the snapshots into a panorama format (Mackie 2002). Though this photograph never circulated outside of the fundraiser (it was purchased by Vancouver curator Scott Watson and hangs in his private collection), Douglas was interested by the results of this project and decided to create a more finished and aesthetically refined version. He returned to the street with his studio assistants from ten in the evening to four in the morning on August 27, 2001, when he blocked off pedestrian and street traffic, lit the block with cinematic lighting and photographed it with his customary, large-format camera set up on a tripod (Mackie 2002). Unlike Ruscha's exercise in depicting the banality of the Sunset Strip, including its pedestrians and car traffic, in snapshots haphazardly taken from a moving car, *100 West Hastings* is instead the result of rigorous aesthetic control and laborious post-production editing.

The erasure of human figures from an economically depressed neighbourhood also recalls Martha Rosler's series *The Bowery in Two Inadequate Descriptive Systems* (1974–75). In Rosler's project, the artist presented depopulated photographs of sites in New York City's impoverished Bowery district alongside a text that listed euphemisms for drunkenness. Just as Rosler's double system of visual and textual descriptions was inadequate for conveying the reality of the lives of the people in the Bowery, Douglas's photograph seems to also be based on the premise that photography cannot be indexical when it comes to representing the lived

experience of the Downtown Eastside. There are, however, important aesthetic differences in Rosler and Douglas's approaches to documenting depopulated cityscapes. While Rosler's project was a direct response to the political inadequacies of social documentary photography and therefore adopted that genre's grainy, minimalist, black and white aesthetic, Douglas's *100 West Hastings* depicts a glossy, richly coloured, almost cinematographic space that is more in line with the formal strategies and concerns of film-making.

100 West Hastings is particularly unsettling to local viewers because of this emptying out of the subjects that usually occupy the sidewalks of the Downtown Eastside streetscape. The people who live and work along 100 West Hastings are often members of marginalized social groups such as the homeless, sex trade workers and drug users who are repeatedly pictured and misrepresented in Vancouver's news media. The neighborhood has not only become synonymous with these issues in public debate, but the Downtown Eastside has also become a hub for community groups, social workers and other services that offer resources for homelessness, addiction and mental health. Douglas's refusal to picture these figures therefore creates an unusual view of 100 West Hastings that is purposefully unfaithful to both popular representations and lived experiences of the landscape.

The location of 100 West Hastings within the city is another important, unrepresented component of Douglas's image. The specificity of the photograph's location is revealed by the work's title, which names the exact address where the photograph was taken.[4] Once designated "the worst block in Vancouver" by the Vancouver Police Department, 100 West Hastings marks the divide between the developed and underdeveloped sections of the city (Sommers and Blomley 2002: 19). One of the most potent markers of this division is the building that once housed Woodward's department store, located directly across the street and behind the viewer

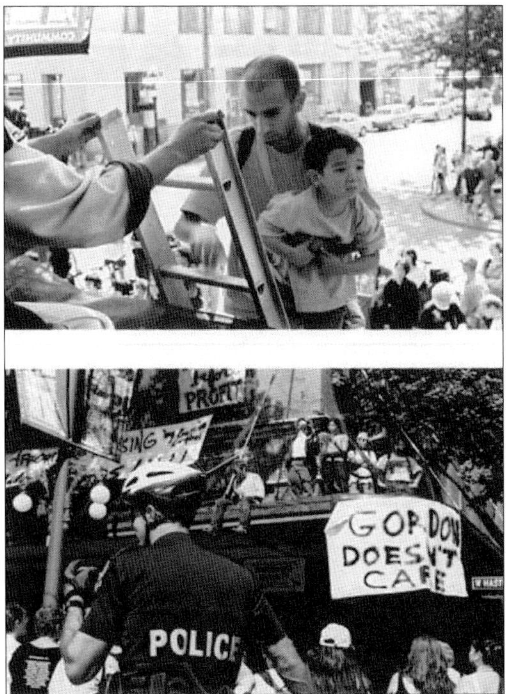

Fig 2 "The Woodsquat," 2002. Photo: Murray Bush, flux photo.

in Douglas's photograph. The store, which closed due to declining business in 1993, has become a highly charged symbol in the ongoing conflict over who owns the physical and intangible rights to the neighbourhood. In 2002, during the planning stages of the Woodward's redevelopment, a public debate between commercial developers aiming to turn the building into condominiums and community groups petitioning for affordable social housing escalated into a four-month live-in staged by squatters on the sidewalk around the building (Figures 2 and 3).

It is difficult to overestimate the impact of the live-in (which became known as the "Woodsquat") on local politics in Vancouver, or the way in which it transformed *Every Building on 100 West Hastings* into a symbol

of this struggle over the built environment in the wake of globalization. Not only did the protest garner significant media attention, but the demonstration also united a variety of countercultural movements—including Olympic Games protestors, advocates for the homeless, and those calling attention to the missing women from the neighbourhood—around one tangible, identifiable issue.[5] More importantly, Woodsquat was successful in resisting some of the seemingly faceless effects of urban gentrification. As a result of the protest, the City of Vancouver relented, agreeing to include both condos and social housing in the renovated building.

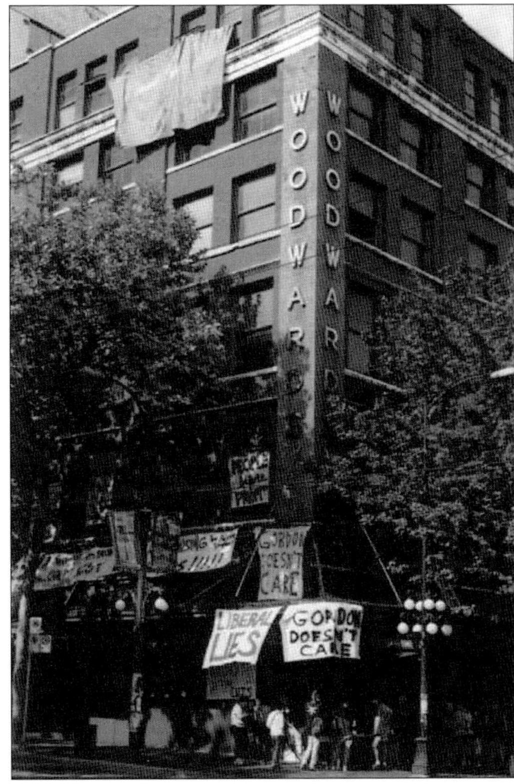

Fig 3 "The Woodsquat," 2002. Photo: Murray Bush, flux photo.

In the meantime, the blocks surrounding the closed department store continued to provide a wide range of social services and, despite ongoing public controversy over its legal and ethical implications, Insite, North America's first supervised injection site for intravenous drug users (Vancouver Coastal Health 2003). Through the squat, then, a local, independently owned department store, forced to close as globalization made suburban "big box" stores and shopping malls more profitable, was rescued from redevelopment as high-end condos and partly transformed into social housing. Though mixed-use housing is by no means an adequate or complete solution to poverty, the Woodward's building, and its neighbouring blocks, represents a site in Vancouver's recent history where local idioms successfully resisted the global forces of gentrification and redevelopment.

With this highly politicized context in mind, I argue that *100 West Hastings* functions as a critique of Vancouver's engagement with the globalized economy for local viewers who can recognize the importance of the place it pictures. This emphasis on the significance of the local context sets Douglas's work apart from photographic production in Vancouver, offering a new strategy for representing place to international art audiences. Douglas's contemporaries in the so-called Vancouver School of photo-conceptualism (an unofficial group of conceptual and post-conceptual photographers including Jeff Wall, Ken Lum, Roy Arden and Ian Wallace) often create large-scale staged and street photography in the same area of the city. But the explicit aim of these representations is to depict scenes in a "non-place": sites that could be anywhere (or nowhere) in a developed, postindustrial, globalized urban landscape.[6] This emphasis on an abstracted "nowhere" setting in the work of the Vancouver School helps to explain its success in the international art market (Wood 2005: 66). Yet *100 West Hastings* reverses this claim by naming the exact

"somewhere" it depicts, implicitly questioning whether a photograph can signify both *somewhere* and *nowhere*, equally and simultaneously: both a distinct, identifiable locale and an abstracted metaphor for a larger global condition.

Rather than prioritizing one local context above all others, Douglas's photograph points to a different conceptualization of place where local and global issues are inextricably linked and decidedly interconnected. Douglas's picturing of the Downtown Eastside reminds viewers that we can no longer disentangle global causes from their local effects, nor distinguish where these causes originated and who is responsible for their repercussions.

Ambiguity and Uncertainty at the Serpentine Gallery

The formal structure of *Every Building on 100 West Hastings* does not immediately disclose its local significance to viewers who are unfamiliar with the social and political history of Vancouver. It is no surprise, then, that when the photograph was exhibited in a public gallery for the first time at London's Serpentine Gallery in 2002, the curatorial team emphasized this "non-place" banality in their interpretations.

Located in the city's Kensington Gardens and free to the public, the Serpentine Gallery's programming focuses on solo exhibitions and small group shows of work by modern and contemporary artists. Displayed alongside nineteen other works, Douglas's photograph was included in the exhibition "Journey into Fear" organized by two resident curators: exhibition organizer Achim Borchardt-Hume and the former chief curator, Lisa G. Corrin (*Stan Douglas: Journey into Fear* 2002: 163). "Journey into Fear" took its name from Douglas's most recent film project, a looping narrative set on a container ship at sea. One of Douglas's now-famous "recombinant narratives" which does not follow a linear progression, the film instead uses a computer system to shuffle the scenes into

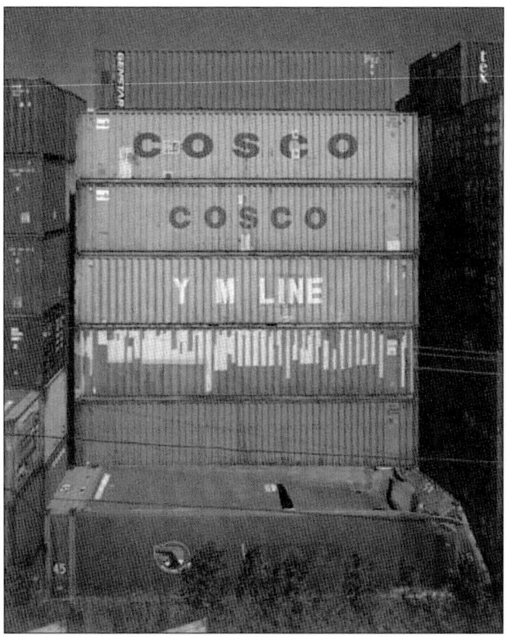

Fig 4 Stan Douglas, *Damaged Containers, Mitchell Island*, 2001. Courtesy the artist and David Zwirner, New York.

endlessly different combinations. The plot follows two characters' argument over the ship's arrival time as it transpires in the pilot's cabin. The male character, Möller, is in charge of safeguarding the ship's containers and wants to delay the arrival of the ship by one day. Due to changing market values, he and his unidentified clients stand to gain US $75 million if the cargo arrives late. Möller is trying to convince Graham, the female character and pilot whose job it is to get the ship to port on time, to delay the ship's arrival. Graham refuses, despite flattery, bribery and eventually death threats, and then exits the cabin. The viewer never finds out who wins the argument, though it is clear through references to American money and Singapore goods that Douglas is alluding to issues of globalization, capitalism, and the shifting ethical implications of speculation and international trade.

Because this was Douglas's first solo exhibition in the UK, and the world premier of *Journey into Fear*, the Serpentine catalogue focuses on the new film and frames Douglas's body of work as a monographic statement from an artist affiliated with Vancouver photoconceptualism; however, the catalog also documents the other works in the show, such as two earlier Douglas films set in Berlin and Detroit, and a series of still colour photographs of sites around these films' settings. This series included four large-scale photographs of Vancouver that were meant to accompany *Journey into Fear* (Figures 4–6), including *100 West Hastings*.

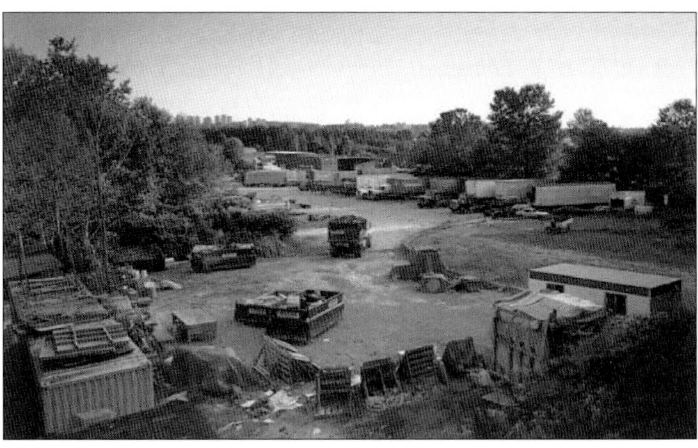

Fig 5 Stan Douglas, *Rookery, Burnaby*, 2001. Courtesy the artist and David Zwirner, New York.

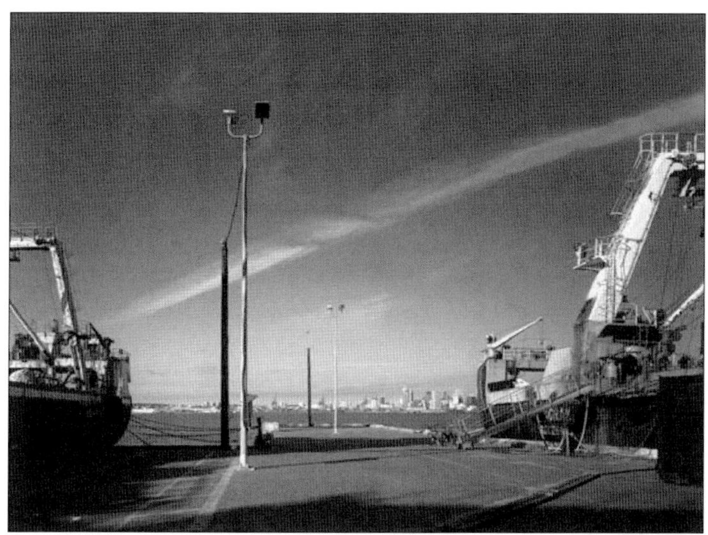

Fig 6 Stan Douglas, *Impounded Fishing Vessels, North Vancouver,* 2001. Courtesy the artist and David Zwirner, New York.

Douglas has produced lush, depopulated photographs to accompany almost every one of his films, and critics and art historians have had difficulty negotiating their role and status in relation to his film work. The general consensus amongst art historians and curators is that Douglas's series of photographs represent a type of research or "site scouting" more common in film production. The Serpentine curator, Achim Borchardt-Hume, takes up a similar line of reasoning in the *Journey into Fear* catalog, describing the photographs in the exhibition as "preliminary site studies" that form the source material for Douglas's films (2002: 10). He argues that the still images in the show document "places whose local histories seem to exemplify monumental shifts in the recent world order: the collapse of Communism [Berlin], the end of the industrial Capitalist era [Detroit], and the rise of globalisation [Vancouver]" (Borchardt-Hume 2002: 8). When Borchardt-Hume moves on to a more detailed discussion of Douglas's *Every Building on 100 West Hastings* (which, at sixteen feet long, is by far the largest image in the show and the only one formatted as a panorama), he

does not miss a beat, continuing to explain that the image represents the globalized nature of contemporary Vancouver: "the cornucopia of shop signs advertising fare from all over the world suggests the effects of global forces converging within a localised situation," he says. "Douglas's Vancouver, then, is a site of transformation, ambiguity and uncertainty" (Borchardt-Hume 2002: 17–18).

There are two problems with Borchardt-Hume's argument: the first is a difficulty that exists in all criticism that positions Douglas's photographs as mere "site scouting" operating at the service of his larger film projects. Although these photographs may document sites that have inspired his final films, Douglas's films are rarely shot on location: they are produced in closed, highly controlled, fabricated sets in a studio.[7] Furthermore, while the act of site scouting implies a hurried and non-aesthetic process of documenting spaces for their artistic use value, Douglas's images are definitely not snapshots. *100 West Hastings* must therefore be examined with the same specificity and eye to detail that is applied to his film work, rather than being relegated to a mode of research or "site scouting." As a tightly controlled image that closely examines the specificity of a particular, locatable streetscape, *100 West Hastings* is not one moment within a larger process of examining a plethora of examples of how globalization affects different cities; it is an image that references the broader issues of globalization that *Journey into Fear* meditates on, but through Vancouver's particular, anomalous engagement with these problems.

The second problem with Borchardt-Hume's argument is his assertion that *Every Building* represents a site of "ambiguity and uncertainty." Set in the Downtown Eastside, Douglas's photograph, as I have outlined, pictures an unambiguous and locatable place in the urban landscape. As urban geographer Nicholas Blomley has pointed out in his book about Vancouver's gentrification process, "the place that is now the Downtown Eastside… has been produced in a complicated and fractured geological layering of material and representational processes" (2004: 32). Although the meanings that are read onto the Downtown Eastside by Vancouver residents may change throughout time, as Blomley's book documents, they are definitely not "ambiguous or uncertain": they are powerful associations that are informed by and rooted in Vancouver's social and political histories.

Catalogs as Instruction Manuals

When the same group of works came to Vancouver to be exhibited in their local context at the Contemporary Art Gallery (CAG) seven months later, the curatorial focus of the "Journey into Fear" exhibition, and its reception, changed drastically. Whereas the Serpentine emphasized the work's relationship to the global forces of capitalism and modernity, the CAG prioritized the local specificity of the image.

Much like the Serpentine, the CAG is a free, centrally located public gallery that focuses on contemporary artistic production. The 2002 exhibition of Douglas's work at the CAG was based on the Serpentine's show, but was re-organized by the gallery's recently hired curator, Reid Shier. Shier chose to present only the works "about Vancouver," which included *Journey into Fear* as well as the suite of four large-scale colour photographs of different locations in Vancouver. Whereas Douglas's work was read by Serpentine viewers as representative of an international artistic development (namely the work of the so-called Vancouver School), at the CAG, the series took on an invigorated local significance for viewers who rarely get to see the work of these photographers in their hometown. Wanting to exhibit the same body of work organized by the Serpentine to a Vancouver public with a different emphasis, the CAG advertised the "Journey into Fear" exhibition by emphasizing the Canadian premiere of Douglas's new film and the "Vancouver set location" photographs. Nonetheless, the catalog that was produced to accompany the exhibition focused exclusively on the photograph *100 West Hastings*. The 100-page volume features a curator's introduction, three commissioned essays on the social and political history of the Downtown Eastside and a pullout, miniature version of Douglas's photograph. Yet the *Every Building on 100 West Hastings* catalog is an unusual monograph in its emphasis on the social and political history of the Downtown Eastside: in fact, only one of the texts, an analysis by artist and art historian Denise Blake Oleksijczuk, directly references the image.

Oleksijczuk tries to place Douglas's photograph within the tradition of documentary photography and brings out similarities between Douglas's photograph and the work of Ruscha and Rosler (2002: 105). Oleksijczuk's essay also points to *100 West Hastings*' relationship to the local issue of the missing and murdered women from the Downtown Eastside when she observes that the "Journey into Fear" exhibition opened at the CAG just six months after Robert Pickton was officially charged with murdering fifteen of these women (2002: 99). Oleksijczuk asserts that the photograph's impact lies in the fact that it forces the viewer into an uncomfortable perspectival position that "demands that we as spectators adopt a staccato-like act of viewing that keeps our eyes moving as if we were engaged in a frantic search for something we have lost." For Oleksijczuk, the things we have "lost" in this landscape are the women who may have ended up on Pickton's farm (2002: 109).

As is clear from this brief survey of the catalog, the focus of the CAG's publication demonstrates a move away from the Serpentine's linking of *100 West Hastings* to Douglas's broader interest in critiquing the effects of globalization, represented by the film *Journey into Fear*, to an attempt to draw out the role this specific photograph plays in the discourses surrounding the local issues of the Downtown Eastside. Advertised as a "monographic publication," the CAG publication used the monograph format to address a specific body of cultural knowledge (Contemporary Art Gallery, n.d.). While monographic publications are usually employed to examine a body of work by one artist in a fine art context, the *Every Building on 100 West Hastings* catalog transfers the "small area" or "single thing" being examined to Douglas's image, which becomes a catalyst for elucidating the local meanings and references in *100 West Hastings* that are entirely specific to Vancouver and which are essential to a full understanding of the photograph's exploration of the globalized city.

Although this socio-historical contextualization of an artist's work is a valid and even established curatorial approach, dedicating an entire exhibition catalogue to one image is not. Yet no one from the CAG explicitly addresses why the gallery felt it was necessary to adopt this strategy. In the "Foreword" to the catalog, CAG director Christina Ritchie observes that, "it rarely happens that an exhibiting institution such as the CAG will focus all of its energy and resources on the

critical exploration and elaboration of a single emblematic work of art" (2002: 8). She then justifies this focus by calling up the "depth and poignancy" of *100 West Hastings*, arguing that the monograph "seems necessary in relation to the artist's remarkable accomplishment" (Ritchie 2002: 8). The CAG's use of the word "poignancy" marks an important shift in the way the political impact of Douglas's image is framed. Common in discussions about the social documentary practices of photographers such as Jacob Riis, "poignancy" invokes a neo-liberal reaction to the "plight" of marginalized groups and communities and evokes a generalized sympathy for the "less fortunate" that works to obscure the specific, racialized and gendered institutional policies and systematic inequalities that create places like Vancouver's Downtown Eastside. While the CAG catalog builds a thorough and convincing case about the specificity and significance of the Downtown Eastside neighbourhood to the photograph and to broader discourses of globalization and gentrification, the way the catalog was promoted and described by the gallery staff, on the contrary, abstracts these subjects and instead focuses on the photograph's general affective qualities.

Explanations from the CAG staff shy away from the image's specific social and political meaning, which is, conversely, exactly what the catalog draws out. This discrepancy between what the gallery *says it is doing* and the work that the catalog *actually does* reveals a slippage that suggests that the CAG catalog was produced as a rebuttal to the Serpentine's reading of the image. The essays in the *Every Building on 100 West Hastings* catalog make what Borchardt-Hume saw as "ambiguous and uncertain," into something emphatic and decided. This prioritization of the social history of the area in the catalog also indicates a desire to somehow re-populate Douglas's image by personalizing the space through a discussion of the lives of the people in the neighborhood. It is a method of augmenting the flow of global capital that the Serpentine's Borchardt-Hume sees in the image with what critic Clint Burnham has termed a flow of "human capital," noting that, "corporate practices are themselves attempts at managing human capital" (2005: 3).

The fact that the CAG's mediation of the image is done in a series of texts in a catalog, which is permanent, portable, and re-readable, rather than on wall panels, is also important; this is not simply contextualization for the viewer, but an instruction manual for other galleries and viewers on how to read this image. This instruction manual format also implies a seemingly paradoxical connection between the local and the global. The CAG's reclamation of *100 West Hastings* as a Vancouver-made image about specific Vancouver issues does not negate other readings of the image by other non-Vancouver publics. Rather, it points to a sense of place in a late capitalist, globalized urban landscape where local and global issues are linked. British sociologist Anthony Giddens perhaps best expresses this relationship between the local and global when he states that:

> in the conditions of modernity, place becomes increasingly *phantasmagoric*: that is to say, locales are thoroughly penetrated by and shaped in terms of social influences quite distant from them. What structures the locale is not simply that which is present on the scene; the 'visible form' of the locale conceals the distanciated relations which determine its nature. (quoted in Wood 1999: 120)

Douglas's picturing of the "phantasmagoric" place that is the Downtown Eastside therefore not only speaks to Vancouver's specific local issues, but also takes a critical stance on the global forces that have created them by depicting a space that has proven resistant to gentrification. The commercial success of the CAG catalog,

now in its second printing, seems to indicate there is a sizeable audience for such a critique.[8] The positive reception of the catalog locally did not go unnoticed by the City of Vancouver, either. When plans for the Woodward's redevelopment were officially released through a report published by Vancouver City Council in 2006, plans for an "interpretive mural" by Douglas that would depict "activity on the ground floor of Woodward's in the mid-1950s, which has been identified as the high-point of retail activity at Woodward's" were announced for the new building's lobby (City of Vancouver 2006: Appendix C, 3). Although no mention is made of why Douglas was chosen to create the mural, the report concludes with a simple statement obviously meant to reference the artist's past experience and suitability for the project: "Stan Douglas created the acclaimed photo-mural [sic], *Every Building on 100 West Hastings*" (City of Vancouver 2006: Appendix C, 4).[9]

By forcefully re-presenting this anomaly in the narrative of global capitalism to viewers, *100 West Hastings*, like many of Douglas's other works, also hints at the yet-to-be-realized radical potential of such a resistance. As anthropologist and art historian James Clifford has explained, with the emergence of feminist and non-Western discourses in contemporary art which offer a radical re-reading of dominant cultural narratives, a new understanding of temporality emerges in which the advancing world system of modernity is not merely challenged or resisted, but rather where new systems and paths through modernity are *produced*. Clifford writes that, in this new paradigm, "[n]on-western [and marginalized] cultural and artistic works are implicated by an interconnected world cultural system without necessarily being swamped by it. Local structures produce *histories* rather than simply yielding to *History*" (1987: 126). The changing curatorial treatments of *100 West Hastings* therefore signal a desire to draw attention to the critical potency of imaging the Downtown Eastside, and, by extension, all urban areas where local idioms produce unique narratives of modernity and globalization in the face of encroaching international patterns.

Appropriation and Implication: *100 West Hastings* as Commodity in the Global Market

If *100 West Hastings*'s critical potential is tied to a recognition of the geographic, social and political space it represents, then how might viewers' interpretations differ when the photograph is seen separately from the Contemporary Art Gallery's catalogue, in the context of the lobby of the McCarthy-Tétrault law firm? The Toronto branch of the law firm, which specializes in business and intellectual property law, purchased an edition of the photograph in 2002 on the advice of their art consultant, Jeanne Parkin, and on the approval of their in-house art collection committee. Their largest purchase to date—both physically and financially—the firm was interested in Douglas's photograph because it fit within an existing collection of predominantly Canadian photography with a strong emphasis on works by the Vancouver School (Jeanne Parkin 2008, pers. comm.). Despite the ways *100 West Hastings* circulated as an effective mode of critique at the Contemporary Art Gallery, Douglas's photograph operates as an example of fine art craftsmanship in the very different, semi-private, corporate setting of a law firm lobby. The content of the image—the fact that the neighborhood pictured is the Downtown Eastside—seems to have been ignored in McCarthy-Tétrault's decision to acquire the photograph. Instead, Brian C. Pel, the head of the art collection committee, emphasized Douglas's incredible skill as a photographer and described the artist's attention to detail in the construction of the photograph, which obscures any evidence of the photographer's presence on the street (Pel 2008, pers.comm.).

The firm's acquisition of Douglas's image seems to have been a success in terms of

aesthetic appeal. While some purchases by the committee had to be returned or relegated to under-used board rooms because of negative reactions by staff and clients, *100 West Hastings* has consistently been displayed in high-traffic areas and has been well-received by visitors and staff.[10] In fact, after a recent re-hanging of the collection, Douglas's image has been given the most prominent place available and hangs just behind the main reception desk in the lobby (Figure 7).

The commercial success and aesthetic appeal of *100 West Hastings* is largely due to Douglas's appropriation of techniques normally used in commercial photography and advertising. In every aspect of the photograph's production, from the total control of the street during photography, to the elaborate digital stitching required to make the image seamless, *100 West Hastings* uses the forms and tactics of dominant commercial forms of representation. As we have seen, the local context of the photograph is so nuanced, specific and uniquely local that, when combined with the image's slick commercial aesthetic, it can be easily overlooked by non-Vancouver publics. Without this context, *100 West Hastings*'s aesthetic seamlessness, monumental scale and dramatic lighting might allow for the consumption of the image in ways that oppose its intended subtext; that is, as a celebratory image of global capitalism that manages to aestheticize even the most unseemly and marginalized spaces of the global marketplace. Without any obvious cues to locate the streetscape as a space of resistance for non-local viewers, *100 West Hastings* becomes unmoored: a placeless locale where Douglas's critique is displaced by aesthetic appreciation.

The artist Tim Lee, working in a generation that has come of age in the wake of Vancouver School photographers like Douglas, wrestles with the conundrum posed by the aesthetic appeal and political polemic of *100 West Hastings* in his essay "Specific Objects and Social Subjects: Industrial Facture and the Production of Polemics

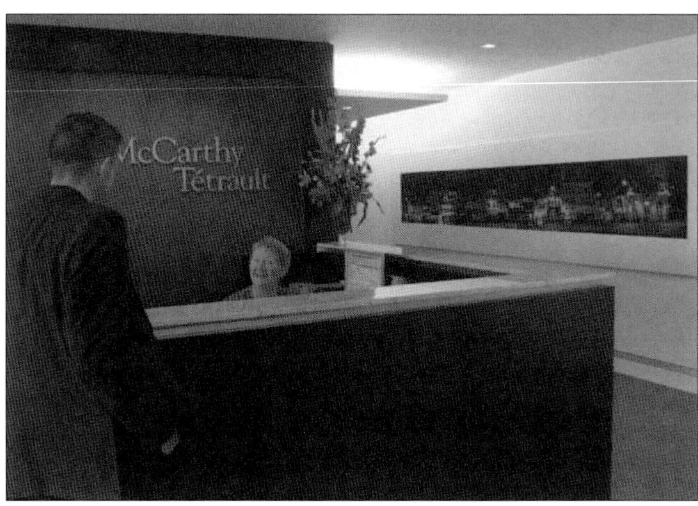

Fig 7 The lobby and reception desk of Toronto's McCarthy-Tétrault law firm. Photo: Brian C. Pel.

in Vancouver" (2007). In it, Lee outlines how Vancouver School images of the city's urban landscape use "a new-found largesse of scale— achieved through large-format commercial techniques—to attach its formalizing will to a painterly rhetoric and an increasingly politicized subjectivity" (2007: 104). For Lee, there is an ideological danger inherent in aestheticizing the poverty and disenfranchisement that have resulted from global capitalism because it risks being misread as a celebration of these forces. Moreover, by manipulating human bodies both physically and digitally, Lee worries such formal strategies might reproduce the conditions of production that are used to maintain this imbalance of power.

The fact that *100 West Hastings* is depopulated and void of human bodies is central in discussions about the critical potential of Douglas's image. On the one hand, we can read the dematerialization of human subjects in the streetscape as a critical mirroring of the active dematerialization of people in the Downtown Eastside; on the other, this depopulation of the landscape is essential to the aestheticization of the streetscape and its appropriation as a high

art image. By presenting an empty landscape, Douglas's image invites viewers to project their own desires onto the photograph. As art historian Abigail Solomon-Godeau argues, "photography communicates affectively, when it does, not because of its truth content, and certainly not by virtue of its explanatory power, but because of its ability to prompt imaginative and transferential projections on the part of the viewer" (1998: 15). This transferral of personal desires and interpretations onto the landscape is particularly problematic when the landscape pictured is the Downtown Eastside, where issues of cultural and literal ownership are central in debates about the future of the neighborhood.

Perhaps more disturbing still is the thought that, for many casual viewers who are pleased with, or overtly benefit from, the effects of globalization and gentrification—surely many contemporary artists and viewers are implicated in these processes—Douglas's photograph might present an empty streetscape ideally suited for redevelopment. Cleaned up and emptied out of the troublesome human figures that could derail the benefits of globalization through demonstrations such as the Woodsquat, the street in *100 West Hastings* is ripe for gentrification, awaiting the next wave of redevelopment and real estate speculation that drives the rest of Vancouver.

Conclusions and Reenactments

Despite the dangers of inviting viewer responses which misread *100 West Hastings* as celebratory of the system it aims to critique, or which invite an affective and aesthetic response at the cost of historical specificity, I believe that Douglas's image might covertly operate as a social document with political potency while disguised as a spectacular and aesthetic panorama. While the public gallery viewers in Vancouver have the semiotic vocabulary and collective visual bank to be able to read *100 West Hastings* as a critique of local politics, and viewers at McCarthy-Tétrault do not, this discrepancy between readings does not necessarily de-value the photograph's critical function. Since the photograph's critique is founded on the viewer's ability to recognize the interrelationship between the rise of corporate and private culture, through the globalization of capitalism, and the decline of marginal and street cultures in areas like the Downtown Eastside, perhaps the lobby of a corporate law firm is one of the most effective settings in which to encounter *100 West Hastings*. In a strange irony, the acquisition and display of private property, in this case Douglas's photograph, intensifies *100 West Hastings*'s demonstration to viewers that the social promises of urban gentrification and global capitalism are impossible to achieve.

The divergent interpretations brought to the photograph and its dialectical movement within the discourses around the effects of globalization seem to indicate that the recent history of global capitalism is still being negotiated and re-written and that the homogenization of difference and the elision of specificity are not necessarily inevitable. Rather, *100 West Hastings*'s circulation and reception seem to reveal that there continue to be opportunities for local structures to produce new, effective histories within the larger history of the triumph of global capitalism.

A similar conclusion is reached by Tim Lee, who argues that visual cues in *100 West Hastings* allow the photograph simultaneously to signify aesthetic appeal and political polemic. For Lee, the very format of Douglas's photograph—its seamless construction, erasure of the human figures and obfuscation of any evidence of the artist's presence—can be interpreted as a critical practice of exaggeration or over-identification with dominant forms of representation: an exaggeration meant to alert the viewer to similar ideological processes that drive global capitalism locally and internationally (2007: 110). By following a commercially inspired system of seamless representation and exaggerating it "in the hopes of revealing its duplicity," Douglas's image therefore draws attention to "an influx of disturbing processes…by making a spectacle of it" (Lee 2007: 107).

Acknowledgments

The author wishes to thank Sarah Parsons, Richard Hill, Sharla Sava, Dan Adler, Cait McKinney and the Toronto Photography Seminar for their feedback on early drafts of this paper, and the two anonymous reviewers for their helpful suggestions. This project was generously supported by the Social Sciences and Humanities Research Council of Canada.

Notes

1 Port Coquitlam, British Columbia resident Robert Pickton made international headlines when he was arrested, charged and tried for the second-degree murders of six women who had gone missing from Vancouver's Downtown Eastside. He is currently serving a life sentence for these murders, and is suspected in another twenty-seven deaths. See "Pickton gets maximum sentence for murders," CBC News website, http://www.cbc.ca/canada/british-columbia/story/2007/12/11/bc-picktonsentencing.html, accessed July 12, 2010.

2　I use the term "global capitalism" throughout this essay to describe current conditions of economic globalization which have seen Western countries move towards a service-based, exchange economy while the global South has become the centre of manufacturing and resource extraction. Importantly, the term "global capitalism" is used by several Marxist theorists to understand globalization as "a new stage in the evolving world capitalist system that came into being some five centuries ago" (Robinson 2004: 2).

3　My interest in examining *100 West Hastings* arose from my experiences living in East Vancouver and working in a government-subsidized childcare program in the Downtown Eastside while studying contemporary art at a Westside university. In my studies in art history at the University of British Columbia and my volunteer work in the public programming department at the Vancouver Art Gallery, the discussions I had with viewers about Douglas's photograph were consistently informed by our lived experiences of the place he pictures. When I moved to Toronto, however, I found that this local context for Douglas's work, and the work of other so-called Vancouver School photographers, was not part of the discourse around these images. The issue of how this kind of situated knowledge, as Donna Haraway terms it, might be translated through visual representations is one of my key concerns as a writer, researcher and curator.

4　It is important here to note that Vancouver's street numbering system is unusually uniform, with each block using a range of 100 numbers that ascend as one travels east or west of Ontario Street (Vancouver's east-west divide). The building at the easternmost corner of the 100 block of West Hastings, for instance, would be 100 West Hastings, while the westernmost building would be 199 West Hastings, with 200 West Hastings continuing on the following block. Block numbers in Vancouver therefore immediately communicate to residents where a building is located in the city's grid system.

5　*West Coast LINE*, a quarterly journal published out of Simon Fraser University, devoted their Fall 2003 issue to a detailed investigation of the context and repercussions of the Woodsquat that provides an excellent account of the demonstration (see Woodsquat. 2003–04. Aaron Vidaver, guest ed., *West Coast LINE*, no. 41/42, 37/2-3, Fall/Winter 2003/04).

6　See Trevor Mahovsky's discussion of non-place in the work of Vancouver artists in "Radical, bureaucratic, melancholic, schizophrenic: texts as community," *Canadian Art*, vol. 18, issue 2 (Summer 2001), pp. 50–56; and Marina Roy's "Adventures in Reading Landscape" in *Vancouver Art and Economies*, Melanie O'Brian, ed., Vancouver: Arsenal Pulp Press/Artspeak, 2007, pp. 69–94.

7　Of Douglas's major film works, only three—*Nut'ka* (1996), *Klatsassin* (2006) and segments of *Vidéo* (2008)—were shot out-of-doors. The rest, including *Der Sandmann* (1995), *Win, Place or Show* (1998), *Journey into Fear* (2001), *Suspiria* (2003), and *Inconsolable Memories* (2005) were filmed on closed, fabricated studio sets.

8　See, for instance, Jill Mandrake's review, "A block unknown," *The Peak: Simon Fraser University's Independent Student Newspaper*, issue 13, vol. 113 (March 31, 2003), no page numbers; and Robin Laurence, "Settling into Unsettling Images," *The Georgia Straight*, Sept 19–26, 2002, p. 110.

9　The photograph Douglas ultimately created for the Woodward's commission, *Abbott and Cordova, 7 August 1971* (2008), depicts actors restaging the 1971 Gastown Riots: a violent clash between Vancouver hippies demonstrating against a string of drug arrests and city police, some of whom had infiltrated the otherwise peaceful protest undercover in an effort to stop the demonstration. The incident, which occurred on the street corner of the Woodward's building only one block north of 100 West Hastings, has been obscured from the city's official history, with Vancouver police frequently denying their involvement in the violence. When the image was recently installed in the newly developed Woodward's building, the public and police reactions to it demonstrated that the event remains an important and contested part of Vancouver's local history. It is, arguably, the first time Douglas has used staged human subjects in his photographs and is likely not what the City or developers expected when they commissioned the image. See Fiona Morrow, "A night to remember (or forget)," *The Globe and Mail*, Thursday, October 30, 2008; Mary Frances Hill, "Beyond the lens, starkly," *Vancouver Sun*, Sunday, November 1, 2008; and Shaun Dacey, "The Gastown Riot as public art," *The Tyee*, February 17, 2010.

10 Pel noted that a work by General Idea and a
    sculpture by David Morris both had to be returned
    to their dealers' galleries because of negative staff
    reactions, while a series of photo collages by Ian
    Wallace has been hung in the smallest board room
    of the firm because it is not a favorite among staff
    and clients (Brian C. Pel, unpublished interview with
    author).

Gabrielle Moser is a critic, curator and PhD
student studying art history and visual culture
at York University. Her writing has appeared
in *ARTNews*, *Canadian Art*, *C magazine*, *esse*,
Fillip, *Invisible Culture* and in Gallery 44's
book *Emergence: Contemporary Photography
in Canada*. Her current research focuses on
the circulation and reception of a series of
photographic slide lectures designed by the
British government to educate English and
colonial schoolchildren about the Empire at the
beginning of the twentieth century

References

Blomley, N. 2004. Property and the Landscapes of
Gentrification. *Unsettling the City*. New York: Routledge:
29–74.

Borchardt-Hume, A. 2002. *Journey into Fear.* An
Introduction. In *Stan Douglas: Journey into Fear*
(exhibition catalogue). London: Serpentine Gallery, pp.
7–18.

Burnham, C. 2005. No Art After Pickton. *Fillip* 1 (1): 1–3.

CBC News, 2007. *Pickton Gets Maximum Sentence for
Murders*. Available at http://www.cbc.ca/canada/british-
columbia/story/2007/12/11/bc-picktonsentencing.html
(accessed July 12, 2010).

City of Vancouver Administrative Report: Woodward's
Heritage Revitalization Agreement - 101 West Hastings
Street (100 West Cordova Street) DE 409942, 2006.
Prepared by Gerry McGeough for the Vancouver City
Council, March 8, 2006.

Clifford, J. 1987. Of Other Peoples: Beyond the
'Salvage' Paradigm. In Hal Foster (ed.), *Discussions
in Contemporary Culture, number 1*. Seattle: Dia Art
Foundation/Bay Press, pp. 121–30.

Contemporary Art Gallery 2002. *Every Building on 100
West Hastings*. Reid Shier, ed. Vancouver: Arsenal Pulp
Press/Contemporary Art Gallery.

Contemporary Art Gallery, n.d. Stan Douglas, *Journey
into Fear*. [Press release].

Dacey, S. 2010. The Gastown Riot as Public Art. *The
Tyee*, February 17, 2010.

Hill, M. F. 2008. Beyond the Lens, Starkly. *The Vancouver
Sun*, Sunday, November 1, 2008.

Laurence, R. 2002. Settling Into Unsettling Images. *The
Georgia Straight*, Sept 19–26, 2002: 110.

Lee, T. 2007. Specific Objects and Social Subjects:
Industrial Facture and the Production of Polemics in
Vancouver. In Melanie O'Brian (ed.), *Vancouver Art and
Economies*. Vancouver: Arsenal Pulp Press/Artspeak, pp.
97–125.

Mackie, J. 2002. Journey into Fear illuminates 100-Block
West Hastings. *The Vancouver Sun*, September 16: B4.

Mahovsky, T. 2001. Radical, Bureaucratic, Melancholic,
Schizophrenic: Texts as Community. *Canadian Art*, 18 (2):
50–6.

Mandrake, J. 2003. A Block Unknown. *The Peak: Simon
Fraser University's Independent Student Newspaper*, 13
(113) no page numbers.

Morrow, F. 2008. A Night to Remember (or Forget).
The Globe and Mail, Thursday, October 30, 2008.

O'Brian, M. 2007. Introduction: Specious Speculation.
In Melanie O'Brian (ed.), *Vancouver Art and Economies*.
Vancouver: Artspeak/Arsenal Pulp Press, pp. 11–26.

Oleksijczuk, D. 2002. "Haunted Spaces." *Every Building on
100 West Hastings*. Reid Shier, ed. Vancouver: Arsenal
Pulp Press/Contemporary Art Gallery, pp. 97–117.

Ritchie, C. 2002. Foreword and Acknowledgements.
Every Building on 100 West Hastings. Vancouver:
Contemporary Art Gallery, 2002, pp. 8–9.

Robinson, W. I. 2004. *A Theory of Global Capitalism:
Production, Class, and State in a Transnational World*.
Baltimore, MD: The Johns Hopkins University Press.

Roy, M. 2007. Adventures in Reading Landscape. In
Melanie O'Brian (ed.), *Vancouver Art and Economies*.
Vancouver: Artspeak/Arsenal Pulp Press, pp.
69–94.

Smith, N. and Derksen, J. 2002. Urban Regeneration: Gentrification as Global Urban Strategy. *Every Building on 100 West Hastings*. Vancouver: Contemporary Art Gallery, pp. 63–92.

Solomon-Godeau, A. 1998. Mourning or Melancholia: Christian Boltanski's *Missing House*. *Oxford Art Journal*, 21 (2): 3–20.

Sommers, J. and Blomley, N. 2002. "The Worst Block in Vancouver." *Every Building on 100 West Hastings*. Vancouver: Contemporary Art Gallery, pp. 19–58.

Stan Douglas: Journey into Fear, 2002. Exhibition catalogue. London: Serpentine Gallery.

Trinh, T. Minh-Ha. 1987. Of Other Peoples: Beyond the "Salvage" Paradigm. In Hal Foster (ed.), *Discussions in Contemporary Culture: Number One*. Seattle: Bay Press, Dia Art Foundation, pp. 138–41.

Vancouver Coastal Health 2003. *Supervised Injection Site – Insite*. Available at http://supervisedinjection.vch.ca/ (accessed July 13, 2010).

Wood, W. 1999. Secret Work. In *Stan Douglas* (exhibition catalogue). Vancouver: Vancouver Art Gallery, pp. 107–20.

Wood, W. 2005. The Insufficiency of the World. In Dieter Roelstrate and Scott Watson (eds.). *INTERTIDAL: Vancouver Art and Artists*. Antwerp: Museum van Hedendaagse Kunst Antwerpen, pp. 63–76.

"Woodsquat," 2003–04. Aaron Vidaver (guest ed.), *West Coast LINE*, 41/42 (37/2-3).

Photography & Culture

Volume 4—Issue 1
March 2011
pp. 73–76
DOI:
10.2752/175145211X12899905861438

On Saturday Afternoons in 1963[1]

Simon Watney

"Years May Go By"

We are in Manhattan and the year is 1963, or thereabouts. A boy in a Sputnik-era sweater is looking out in profile from a Chelsea rooftop with the Empire State Building far behind him, many blocks uptown and to the east and half shrouded in mist. His hair is greased back in the then fashionable bouffant quiff of early rock-and-roll stars such as Ricky Sands and Ricky Nelson, and actors including Rock Hudson. It is a look which is still much imitated by later rockabillies. He looks to be about eighteen and has the preppy good looks of many of the younger stars of popular contemporary American TV shows such as 77 *Sunset Strip*, and indeed he rather resembles the actor Edd Byrnes who played the role of the painfully hip character Kookie from 1958 to 1964, albeit in a much more wistful minor key. Just visible on the third finger of his left hand is what looks like a High School class ring, big and shiny. Behind him on the left is a generic water-tower with the stenciled text "Ardin For Manhattan" and a distant hoarding advertises a used car branch of the Knickerbocker Ford company—knickerbocker being a generic term for New Yorkers of Dutch descent, and indeed for New Yorkers in general. Not, of course, that we know where he came from, only where he'd arrived. He is staring straight ahead, and he looks very sweet and vulnerable and young, though this is partly the composite effect of another photograph I also own of him taken just a few feet to the left and only moments earlier or perhaps later, in which he's wearing a skimpy cheap-looking pin-striped jacket with wide lapels. He's not a rich kid.

"So Hold on to Your Special Friend"

It would be difficult to exaggerate the glamour exerted by the idea of New York in my suburban London childhood and adolescence, maybe five or six years younger than him, and long before Sir Freddie Laker's enterprising low-cost Skytrain flights arrived on the scene in 1977, making America easily accessible even to council estate boys like me. I bought both photographs at a shop called "Gay Treasures" which for a decade or more was at 546 Hudson Street between Charles and Perry in Greenwich Village from some

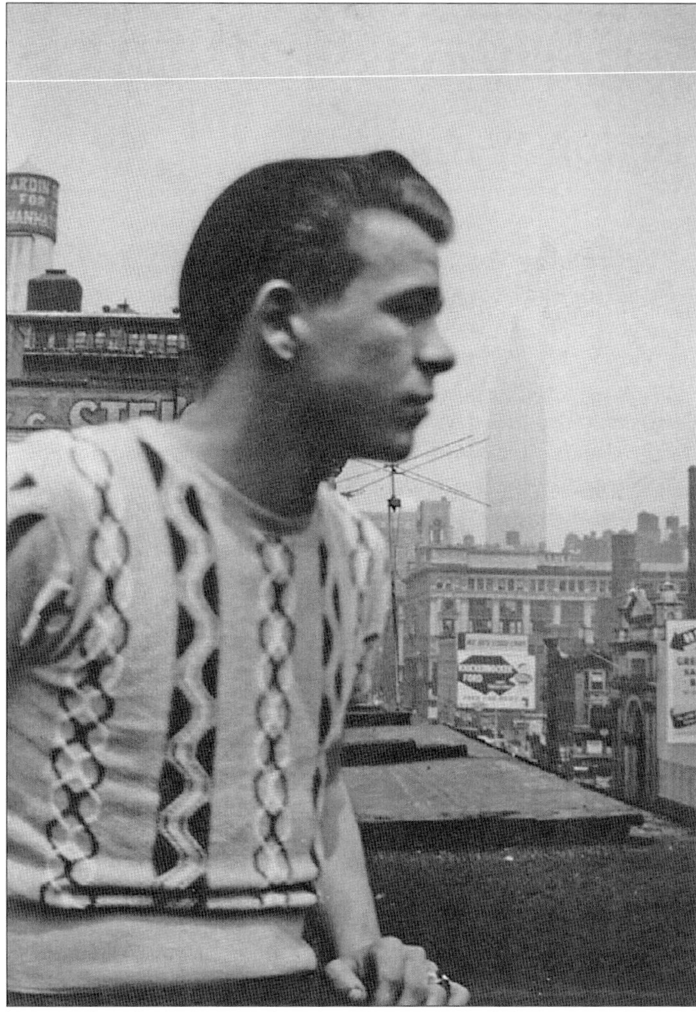

Fig I New York, c. 1963, anon.
7.7 x 11.4 cms. Private Collection.

time in the 1980s onwards. I think there was also another branch in San Francisco. Anyway, as the name suggests it was a store which specialized in vintage gay erotica, with huge stocks of old American photo magazines with titles such as "Grecian Guild Pictorial", "Star Models", "Male Classics" and most famously "Physique Pictorial" which was published by Bob Mizer—the Diaghilev of post-war US gay erotica. They also sold good prints by studio photographers such as Bruce

of Los Angeles, which were originally marketed by mail to collectors from named model-based catalogs. To a greater or lesser extent these all reflected the impact of harsh obscenity legislation in their style and lay-out, delightfully (to our jaded eyes) camouflaging homosexual desire amid the *papier-mâché* props of classical antiquity, cowboy movies, and other foundational legitimizing visual myths of mainstream American identity, thereby simultaneously slyly acknowledging and outwitting censorship, and enabling them to be sent legally via the US postal system.

There were also racks of single photos classified by size and price, extending as the 1980s drew on into a vast array. They only cost one or two dollars and I bought lots, both for myself but also for my older friend Derek Jarman who used many in his collage pictures over the years. Comparatively few were commercially produced and it took me a while to realize that this growing flood of available photographs had another darker, sadder significance. Wandering around Manhattan in the mid-eighties one got used to the increasing sight of great heaps of people's belongings slung out on the street, and as the decade wore on it was increasingly obvious that a high proportion of this social detritus was not simply stuff being chucked out by people casually editing down their possessions as they moved between apartments, but was on the contrary one outward and visible register of lives cut short before the luxury of any such voluntary editing could ever have taken place. The swelling racks of old photographs for sale at "Gay Treasures" provided a still more poignant reflection of the lives of those who had not lived to edit their own histories, and whose anonymous photo albums

had simply ended up here for sale, as HIV swept through the city, leaving this tide of photographic flotsam in its wake, whilst countless more albums doubtless went up in smoke. Needless to say I have no idea who the boy in the photograph was, or possibly still is. He looks incredibly young to me now, but then after all these years so do almost all my New York friends who died before the availability of anti-retroviral drugs in the early 1990s, the drugs that now keep me alive, and able to age, if not gracefully. I hope my boy in his Sputnik-era sweater with his Chet Baker looks was spared the ghastly fate of so many of his now largely forgotten generation of young long-since-dead gay men. He was just the kind of boy I first went to America to find, and now I could be his grandfather. "Years may go by"…

Notes

1 Rickie Lee Jones, On Saturday Afternoons in 1963, 1979.

Simon Watney is a widely published independent critic and art historian who writes regularly in The Burlington Magazine and The Art Newspaper. He currently teaches part-time at the University for the Creative Arts (UCA) at Farnham, Surrey.

Photography
The Key Concepts

David Bate

Since its introduction nearly 200 years ago, photography has become part of everyday life, a position consolidated by the recent development of digital imaging and manipulation. Used to confirm identity, to sell products, to reshape the real, to visualize the news, to record and communicate the personal moment, and as an art form in its own right, photography is now one of the most accessible and pervasive of media.

Photography: The Key Concepts provides an ideal guide to the place of photography in our society and to the extraordinary range of photographic genres. Outlining the history of photography and explaining the body of theory which has built up around its use, the book guides the reader through the genres of documentary, portraiture, landscape, still life, art and global photography. Illustrated with a range of historical and contemporary images and case material, this book is essential reading for anyone interested in photography.

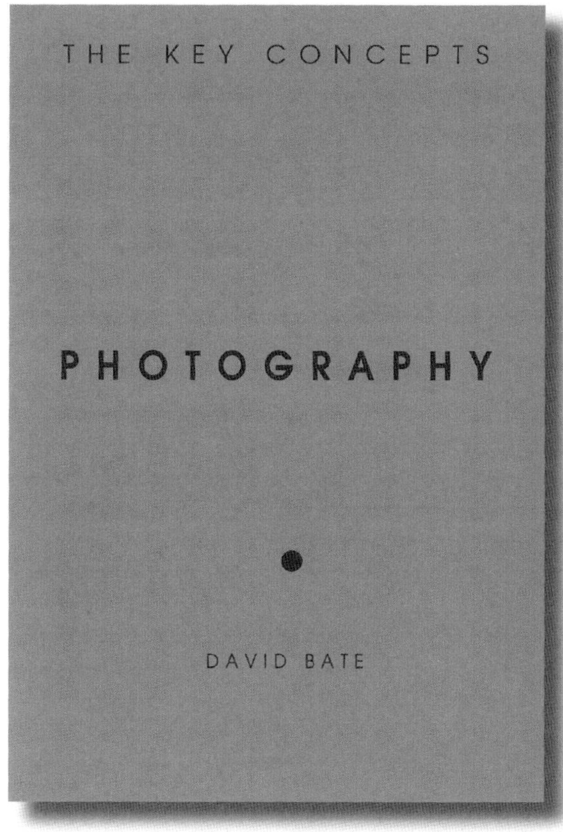

July 09 • 20 bw illus • 224pp
PB 978 1 84520 667 3 **£14.99 $24.95**
HB 978 1 84520 666 6 **£50.00 $99.95**

David Bate is a photographer and writer on photography. He is currently Reader in Photography and Course Leader of the MA Photographic Studies programme at the University of Westminster. His theoretical writings include the book *Photography and Surrealism* and his photographic works have been exhibited in Europe and North America.

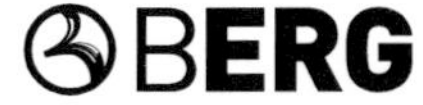

**Photography
& Culture**

Volume 4—Issue 1
March 2011
pp. 77–84
DOI:
10.2752/175145211X12899905861474

A Cold War Tourist and His Camera

Martha Langford and John Langford

For almost fifty years, between the end of World War II and 1991, Canada played its part in the Cold War. Collective memories of this period are sparked by news photos of nuclear testing and tanks at the Berlin Wall, while private life is enshrined in slide shows of family milestones and sun-drenched vacations. *A Cold War Tourist and His Camera* belongs to both these image worlds as an interdisciplinary study of vernacular photography conducted close to home by the children of an amateur photographer whose apprenticeship took place in those interesting times.

Our narrative is a rediscovery of photographs taken by Warren Langford (1919–97), while studying at Canada's National Defence College (NDC) in 1962–63. Modeled on the Imperial Defence College in London, the NDC program was designed to sensitize thirty participants to the global context in which they worked and to prepare them to do their jobs effectively if the Cold War became hot—not a theoretical prospect during the Cuban Missile Crisis of October 1962. Travel was a key component of NDC training. In North America, students visited military installations from the Arctic to San Diego. The Afro-European itinerary included non-aligned and NATO allied countries, as well as the embattled Berlin. Never before much interested in photography, Warren Langford bought a camera and produced some 200 Anscochrome and Kodachrome slides of his domestic and foreign tours. He also posed for other people and accepted their duplicate slides as gifts. Returning home, he set up the screen and projected his slide shows for the family.

Reviewing these images, we have grown interested in the curriculum of the NDC and its often oblique photographic representations. From a geopolitical perspective, John has reconstructed some of the backstory to the photographs, seeking to understand how the various participants might have experienced visual evidence of the Cold War, as well as its framing by and staging for the camera. Martha's role has been to situate this private travelogue in relation to the mass media—*National Geographic* and *Life*—and reflexively to consider the function and value of such a particular collection. These disciplinary perspectives are preserved in the body of the text, which also reflects the degree to which our voices have mingled throughout the recreation of the slide show and its thick histories.

A Cold War Tourist and His Camera makes no claims for Warren Langford as a photographer— he was a snapshooter with no greater ambition than putting together a slide show, a projected album, to preserve his memories and show to his family. But as a 'taker' of Cold War positions and 'maker' of photographic impressions, his collection of slides reflects both the nightmare of nuclear annihilation and the dream of world travel. Inside and outside these largely touristic frames are potential theatres of war and sites of ideological conditioning. And the witness/photographer is no less complex a construction: family man and public official; an apprentice snapshooter on an itinerary of photographic opportunities; a professional tourist "seeing through the lens" of iconic Cold War photographs and popular photo stories.

Martha Langford is a Concordia University Research Chair in Art History who has published extensively on photographic history and theories of memory, including studies of photographic albums and contemporary photographic works of art. John Langford, a professor in the School of Public Administration, University of Victoria, did graduate work in international relations in the 1960s before focusing on public service reform, an area in which he has published widely. *A Cold War Tourist and His Camera* is forthcoming from McGill-Queen's University Press in Spring 2011.

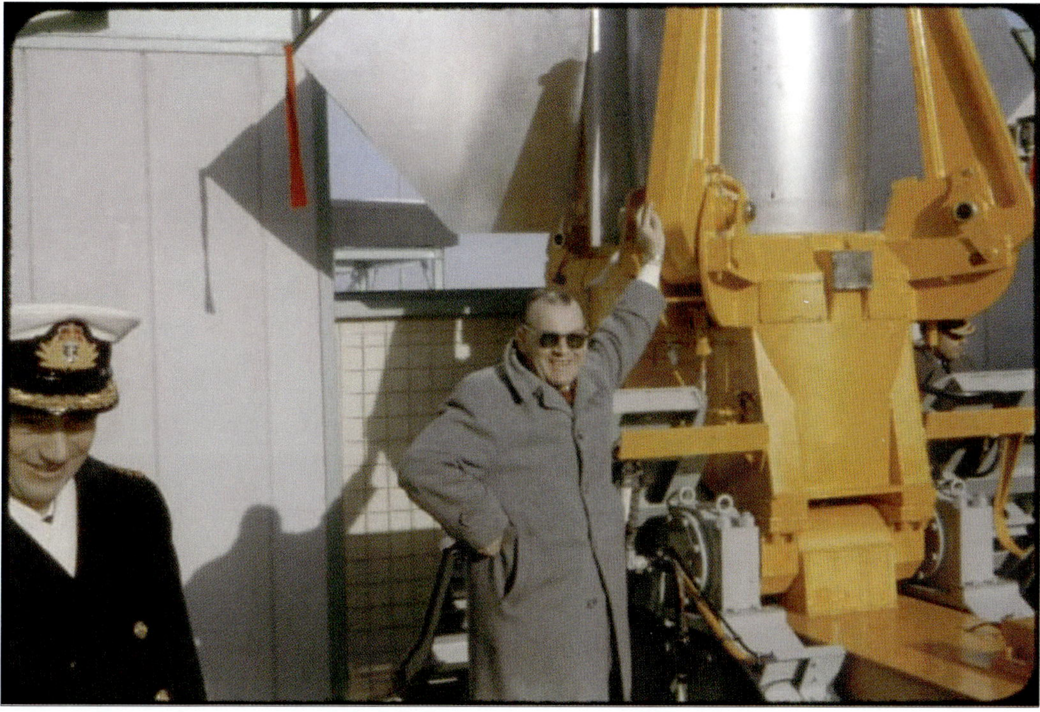

Fig I North Bay, Ontario, January 1963. In a demonstration of Canada's conflicted commitment to nuclear weaponry, an unarmed Bomarc missile is raised to its ready-to-fire position. Horsing around for the camera, a civilian member of the group reaches up to touch the erector. Would a picture like this have been allowed if this missile had been fitted with its required nuclear warhead? One member of the group quipped: "Now I've seen my first eunuch!"

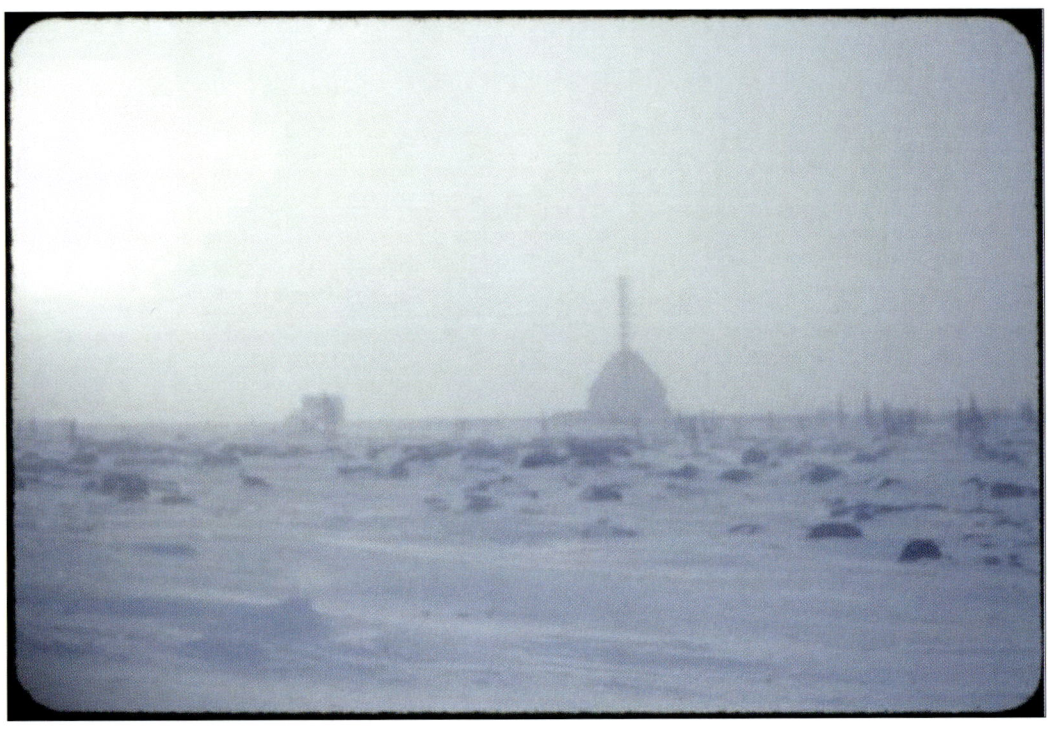

Fig 2 Fort Churchill, Manitoba, January 1963. At an American military installation in the Canadian North, the Aerobee Rocket Launch Tower and the blockhouse from which it was controlled are silhouetted against the horizon. The Anscochrome slide gives a subtle rendering of the North's disorienting terrain; distance and scale are difficult to determine (the Launch Tower was 53 metres high).

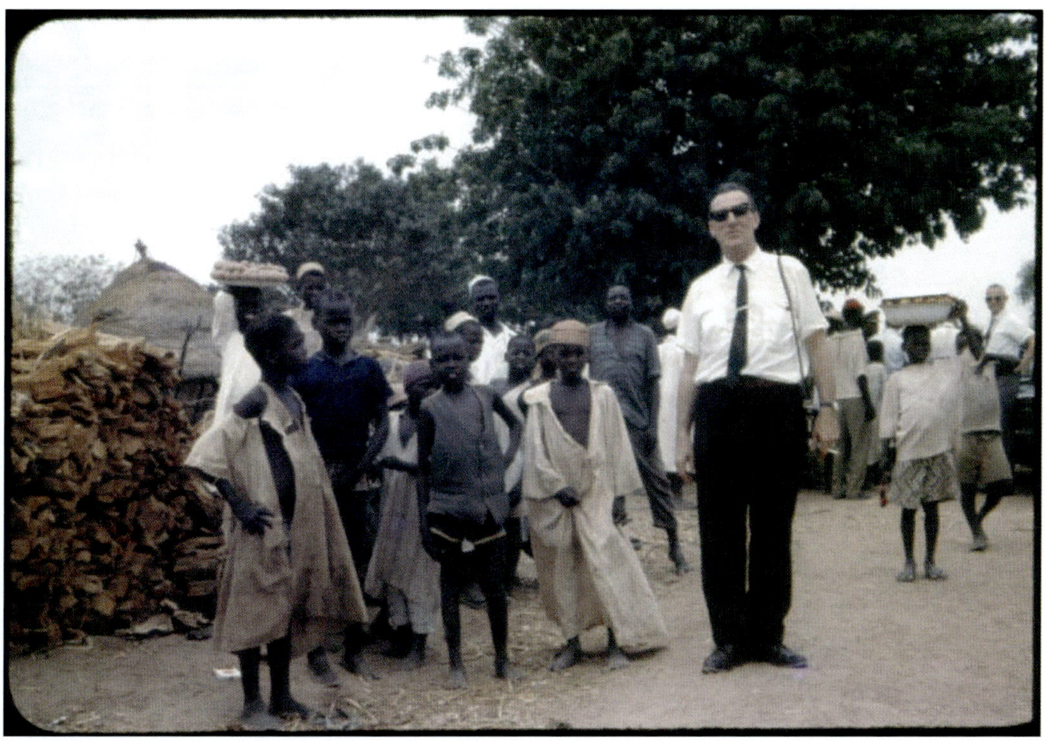

Fig 3 Near Kano, Nigeria, April 1963. The African itinerary included Morocco, Nigeria, Kenya, and Egypt, then known as the United Arab Republic—decolonizing nations struggling to avoid Cold War alignment. For the Cold War tourists, the novelty of Africa and the pure spectacle of its economic, political, and ethnic challenges seem to have displaced some of NDC's focus on ideology and defense. A tour of northern Nigerian markets is pictured as a series of brief ethnographic encounters.

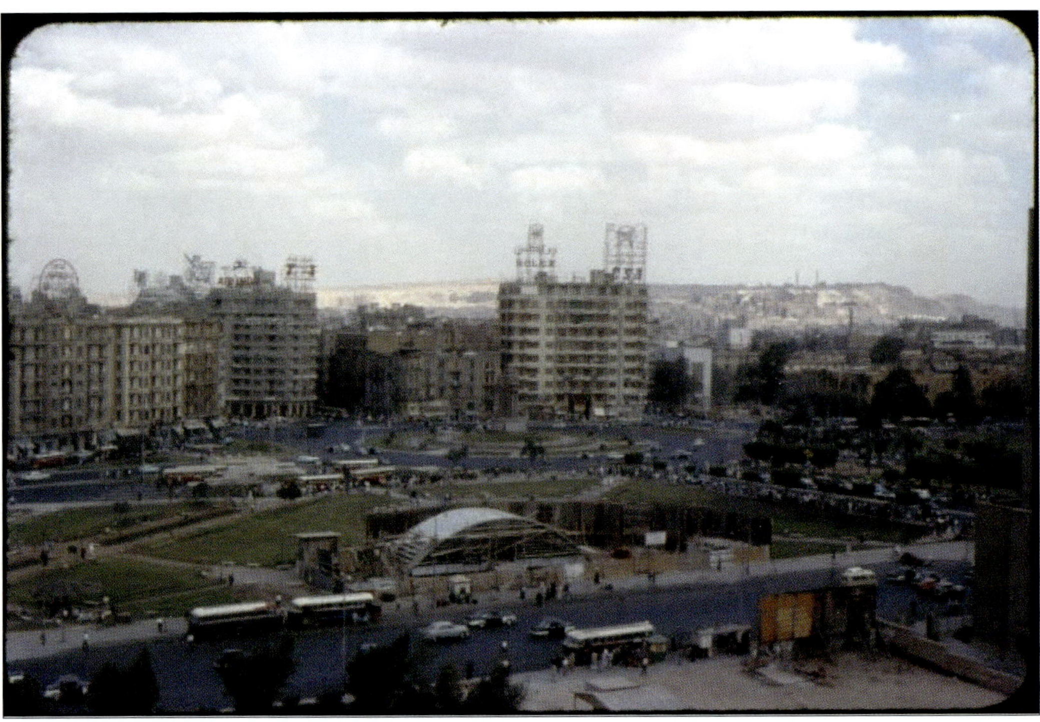

Fig 4 Cairo, United Arab Republic, April or May 1963. In Egypt, the base of the tour was the Cairo Hilton, built on the site of the former British barracks, between Midan Al-Tahrir (Liberation Square) and the Nile. A view from the back of the Hilton captures three stages of Egypt's modernization: on the horizon, the Alabaster Mosque of Turkish patriarch Mohammed Ali Pasha; the square itself, built by Khedive Ismail, the Francophile visionary behind the Suez Canal; and first signs of the square's reconstitution as a commuter hub in the time of Nasser, builder of the Aswan High Dam.

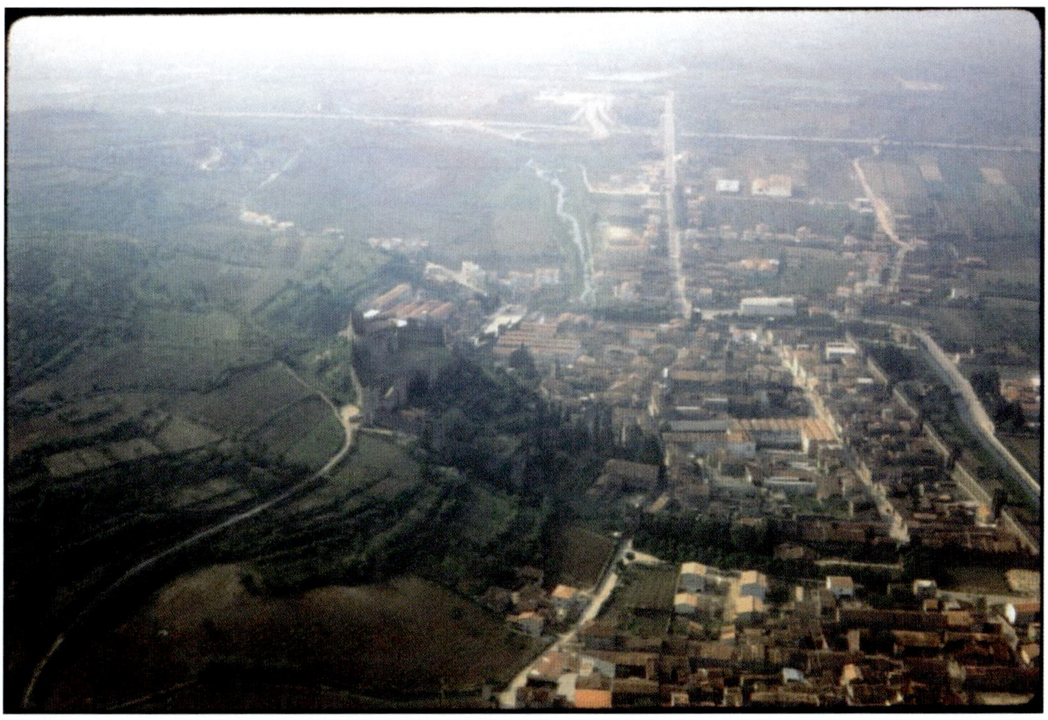

Fig 5 Northern Italy, May 1963. At military bases near Verona and Vicenza, the group focused on the tactical and defensive nuclear missile weaponry being operated by US and Italian armed forces in support of NATO—dangerous "flexible response" elements of the nuclear deterrence toolkit. Having considered the possibilities of turning Europe into a Dantesque inferno, the Cold War tourists were ferried into Venice on an American military helicopter, the Sikorsky S-58, heavily used by the Marine Corps during the Vietnam War.

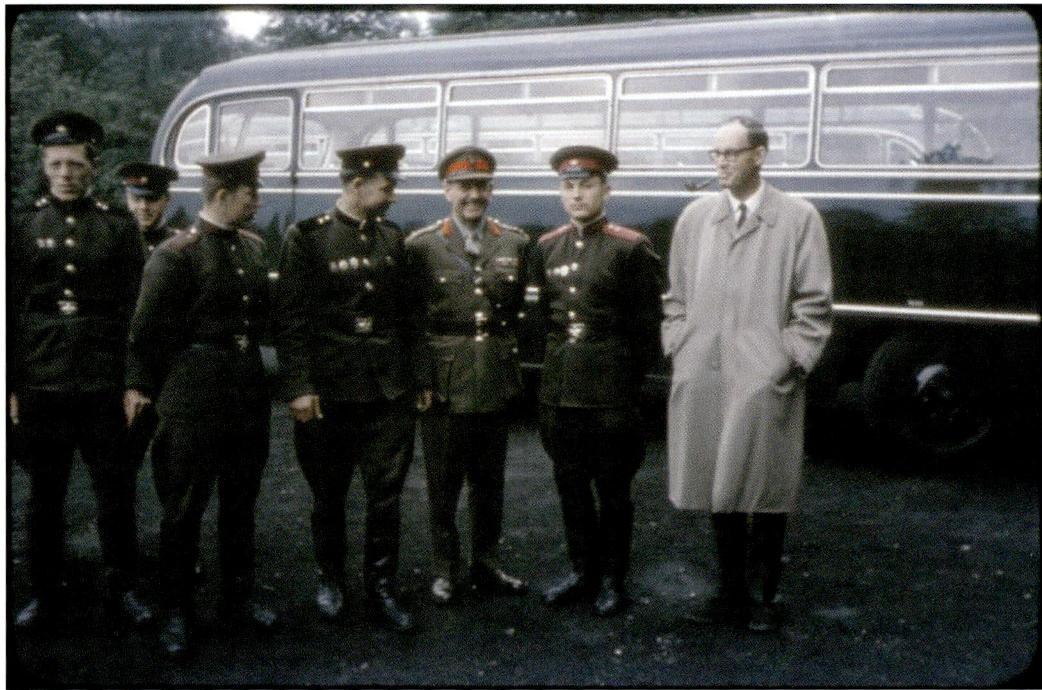

Fig 6 East Berlin, May 1963. Dark tourism in Berlin featured the Wall, still very much a work-in-progress, as well as World War II ruins and monuments. Photographs taken at the Treptower cenotaph hint at the possibility that East-West confrontation was more nuanced than Cold War posturing might insist. Warren Langford appears, grinning and smoking his pipe. This is strange territory for a supposedly well-trained Cold Warrior: here, on Soviet sanctified ground, he and his military colleagues are standing peaceably with former allies, now enemies, in what seems to be a very relaxed moment for everyone.

**Photography
& Culture**

Volume 4—Issue 1
March 2011
pp. 85–92

DOI:
10.2752/175145211X12899905861519

Reprints available directly from
the publishers

Photocopying permitted by
licence only

Portfolio

The New Pre-Raphaelites

Sunil Gupta

Keywords: Saleem Kidwai, Section 377, homosexual, morality, portraiture, queer, Bollywood, sexuality

Section 377 of the Indian Penal Code, which criminalized "unnatural" sex between consenting adults in India, was successfully challenged by a landmark ruling at the Delhi High Court on July 2, 2009. It was not of indigenous origin as a piece of legislation; its origins lay in the period of British Colonial rule. A consequence of this is that there is no visibility for homosexual relationships in the sub-continent. What the court ruled in 2009 was that there was a difference between constitutional morality and private morality, and that the human rights of the individual to choose his or her own partner were being violated.

Now that it's been a year since the law changed and there has been a great deal of media debate, it's possible to see that legal change can precede social change. However long it will take for the majority of the population to change its moral stance, the individual has become free to pursue an alternative lifestyle. From this basic premise further reforms are possible in employment, property and family structures.

I've been using portraiture for a while as a means of gaining same sex desire some visibility in the form of a photo documentation of individual people. In my series titled *Exiles* (1986–87) it was framed in a period of intense repression, where even the faintest image seemed non-existent. *Mr. Malhotra's Party* (2006–) is about locating the new Indian queer family in a public space.

In this series of pictures I wanted to address the problem of the lack of an easily accessible iconography of same sex desire involving women and men in India. Indian history has only just begun to recognize the contributions of same sex desire in literature. Co-editors Saleem Kidwai and Ruth Vanita produced the first anthology of texts sourced from across the sub-continent in a variety of languages and historical periods. Art history has yet to produce such published research.

Therefore one looks for subjective interpretations amongst the examples of art in the public realm, which historically have been in sculpture and painting. Classical Indian art, particularly before the Islamic period (12th century onwards), referred to gay sex. But the later 19th and 20th centuries produced no schools of discourse, and very few known examples. It is only now in the fledgling arena of postmodern queer film and video that a body of work is emerging that takes on this subject, fueled in part by the Diaspora experience.

There is a well charted trajectory that informs Western traditions in photography from 19th-century French painting via Baron Von Gloeden through to Robert Mapplethorpe to the more hybrid forms of desire documented by Rotimi Fani-Kayode. However, there is also a tradition of camp that exists in the sub-continent that is referred to extensively in Bollywood cinema. Likewise the early modern European tradition of homo-erotic images for private circulation is equally well established in India.

In making this body of work I used well known references to "Western" art history since it has gained a certain international recognition. This same Western tradition has already incorporated elements of Aboriginal, African and Asian art within it. One of the images seen in New Delhi resonates for an audience here even though it is based on Manet's "Olympia", a painting that few people here would actually have seen. Similarly the Pre-Raphaelite

movement in England was contesting the stifling norms of their world, especially assumptions around sexuality and gender. I've chosen to adapt their focus on camp and sensuality and the arrangement of the body, and update it to visualize a modern Indian queer identity using the language of exoticism taking an assertive stance.

Politically the very identity of same sex desire is contested in India. The notion of "gay" used very casually by urban men across the country doesn't seem to fit the wider extent of actual practice bound as it is to Western social norms. The term "kothi" has come to be used to refer to the indigenous Indian homosexual man. This is now widely used in the literature to fight AIDS. Literally it describes an effeminate man in search of an ideal masculine (heterosexual) partner. So by definition it is a search that cannot be fulfilled, similar to the position adhered to by Quentin Crisp in England in the early and mid-twentieth century. This idealized unfulfilled desire is the subject of these pictures, set in the wider context of the current struggle for human rights and a continuing change in the law, in India and elsewhere in the world today.

Sunil Gupta was born in New Delhi in 1953 and is a Canadian citizen who now lives and works in London and Delhi. His work is represented by Vadehra Art Gallery, Delhi.

This project was originally commissioned by Autograph – ABP, London.

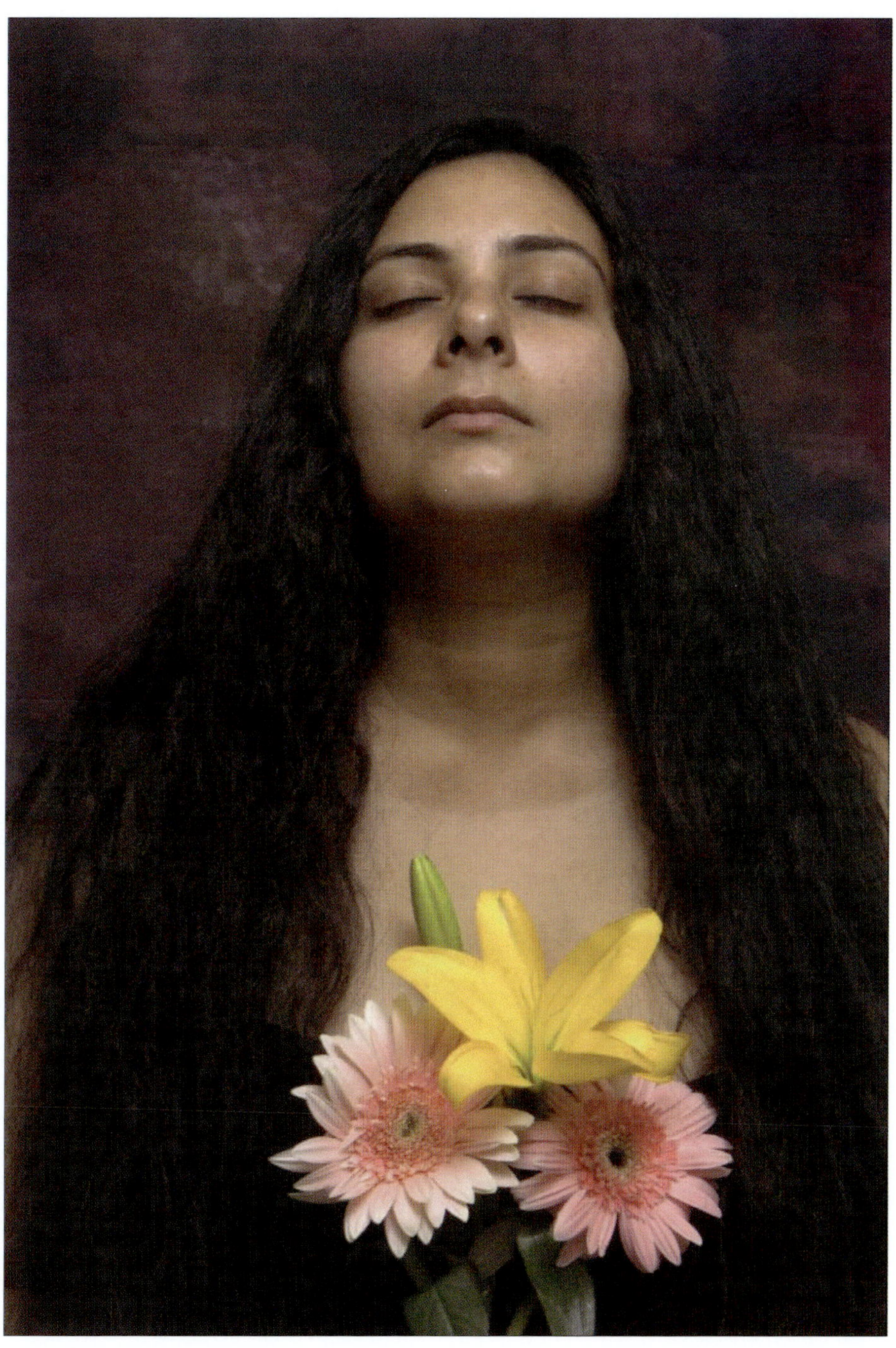

Fig I The New Pre-Raphaelites, Untitled #4. © Sunil Gupta/Vadehra Art Gallery, New Delhi, India.

Photography & Culture   Volume 4   Issue I   March 2011, pp. 85–92

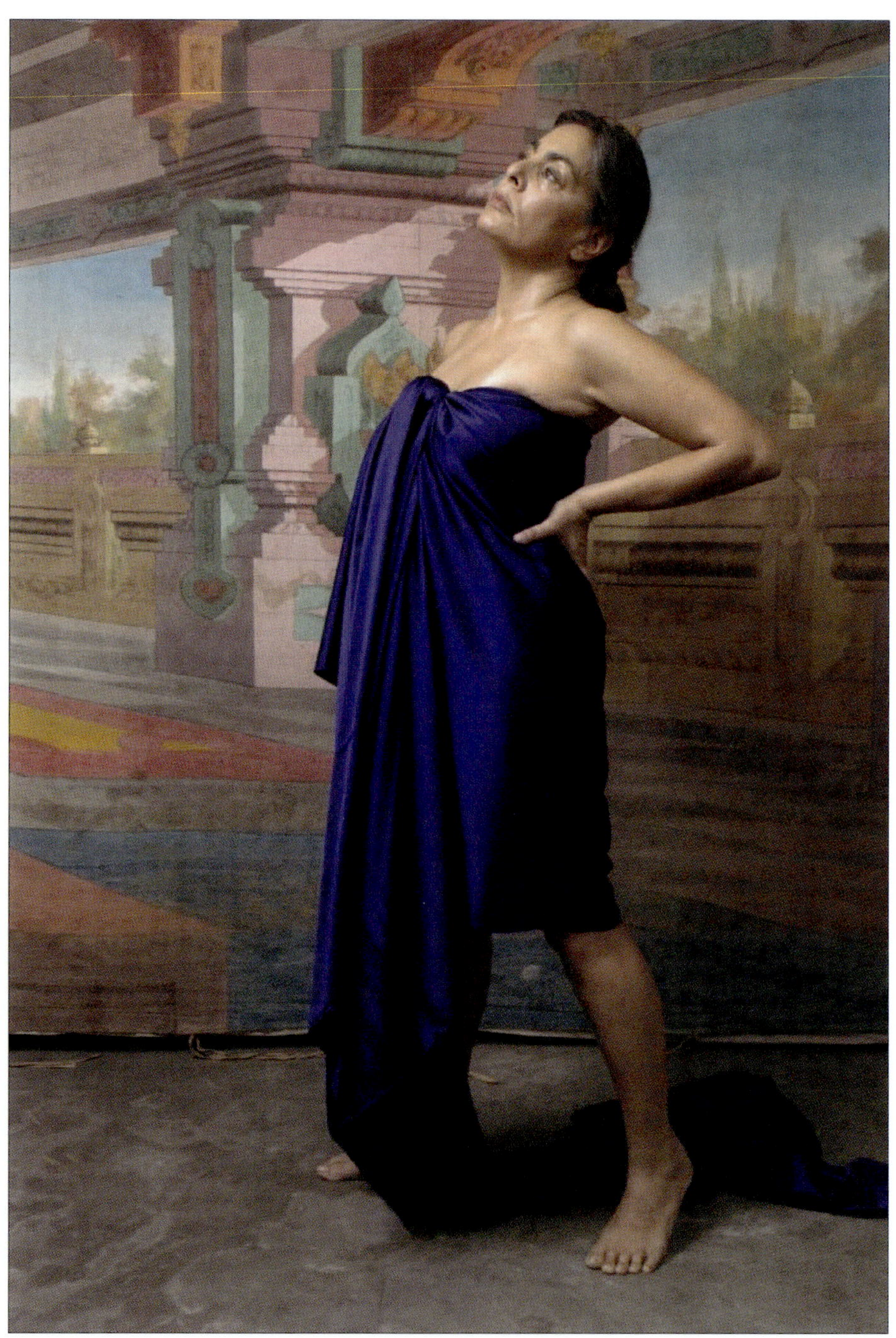

Fig 2 The New Pre-Raphaelites, Untitled #6. © Sunil Gupta/Vadehra Art Gallery, New Delhi, India.

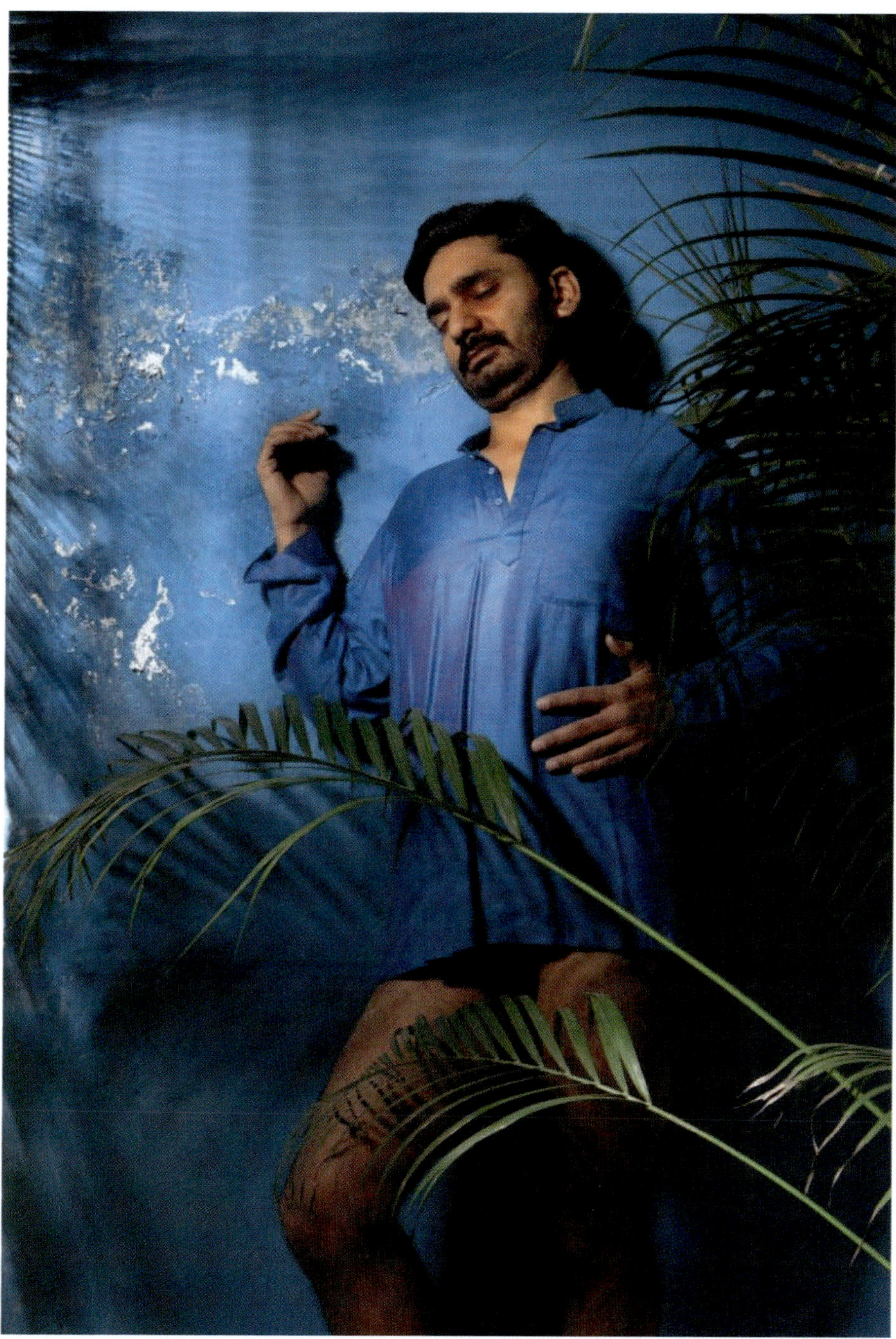

Fig 3 The New Pre-Raphaelites, Untitled # 15. © Sunil Gupta/Vadehra Art Gallery, New Delhi, India.

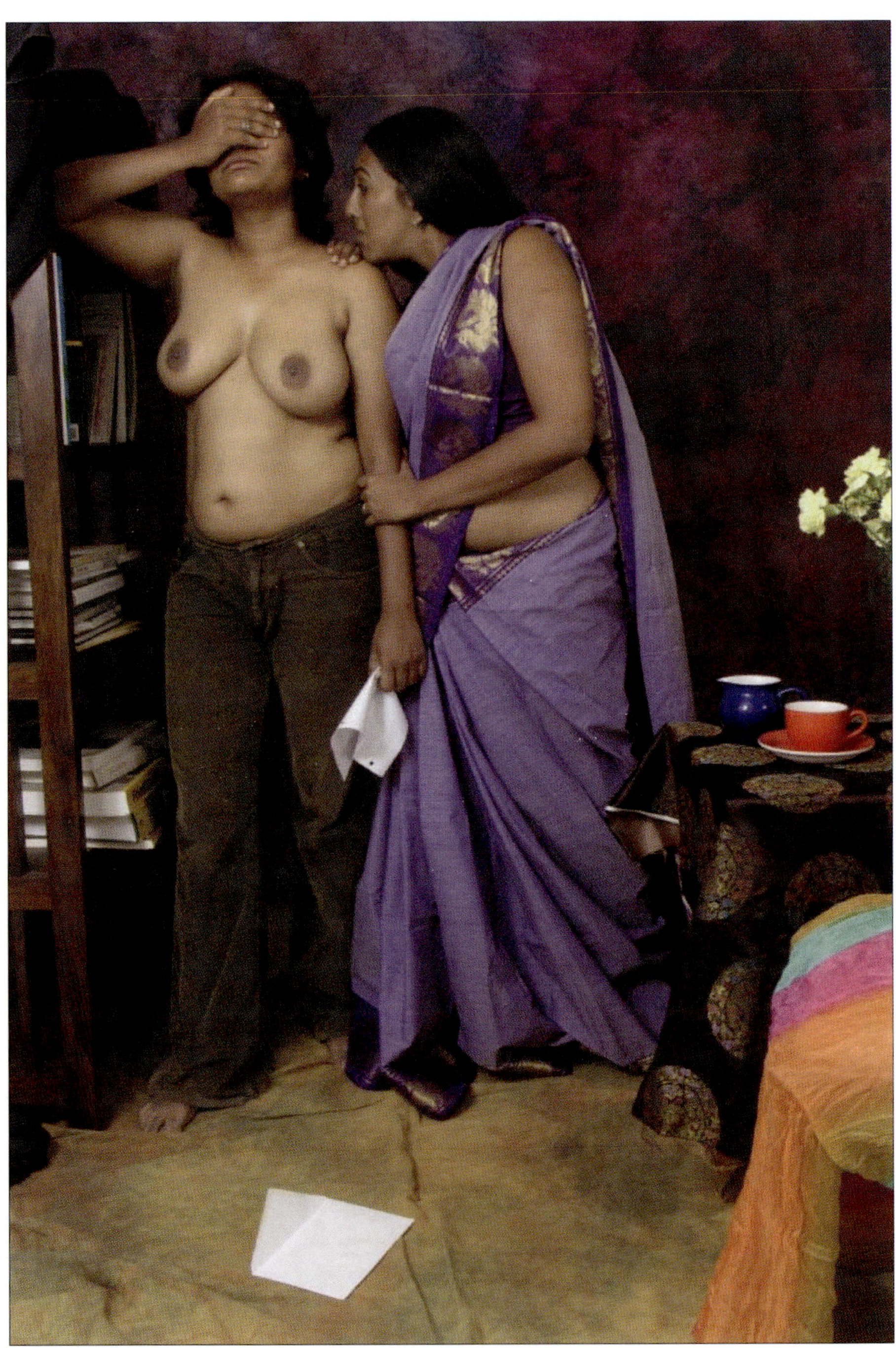

Fig 4 The New Pre-Raphaelites, Untitled #10. © Sunil Gupta/Vadehra Art Gallery, New Delhi, India.

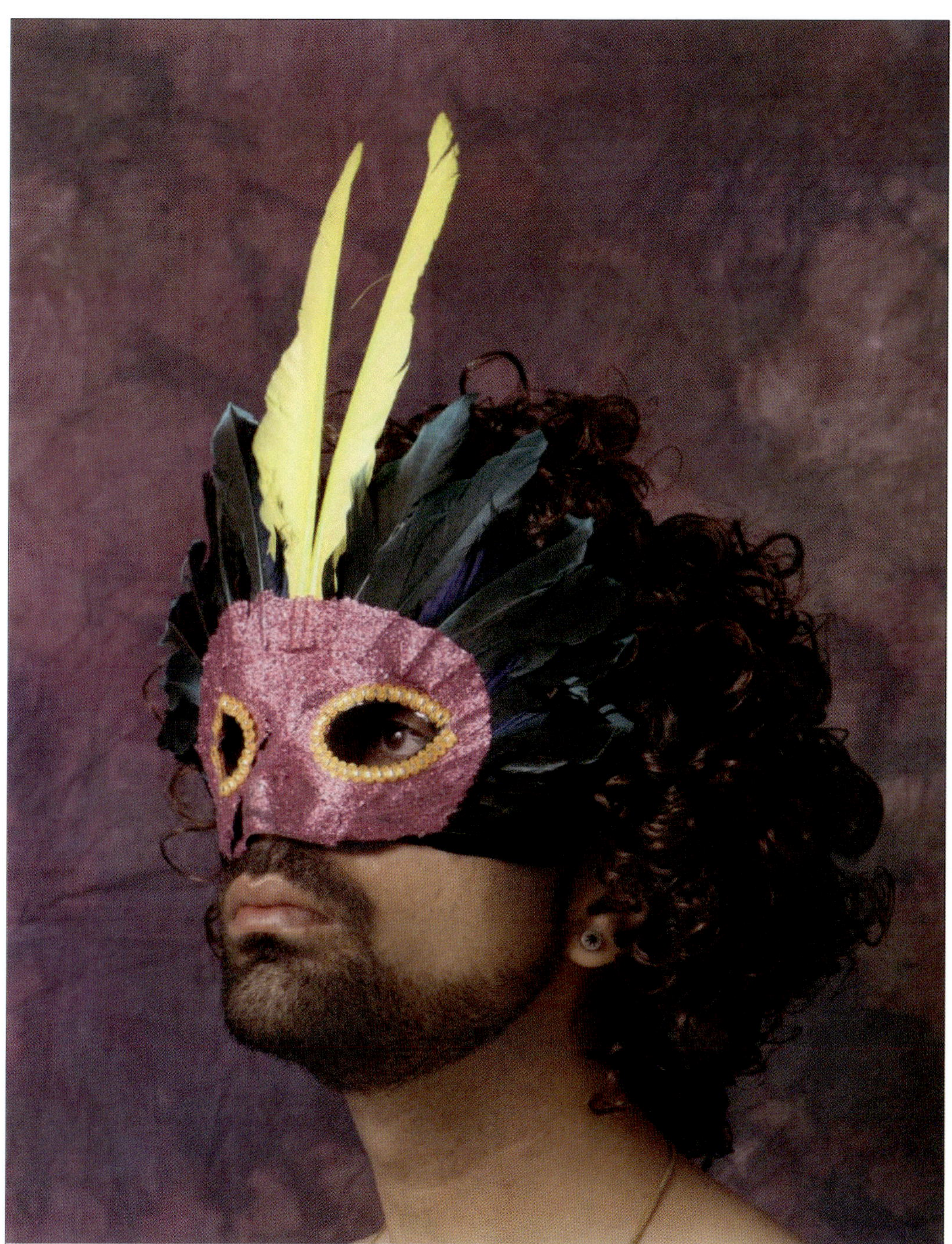

Fig 5 The New Pre-Raphaelites, Untitled # 11. © Sunil Gupta/Vadehra Art Gallery, New Delhi, India.

Photography & Culture   Volume 4   Issue 1   March 2011, pp. 85–92

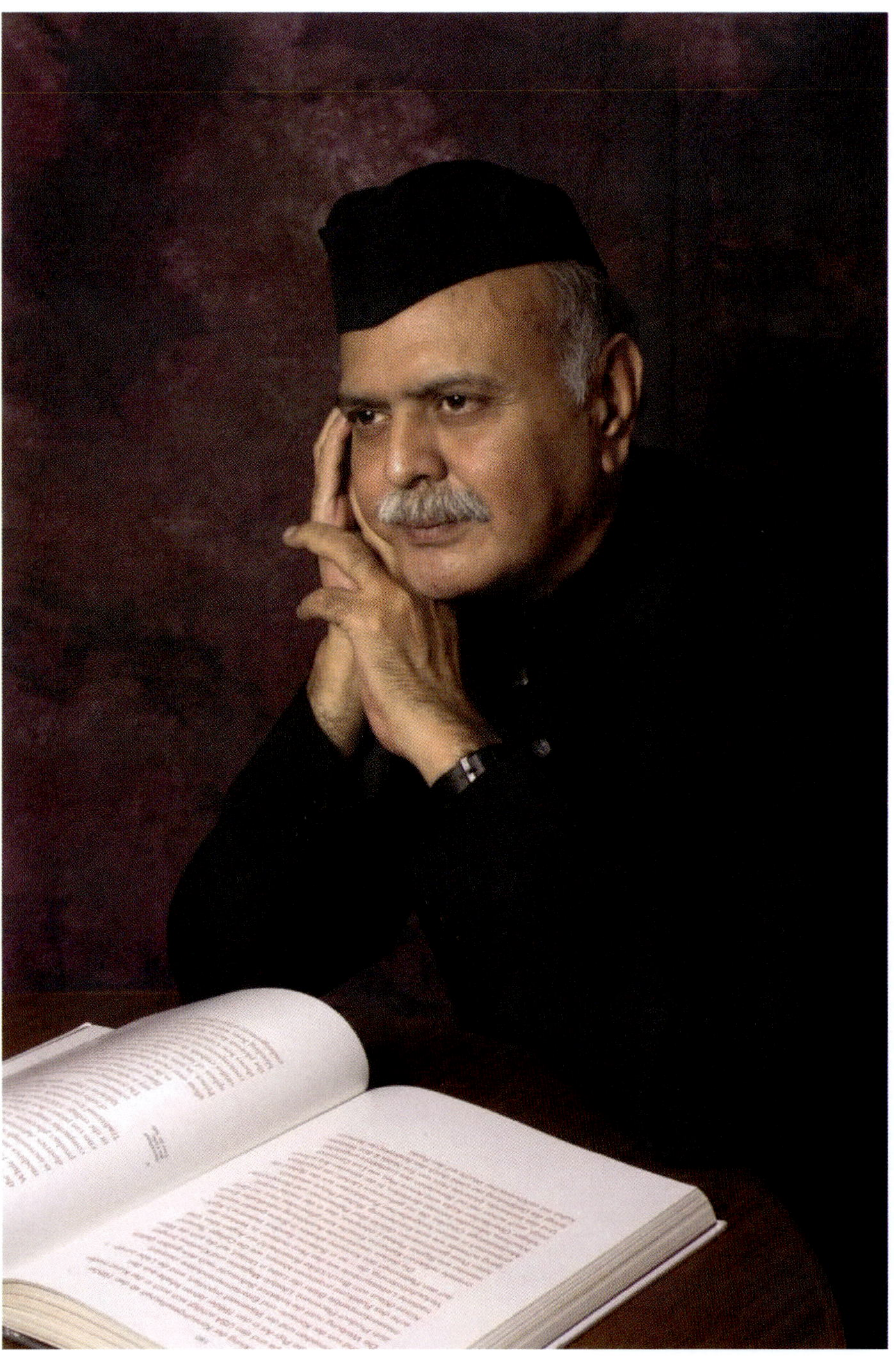

Fig 6 The New Pre-Raphaelites, Untitled #14. © Sunil Gupta/Vadehra Art Gallery, New Delhi, India.

Photography & Culture   Volume 4   Issue 1   March 2011, pp. 85–92

**Photography
& Culture**

Volume 4—Issue 1
March 2011
pp. 93–102

DOI:
10.2752/175145211X12899905861555

Review Essay

The Americans at 50: A review of the exhibition and related
publications of *Looking In: Robert Frank's* The Americans.[1]

Reviewed by David Harris

Abstract

In celebration of the fiftieth anniversary of the first American
edition of Robert Frank's seminal publication *The Americans*,
the National Gallery of Art circulated an exhibition in
2009, accompanied by two related catalogs that provide a
comprehensive and exhaustive examination of the genesis,
creation, and critical reception of the book. This review analyzes
the curatorial issues raised by both the exhibition and the
publications in representing *The Americans* as a physical object and
cultural entity.

Keywords: Robert Frank, The Americans, photographically
illustrated books, photography exhibitions

It is a relatively small *quarto* book, measuring 7 ½ x 8 ½ inches (18.5
x 21 cm), one which we, as readers, can hold open comfortably
with one hand, balancing and cradling it while the other hand turns
the pages. Or it can be placed on a table or desk where, because
of its sewn binding, it lies flat and we can flip the pages using either
one or both hands. A white dust jacket bearing the image "Trolley –
New Orleans" with the book's title, *THE AMERICANS*, printed
above the image, and *PHOTOGRAPHS BY ROBERT FRANK* and
INTRODUCTION BY JACK KEROUAC printed on the lower section
of the image, wraps around the cover. In opening the volume, we
move through the half-title and title pages, the colophon, a seven-
page introduction, a further half-title page, before reaching the
photographs, reproduced as an unbroken sequence of eighty-three
gravure plates, on the right-hand page with the title in the lower left
corner of the facing page. The book ends with printing information.
In 1959, when first published in English, it sold for $7.50.

To immerse ourselves in *The Americans* is a private and intimate
experience, the quiet engagement of a single reader with a book.
In the presentation of the plates, only one image is ever visible at
a time, and this shapes the experience of "reading" the book as a
succession of discrete photographs.[2] We must absorb the contents
of one image, while holding the latent memory of previous or
successive images in mind (particularly if we are already familiar

with the book). In this way the book's narrative is slowly constructed, its meaning created plate by plate. With each successive reading, the "original" experience is recreated, but subtly modified and altered, deepened and enriched; previously overlooked details—the quality of light, the expression on a face in the background, the tilt of the composition—may be noticed for the first time, with certain effects recalled afresh from previous encounters. The most salient aspect of this experience is that the process of reading is never exhausted; the images are hidden, revealed, and then hidden again in the physical activity of turning the pages. The meandering sequence of plates moves through to the final photograph of Frank's family nestled in a rented automobile on the side of a Texas highway. It is an image of transience, not of finality, and one that functions as an invitation to return to the beginning of the book.

Originally published in Paris in 1958 as *Les Américains*, the sequence of eighty-three plates was accompanied by extensive excerpts from sociological and travel writing by both French and American authors, selected and edited by Alain Bosquet.[3] The book was published the following year in its definitive, English-language form, with Kerouac's text followed by the eighty-three plates with succinct titles only. When it was released in an edition of 2,600 copies on January 15, 1960, *The Americans* was greeted by howls of derision, by caustic and, for the most part, sour reviews, which castigated the book as a skewed view and biased assault on America, one that lacked even the beauty of technically well-made photographs.[4] Slightly more than 1,100 copies were sold before December 1960, at which time the book was withdrawn by the publisher and declared out of print. By the time that Aperture, in association with the Museum of Modern Art and Grossman Publishers, released an "expanded edition" in 1968 and 1969,[5] *The Americans* had quietly secured a cult status as a celebrated but rarely seen volume; it was now heralded as a

poetic, insightful critique of American society, a set of beautifully printed images distilling one man's view of America.[6] Subsequent English-language editions in 1978, 1986, 1993, and, most recently, 2008, in addition to French, German, Japanese, and Chinese editions, have ensured that the publication has remained widely and readily available, and it has gradually assumed the mantle and authority of an unassailable "classic", seen as a pivotal and highly influential body of work that both represented an era and transcended it in the uncompromising clarity of its vision.

The Americans is now included in all histories of photography and in every survey of the period. In his 1964 edition of *The History of Photography*, Beaumont Newhall included Frank as one of only four photographers in his final chapter "Recent Trends,"[7] and in 1978, John Szarkowski in his introduction to a survey of recent American photography, *Mirrors and Windows*, hailed the publishing of *The Americans*, together with the founding of *Aperture* magazine in 1952 and Edward Steichen's 1955 exhibition *The Family of Man* as "the three most important events in American photography during the fifties."[8] More recently Martin Parr and Gerry Badger, in their highly opinionated survey of the history of the photographic books, describe *The Americans* as "arguably the most renowned photobook of all."[9] The work has also permeated the photographic art market; to cite three recent examples of auction sales, in October 2009, an enlarged contact sheet from *The Americans* sold for $40,000; in April 2010, a print of "Butte, Montana" (plate 26 in *The Americans*) went for $146,500; and in May 2010, a first edition of *The Americans* sold for £43,250 (US $62,194).[10]

In examining the extensive writings on Frank's work, it is not always clear what an author means by the phrase "The Americans:" is this a reference to a book, a group of photographs, or a few individual images? Many writers elide all three as though they were interchangeable and, in essence, all part of a single entity. Critics and commentators describe the book as a whole, but use individual images to illustrate their points. If the meaning of the work resides in the overall sequence, as most writers have argued, what happens when individual images or clusters of images are removed from their position in the sequence and shown separately in exhibitions or are used as illustrations in essays and exhibition catalogs? By now, many of the images, including the book's cover image, have become iconic, and are treated as representative, even emblematic, of the entire body of work. Their pervasiveness is certainly indicative of the fame of *The Americans* now circulating well beyond photographic circles, and the book is seen by many as a touchstone of American culture in the 1950s.

To celebrate the fiftieth anniversary of the book's first American edition, the National Gallery of Art in Washington undertook an enormous, collaborative research project under the direction of Sarah Greenough, the museum's senior curator of photography, that has resulted in both an impressive exhibition and two related publications, all titled *Looking In: Robert Frank's* The Americans. The exhibition opened in Washington in early January 2009, and was subsequently shown at the San Francisco Museum of Modern Art and the Metropolitan Museum of Art in New York, where I saw the exhibition later that same year. Accompanying it was an impressive 374-page catalog with twelve essays by nine authors, plates of the entire exhibition, a checklist, bibliography, and index. In addition, the gallery published an even more lavish *Expanded Edition* of the catalog, as an independent publication, running to 504 pages. As well as all of the material found in the exhibition catalog, this massive publication includes reproductions of all eighty-one related contact sheets, detailed comparative reproductions of the original maquette of the book and the cropping of the images in all the French and American editions of the publication, correspondence and

archival material, a map of Frank's travels in 1955 and 1956, and a comprehensive chronology of his life and career.

The National Gallery is ideally suited to initiate and carry out this project because of its close relationship with Frank that has developed over the past twenty years. In 1990, Frank donated "a large gift of his work, including an important group of exhibition prints, a bound volume of original photographs titled *Black White and Things*, and a substantial archival collection of all of his negatives and accompanying contact sheets made before 1970 and more than a thousand work prints,"[11] an initial donation that was augmented by Frank in 1994 and 1996 with additional exhibition prints and archival material. With further acquisitions and gifts from other donors, including all of the photographs included in the 1989 edition of *The Lines of My Hand*, the museum's online catalog now lists 4,859 acquisition records of work by Robert Frank.[12] In addition, the museum co-published the 1993 and the 2008 English editions of *The Americans*, the 2008 Chinese edition, and the 1994 edition of *Black White and Things*. In 1994, the museum mounted and circulated the exhibition *Robert Frank: Moving Out*, which provided an overview of Frank's career and, in the accompanying catalog, included an extensive essay by Greenough on *The Americans*. The museum holds the primary material with which to carry out a thorough and comprehensive study of this book and, equally crucial to the success of this project, the agreement and good will of Frank himself, who is in a position to supply details and verify what actually happened.

In her introduction to the publications, Greenough succinctly sets out the context and ambition of the project:

Only now, as *The Americans* marks its fiftieth anniversary and the artist himself is in his eighties, has Frank permitted an in-depth examination of the publication: one that studies its roots in his earlier books as well as those of his contemporaries; one that provides an extensive analysis of its creation, through a presentation of his contact sheets, work prints, and the book's preliminary sequence and maquette; and one that includes an explication of its sequencing and a discussion of the impact of *The Americans* on his later art. That is what this book and its related exhibition seek to do.[13]

The most telling word in this passage is "permitted," with the implication that such an investigation may not have been welcomed earlier or, without Frank's agreement, even been possible. The project centred on the messy creative process, with the hundreds of contact sheets, work prints, and the maquette, in order to reconstruct how *The Americans* was created and the publication conceived and produced, rather than, as has been done in previous exhibitions, with a celebration of the final group of eighty-three images. This change in emphasis in itself is noteworthy and indicative of the serious commitment of resources, both human and financial, by the National Gallery. This is surely the most thorough study of a single photographic book ever undertaken, and it marks an enormous contribution to photographic history and, in particular, to our knowledge of photographic books. However, as Greenough's text makes clear, this study focuses on Frank, *his* relationship to the publication, and its significance within Frank's earlier and later work. While Frank's relationship with other photographers and writers and with other photographic books is acknowledged and documented, the emphasis rests firmly on him. This is a study that privileges the creator and the process of creation from his point of view, and offers an interpretation that is sympathetic to Frank's own understanding of *The Americans*, rather than proposing a radically new reading.

The main curatorial problem facing Greenough in conceiving both the exhibition and its related publications was essentially the same: how to represent the genesis and form of *The Americans*. As Greenough explained in her introduction to the publications, "both the catalogue and the exhibition are divided into four sections that address Frank's early years, his Guggenheim fellowship, *The Americans* itself, and its impact on his later career."[14] Having made the decision to organize and present the material in four chronological sections, she then had a number of further questions to resolve: how could Frank's creative and editorial process be revealed; how could the significant moments and stages in his decision-making process be represented; and how could the specific qualities of the publication, in particular the sequencing of single images, be shown?

Of the two, the exhibition, as I encountered it at the Metropolitan Museum of Art, seems the least satisfying in the sense of its ability to address these questions. The allocated space was far too small for the volume of material, and the exhibition's four sections fitted awkwardly within the overall configuration of the museum's sequence of five elegant, but relatively modest galleries. The introductory panel, a display case with copies of the French edition of *Les Américains* and Walker Evans's copy of *The Americans*, and an enormous enlargement of a contact sheet (Americans 18/19) framed the entrance. The first two sections—"Zurich to New York, 1924–1954," "Guggenheim Fellowship, 1955–1957"—and the first six photographs from the third section, "*The Americans*, 1958–1959," began in the outside corridor and filled the first gallery, a total of seventy-two photographs. The remaining seventy-seven photographs forming the rest of the third section, "*The Americans*, 1958–59," occupied the second, third, and fourth galleries. The final section, "Destroying *The Americans*, 1960–2008" and comprising only two works, was presented in the last room. In the first, second, and fifth rooms of the galleries were display cases with Frank's and other photographers' publications, letters, and archival documents; in the second room were two display cases with a sampling of twenty-two contact sheets. Throughout the exhibition, informative didactic panels and extended labels, derived from Greenough's essays in the publication, accompanied the objects.

Imposing a chronological structure will pose certain difficulties, and some of the problematic aspects of the exhibition's presentation were clearly the result of limitations of space at the Metropolitan Museum. The thirty-three prints comprising *Black White and Things* that Frank sequenced in a handmade book of original photographs in 1952, for example, were displayed in the corridor outside the formal entrance to the galleries. This meant that the work was presented before the exhibition's introductory panel and thus out of its chronological sequence (these prints are numbers 26–59 in the exhibition's checklist). Were visitors meant to return to these images after viewing the earlier photographs in the first gallery? A second problem concerned the relative size of the photographs and the nature of looking. The contact sheets, shown in the second gallery, are relatively small objects, which require very close, sustained scrutiny to absorb the information found in them; this represents an inherently different kind of looking from that which the larger prints of *The Americans* shown on the walls of the gallery demand of viewers. In this gallery, the beautifully framed photographs dominated the space, and, not surprisingly, most visitors gravitated to these images, largely passing over the contact sheets. Finally, and at another level, there are interpretive questions concerning how best to represent *The Americans* as a publication. Enormous efforts had clearly been made to assemble a graphically powerful set of the eighty-three images, and these were drawn from at least twenty-two institutional and private collections. Since Frank printed the work over a period of time, the photographs varied both in printing quality and size (ranging from

6 x 10 inches to 16 x 23 inches).[15] While these differences would normally have been welcome, providing variety and giving energy to this large group of photographs spread over four rooms, the effect was slightly unsettling for two reasons. First, the prints followed the same order as the images in the book, but the varying sizes of the photographs on the walls imposed their own hierarchy and rhythm on the sequence, thereby creating an entirely different effect from that generated by their uniform and consistent size in the publication, in which each image is accorded equal importance. Second, the images in the book are presented individually, one on each page-spread; in the exhibition, however, visitors were able to survey, depending on where they stood in a room, not merely single prints but clusters and runs of prints along one or more walls. As a public experience, as opposed to the private experience of reading the book, viewing the prints in this way allowed visitors to savor the beauty of individual photographs, to compare them with one another, and to see more easily the formal and iconographic relationships between images that could never be perceived in the same way in the book. Presumably, this form of presentation would have been closer to what Frank experienced in envisioning and laying out the sequence of photographs for his publication.

The accompanying catalog and the *Expanded Edition* are similarly divided into the same four chronological sections as the exhibition. In each section, Greenough provides a substantial, chronologically based essay, which can be read as one long, continuous text. Complementing Greenough's narrative are shorter essays by eight authors, devoted to Frank's friendships and pivotal relationships with photographers (Louis Faurer, Gotthard Schuh, Walker Evans), curators (Edward Steichen in his capacity as Director of Photography at the Museum of Modern Art, and Philip Brookman, who has curated several Frank exhibitions since 1978), a publisher (Robert Delpire, who published the first French edition of the book), and a writer (the novelist Jack Kerouac, who wrote the introduction to *The Americans*). In each section, the essays, which are also heavily illustrated, precede the presentation of the corresponding plates.

If the objects predominated in the exhibition, with words playing a supportive role, this relationship is substantially reversed in the related publications: the books are structured so that we are encouraged to read the essays in conjunction with an examination of the plates. Words establish the temporal narrative, re-create the circumstances of Frank's choices and decisions, make links between bodies of work over time, describe relationships between different photographers, and analyze specific images. While the number of pages devoted to the plates and the quality of the reproductions endows them with a substantial weight and presence, an informed response to them is largely predicated upon a familiarity with the ideas and interpretations found in the essays.

What was unsatisfactory in the exhibition is largely resolved in the publications. *Black White and Things* appears in its proper sequence in the plate section, and there is no longer such a discrepancy in size between the contact sheets and the plates from *The Americans*. The contact sheets are reproduced at a scale that is both inviting and conducive to study—indeed, it almost seems as though the dimensions of the publications were determined by the proportions of the contact sheets. The section of plates reproducing the entire sequence of *The Americans*, however, remains open to the same criticism as its presentation in the exhibition. Some of the images are reproduced alone on the right-hand page, but most appear as facing images across a page-spread, again setting up comparisons that were not part of the original concept of the book.

Scholarship consolidates and builds upon earlier research, and draws upon material not previously known or available, in order to offer new interpretations and alternative perspectives.

In this case, it is the contact sheets, the work prints, and the original maquette that comprises this new material.

The existence of the contact sheets had been known previously, but only in an incomplete and fragmentary form. In the 1972 Japanese edition of *The Lines of My Hand*, Frank created a four-page fold-out that reproduced twenty-eight separate negative strips, each of which included an image of one of the plates from *The Americans*.[16] In the 2004 exhibition at Tate Modern in London, England, *Robert Frank: Storylines*, twelve enlarged contact sheets, similar but not identical to those reproduced in *The Lines of My Hand*, were displayed at the beginning of the exhibition, and included the negatives of all eighty-three images from *The Americans*.[17] While the number of rolls that Frank shot had remained uncertain,[18] Greenough has now clarified that Frank shot 767 rolls of film related to the project. She details when the contact sheets were made and how they were used,[19] and the *Expanded Edition* reproduces eighty-one contact sheets corresponding to the final selection of images in the publication.[20]

While the strips reproduced earlier in *The Lines of My Hand* and *Storylines* encouraged viewers to engage with the moment of creation through seeing the immediately adjacent images, as a reflection of how photographers work, this is misleading. Viewing the entire contact sheet reveals a far more complex and unpredictable process of photographing, consisting of hard work, intuition, and, at times, fortuitous happenstance. Only two sheets yielded more than one of the final selection of images (*Americans* 18/19 and 77/78). Although his trip to the Democratic convention in Chicago in August 1956, for example, yielded three images (*Americans* 3, 51, and 58), these were culled from fifty rolls of film.[21] While some sheets reveal Frank immersing himself in an event, such as the roadside fatality along US 66 in Arizona, where he exposed an entire roll of film (*Americans* 35), other rolls show a more immediate response to a situation, with Frank taking only one or two images. The most famous of these is his photograph of the African American nurse with the white baby (*Americans* 13). The publication of the contact sheets enormously enhances our knowledge of Frank's method of photographing, but this understanding still feels provisional, and awaits a full study of all 767 sheets, which will also situate Frank's method of working within the history and uses of contact sheets by earlier and contemporary documentary and artistic photographers.[22]

After developing his negatives and printing contact sheets, Frank selected approximately one thousand images and enlarged these as 8 × 10-inch work prints. Over the summer and autumn of 1956 and the winter of 1957, he gradually distilled these, editing them down to the final sequence of eighty-three images. Three enormous frames in the exhibition and three double-page spreads in the publications presented 119 work prints as a partial reconstruction, a simulation of a portion of his studio wall, with the rough grouping of images into themes that Frank was then considering.[23] His original maquette of *The Americans*, the next stage in the process of creating the publication, was probably made in the spring of 1957, and comprised a sequence of ninety-two images, including all of the final images. This sequence has been meticulously re-constructed and published for the first time in the *Expanded Edition*.[24] The contact sheets, the work prints, and the maquette separately and together mark intermediary stages and pivotal moments in the selection and editing process, and allow us, for the first time, to enter into a much fuller understanding of the genesis of the publication. The creative process will always remain mysterious and in part unknowable, and will elude all attempts at a complete explanation. The significance of this important exhibition, and particularly its related publications, lies in assembling the surviving artefacts and documentation, and in meticulously and exhaustively reconstructing this process, while at the same time preserving its essential mystery.

Events, dates, and circumstances can be recovered to a large extent, but the interpretations of the book, its interior life, will continue to touch and affect future readers.

This brings us back to the publication, *The Americans*. The current edition was co-published by Steidl and the National Gallery of Art with Frank's full participation in 2008.[25] After the various sizes and printing permutations of the previous five editions, this volume appears at first as though it were a facsimile of the 1959 English-language edition, replicating its overall size and the appearance of the photogravures. However, on closer study, this edition takes its place as yet another version, a further variant and interpretation of the original book: the dust-jacket and the typography have been redesigned, the book bound in black matte linen, Kerouac's introduction re-set, and the plates printed in tritone on thicker, whiter paper.[26] In comparison with the first edition, this book is more substantial and slightly heavier to hold. The paper stock gives the images, which are beautifully printed with a luminous, sooty opacity, a weightier presence, endowing the process of turning the page with a more deliberate finality. After handling the bulk and weight of *Looking In: Robert Frank's* The Americans, either the catalog and especially the *Expanded Edition*, it is almost as a relief to pick up the comparatively tiny book, *The Americans*, and enter immediately into a different world, the book and plates perfectly scaled to the imaginative needs of a reader encountering and discovering Frank's vision of America.

Notes

1 Sarah Greenough, curator. *Looking In: Robert Frank's* The Americans.

Itinerary: National Gallery of Art, Washington, D.C., January 18–April 26, 2009; San Francisco Museum of Modern Art, San Francisco, May 16–August 23, 2009; The Metropolitan Museum of Art, New York, September 22, 2009–January 3, 2010.

Robert Frank. *The Americans*. Göttingen: Steidl; Washington: National Gallery of Art, 2008. 180 pages.

Sarah Greenough, with contributing essays by Stuart Alexander, Philip Brookman, Michel Frizot, Milton Gasser, Jeff L. Rosenheim, Luc Sante, and Anne Wilkes Tucker. *Looking In: Robert Frank's* The Americans. Washington: National Gallery of Art; Göttingen: Steidl, 2009. 374 pages.

Sarah Greenough, with contributing essays by Stuart Alexander, Philip Brookman, Michel Frizot, Milton Gasser, Jeff L. Rosenheim, Luc Sante, and Anne Wilkes Tucker. *Looking In: Robert Frank's* The Americans. *Expanded Edition.* Washington: National Gallery of Art; Göttingen: Steidl, 2009. 506 pages.

2 While it is possible to hold the corner of one or more pages and flip forward or backwards, thereby making the process of comparing one or more images easier, it is still only possible to view a single image at one time.

3 Frank's book formed the fifth publication in the series *Encyclopédie essentielle* by Robert Delpire. Details are now available in Michel Frizot's essay, "Robert Frank and Robert Delpire," in Sarah Greenough's *Looking In: Robert Frank's* The Americans. *Expanded Edition* (Washington: National Gallery of Art; Göttingen: Steidl, 2009), pp. 190–98.

4 The initial reviews are listed, with excerpts, in Stuart Alexander's essential *Robert Frank: A Bibliography, Filmography, and Exhibition Chronology, 1946–1985* (Tucson: Center for Creative Photography, University of Arizona, in association with the Museum of Fine Arts, Houston, 1986), pp. 24-26.

5 The 1968 and 1969 editions of *The Americans*, which are virtually identical, include twelve additional pages that are devoted to Frank's films. These editions are described in Alexander, *Bibliography*, pp. 55–56 and 59. See also Sarah Greenough, "Blowing Down Bleecker Street: Destroying *The Americans*," in *Looking In*, pp. 316–20.

6 See Greenough, "Blowing Down Bleecker Street," in *Looking In*, p. 316.

7 Beaumont Newhall, *The History of Photography From 1839 to the Present Day* (New York: The Museum of Modern Art, 1964), p. 200.

8 John Szarkowski, *Mirrors and Windows: American Photography Since 1960* (New York: The Museum of Modern Art, 1978), p. 16.

9 Martin Parr and Gerry Badger, *The Photobook: A History*, Volume 1 (London and New York: Phaidon, 2004), p. 247

10 The contact sheet was sold at Christie's New York, Photographs, Sale 2206, October 8, 2009, lot 793; the print of "Butte Montana" was sold at Sotheby's New York, Photographs, Sale 8624, 13, April 2010, lot 160; and the first edition of *The Americans* at Christie's South Kensington, Photobooks, Sale 5456, 21 May, 2010, lot 261.

11 Earl A. Powell III, foreword to *Robert Frank: Moving Out*, by Sarah Greenough and Philip Brookman (Washington: National Gallery of Art; Zurich: Scalo, 1994), p. 19.

12 The website for the National Gallery of Art's collections is http://www.nga.gov/collection/index.shtm

13 Greenough, introduction to *Looking In*, p. xx.

14 Ibid., p. xx

15 Although printing dates are not included in the catalog, Greenough discusses Frank's printing of this work in "Blowing Down Bleecker Street," in *Looking In*, pp. 316–17.

16 Robert Frank, *The Lines of My Hand* (Tokyo: Yugensha, Kazuhiko Motomura, 1972), pp. 86–90. Frank also included twelve negative strips, of which five were different from those published in the Japanese edition, in the first American edition of *The Lines of My Hand* (New York: Lustrum Press, 1972), n.p. These strips were omitted from the 1989 revised edition.

17 Eight of the twelve are reproduced in the accompanying catalog, Robert Frank, *Storylines* (Göttingen: Steidl, 2004), pp. 2–7, and pp. 206–207. An exhibition featuring eight "contact sheet enlargements" was shown at Pace/MacGill Gallery, October 29–December 5, 2009; see the gallery's website http://www.pacemacgill.com/exhibitions_frank09.html.

18 For example, in 1986, Anne Tucker estimated that Frank had shot and contact printed "almost 800 rolls of film"; see "It's the Misinformation That's

Important," in *Robert Frank: New York to Nova Scotia* (Houston: Museum of Fine Arts; Boston: New York Graphic Society, 1986), p. 95.

19 See Greenough, "Disordering the Senses: Guggenheim Fellowship" and "Blowing Down Bleecker Street" in *Looking In*, pp. 121, 123, 128, 133, 341 (note 4), and 342 (note 54). All the contact sheets are included on the National Gallery of Art's collections website, cited in note 12.

20 Two of the contact sheets include two images that were selected for the final publication (*Americans* 18/19 and 77/78). See also Greenough, "Disordering the Senses," in *Looking In*, p. 134.

21 These are listed on the National Gallery of Art's collections website under "Convention" and "Convention hall – Chicago."

22 In addition to Greenough's comments (cited in note 19 above) and pending a full study, a few preliminary observations can be made. While the majority of the sheets represent complete rolls of 35mm film (such as *Americans* 2, 3, 4, 5, 6, etc.), there are others that are either partial rolls (*Americans* 1, 9, 18/19, 21, 38, 44, 47, 52, 54, 55, 57, 59, 71, 74, 76) or, in a few cases, a mixture of more than one roll (*Americans* 22, 25, 34, 68, 73, 82). Moreover, the rolls are seldom organized to replicate the order in which the negatives were taken but laid out randomly, which makes the process of following the order in which Frank shot the roll cumbersome. The various orange, red, and blue annotations allow one to follow Frank's editing process, as he considered various images, hesitated with question marks (*Americans* 34), and occasionally indicated cropping marks (*Americans* 25).

23 Greenough does not specify whether this "reconstruction" was intended as a record of a particular moment or to reveal Frank's general editing method during the summer and autumn of 1956, beyond indicating that it was re-created in 2007 and 2008. See "Disordering the Senses," in *Looking In*, p. 133 and plates 64–66.

24 The actual maquette does not survive in its original form. See Greenough, "Disordering the Senses," in her *Looking In*, pp. 134–35, Andrea Nelson, "Making and Remaking *The Americans*," in *Looking In*, pp. 459–83.

25 Information about the printing of the 2008 edition is taken from the brochure, *Robert Frank, Published by Steidl*, accompanying the book.

26 This is not intended as a complete account of all the differences between this and the first English-language edition. For cropping differences, see Nelson, "Making and Remaking."

David Harris is Associate Professor, School of Image Arts, Ryerson University, Toronto. His publications include *Eadweard Muybridge and the Photographic Panorama of San Francisco, 1850–1880* (Canadian Centre for Architecture), *Eugène Atget: Unknown Paris* (The New Press), *Of Battle and Beauty: Felice Beato's Photographs of China* (Santa Barbara Museum of Art) and, most recently, *Gabor Szilasi: The Eloquence of the Everyday* (Musée d'art de Joliette and Canadian Museum of Contemporary Photography).

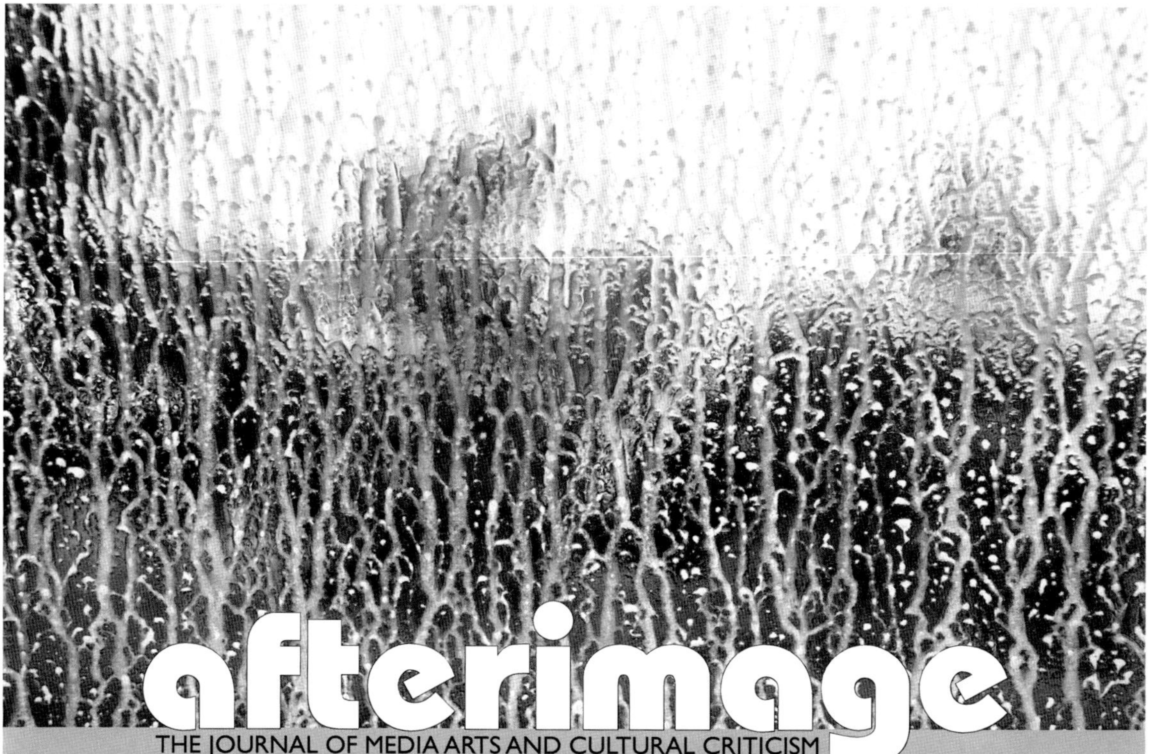

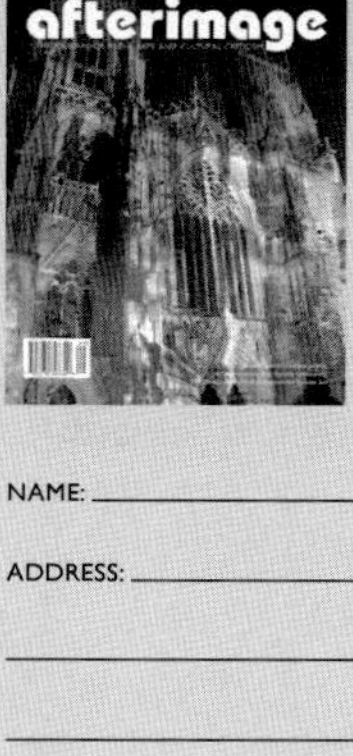

Photography & Culture

Volume 4—Issue 1
March 2011
pp. 103–106
DOI:
10.2752/175145211X12899905861591

Reprints available directly from
the publishers

Photocopying permitted by
licence only

Exhibition Review

The Silent Village: Humphrey Jennings/Peter Finnemore/
Rachel Trezise/Paolo Ventura.
January 16–February 27, 2010, Ffotogallery,
Turner House Gallery, Penarth, Wales.

Reviewed by Paul Gough

On the morning of Wednesday June 10, 1942, the village of Lidice,
about 20 kilometres north-west of Prague in Czechoslovakia, was
destroyed in retaliation for the assassination of Reinhard Heydrich,
controller and highest ranking Nazi official in the Protectorate of
Bohemia and Moravia. Acting on Hitler's direct order, the men of
the small mining village were rounded up and shot in groups of five,
until the SS Commander in charge, irritated by the delay in carrying
out the executions, ordered that ten be shot at a time. By mid-
afternoon 173 men lay dead around Horak's farm; a photograph
taken later that day shows them strewn in lines across the ground,
the walls of the farm lined with mattresses to absorb the bullets
and limit ricochet fire. Two days later 184 women from Lidice were
deported to the concentration camp at Ravensbruck, from where
less than half survived. Separated from their parents, 105 children
were sent to Lodz where they were imprisoned and maltreated.
A few weeks later they were shipped 70 kilometres away to an
extermination camp at Chelmno and gassed to death. Only a few
survived the war. In all, some 340 villagers died as a result of the
Nazi reprisal.

The village was not spared. Its buildings were set ablaze, the
remains then knocked to the ground and smashed until not a
trace of the village was left. The act was systematic, thorough and
dispassionate, the desecration industrial in its method. Unsuprisingly,
the entire process was filmed by Franz Treml, the proprietor of
a Zeiss-Ikon shop in Prague who later became a film adviser
for the National Socialist German Workers' Party. His footage
and photographs show a small group of German soldiers busily
destroying the farmsteads, the mining gear and the industrial units;
others show teams of Nazis posing in front of the shambles that
was once Lidice.

Such is the bald historical context for this provocative exhibition
in Ffotogallery, Penarth. Intelligently curated by Russell Roberts,
Reader in Photography at the European Centre for Photographic
Research, University of Wales, Newport, the centerpiece of the
show is the remarkable film made by Humphrey Jennings soon after
the atrocity. Its awesome soundtrack penetrates the very heart of

the fine gallery building in Penarth, adding a grim backing track to the work of Paolo Ventura and Peter Finnemore, which hangs in the gallery and the writings of Rachel Trezise, David Berry and Roberts himself which accompanies the exhibition in a well produced boxed-catalog.

Jennings's film may dominate the space, both aurally and physically, but it is the haunting iconography of Ventura and Finnemore that lingers long after. The film is a stunning piece of responsive documentary, passionate in its anger and heartfelt in its vicarious identification with the doomed Czech villagers.

As the Lidice reprisal became known across Europe, the atrocity was met with outrage and instantaneous acts of commemoration: towns across the world were renamed after Lidice to ensure that its name would not be forgotten; coal miners in Stoke-on-Trent founded an organization "Lidice Shall Live" to raise funds for its rebuilding; American poets and European composers created original works to remember the massacre. In England, artist, poet and filmmaker Humphrey Jennings set out with the Crown Film Unit to make a short film that recreated the fate of Lidice. In autumn 1942 his crew arrived in the Upper Swansea Valley at the small village of Cwmgïedd, close to the town of Ystradgynlais, to create the film that would become *The Silent Village*. Using local villagers as the "actors", the thirty-six minute film traces the inevitable tale of a population being insidiously overwhelmed by largely invisible oppressors. Skillful montage helps build the tension as the film isolates objects and certain details; loudspeakers, radios, the voice of command announcing first a "Protectorate State" and then cumulatively menacing messages; deep shadow and restrained movement only serves to underline the threat that gradually pervades the film and overwhelms the villagers. Although a constant fear of reprisal dominates its second half, there is little overt violence, even the mass killing at the close of the film takes place off camera. A stirring rendition of "Land of my Fathers" closes

the film and reverberates around the galleries, an uncomfortable reminder of the perils of "lost liberty, untimely death and savage oppression." A number of stark silhouette sequences in the film—mostly those that show a castle built by English invaders under Edward the First—adds a further layer of intention, drawing uncomfortable parallels with the history of English dominance in Wales.

Ventura's carefully recreated and honed images would appear to revisit the morbid portraits of the Nazi soldiers and officers that destroyed the village; their distressed surfaces and scoring-out suggest denial and decay but these are clearly reconstructions, careful fabrications of toy soldiers, miniature farm buildings and the occasional model animal re-presented as "authentica," retrieved decades later and presented as contemporary images. Their very artifice and their exacting craftsmanship seems acutely appropriate in this setting, drawing uncomfortable resonances with the systematic destruction of Lidice and the many still photographs of Nazi soldiers posing proudly for the camera amidst the maelstrom of the burning village. Ventura's images toy cleverly with the fetishization of the military past and the fascination of battle re-enactments, with its strange mix of vicarious pleasure and exacting simulation.

Finnemore's work, by comparison, appears to offer only a very oblique take on the Lidice incident, but like much of his corpus of work addressing memory retrieval, his photographs benefit from close and slow scrutiny. Typically mournful, accidental, and occasional, they approach their subject indirectly; tucked away amongst the stacked pile of shabby video-cassettes and tapes in one photograph, for example, is a copy of Jennings's film; in another an old tin for a roll of Agfa film is stamped "Made in Germany", its contents unknown and more ominous for that fact. More obvious references to the doomed village are represented through images of commemorative stamps and souvenirs such as fridge magnets and ornaments. There is a profound visual intelligence here, but also, as Roberts comments in a penetrating catalog essay, an impish humor is at work. It sits uneasily alongside images of decay and dustiness, caught in a tense dynamic of unwanted occupation, colonial dominance and contested histories.

Along with Ventura's discomforting portraits, Tresize's necessarily awkward short story, and Roberts's insightful analyses, this show adds immensely to Finnemore's standing and to his continuing engagement with familiarity and obscurity, a gentle mapping of personal circumstance bought into shocking and sharp relief by the grim events at Lidice and its lingering aftermath.

Paul Gough is Deputy Vice-Chancellor (Academic) at UWE, Bristol. For ten years he was Executive Dean of a large Faculty of Creative Arts, Design and Media. A painter, broadcaster and writer, he has exhibited widely in the UK and abroad, and is represented in several art collections. His research interests lie in the processes and iconography of commemoration, the cultural geographies of battlefields, and the representation of peace and conflict in the 20th and 21st century. Amongst his recent publications is a monograph on the British artist Stanley Spencer, and *A Terrible Beauty*, an extensive study of British art of the Great War.

American Visual Culture
Mark Rawlinson

Visual culture – art, advertising, architecture, cinema, television, cartography, video, the internet, and images of science – has shaped American national identity more than that of any other country. Covering the period from the late nineteenth century to the present day, the book explores how visual culture has at once transformed and consolidated the image of the United States.

American Visual Culture *presents both an analysis of the diversity of American visual media and a critical introduction to the study and interpretation of visual culture. Thematic chapters – on American urban and rural landscapes, icons, popular culture, art and photography, as well as on crime, anxiety and sex – describe the cultural, intellectual and historical context. Throughout, these themes are discussed in conjunction with clear and concise explanations of key visual theories and methodologies.*

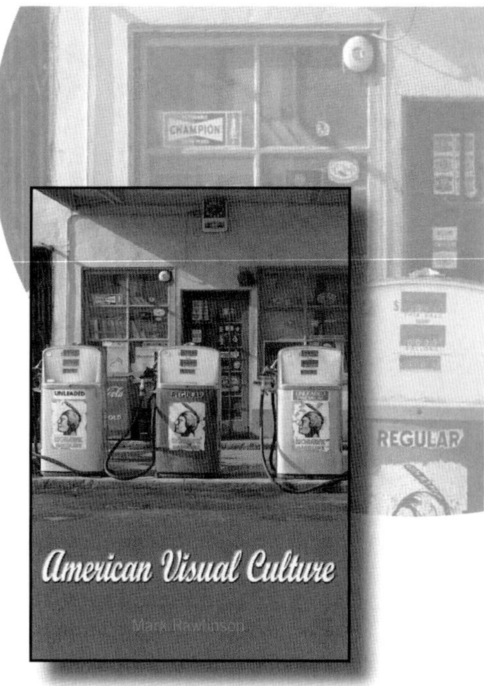

July 09 • 248pp • 40 bw illus
PB 978 1 84520 217 0 **£17.99/$29.95**
HB 978 1 84520 216 3 **£55.00/$109.95**

American Science Fiction Film and Television
Lincoln Geraghty

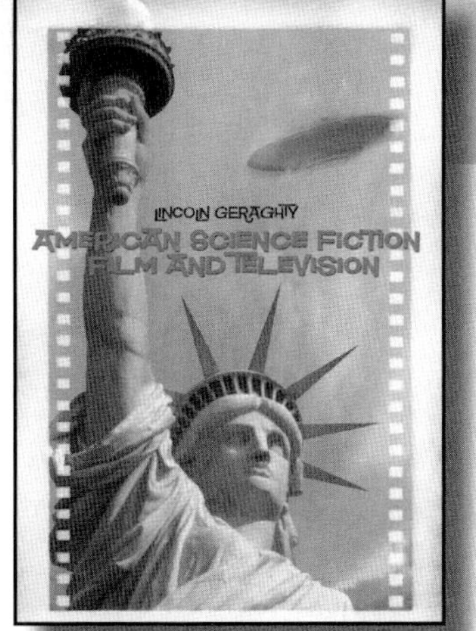

American Science Fiction Film and Television *presents a critical history of late 20th Century SF together with an analysis of the cultural and thematic concerns of this popular genre. Science fiction film and television were initially inspired by the classic literature of HG Wells and Jules Verne. The potential and fears born with the Atomic age fuelled the popularity of the genre, upping the stakes for both technology and apocalypse. From the Cold War through to America's current War on Terror, science fiction has proved a subtle vehicle for the hopes, fears and preoccupations of a nation at war. The definitive introduction to American science fiction, this is also the first study to analyse SF across both film and TV. Throughout, the discussion is illustrated with critical case studies of key films and television series, including* The Day the Earth Stood Still, Planet of the Apes, Star Trek: The Next Generation, The X-Files, *and* Battlestar Galactica.

Oct 09 • 160pp
PB 978 1 84520 796 0 **£14.99/$24.95**
HB 978 1 84520 795 3 **£50.00/$94.95**

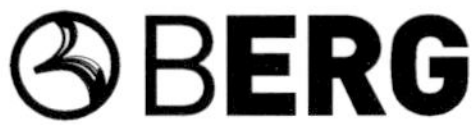
BERG

Order now at www.bergpublishers.com

Photography & Culture

Volume 4—Issue 1
March 2011
pp. 107–110
DOI:
10.2752/175145211X12899905861672

Reprints available directly from
the publishers

HELIOS: Eadweard Muybridge in a Time of Change

Edited by Philip Brookman

Essays by Marta Braun, Andy Grundberg, Corey Keller, and Rebecca Solnit (Göttingen, Germany: Steidl/Corcoran Gallery of Art, 2010)

Reviewed by Elizabeth Hutchinson

In 1873, the San Francisco publishing firm Bradley and Rulofson issued a catalog of photographic views by the British immigrant Eadweard Muybridge. Soon to be famous for his experiments recording human and animal locomotion conducted at the University of Pennsylvania, Muybridge was best known at the time for a recent series of mammoth-plate views of Yosemite. The catalog traces other series Muybridge had produced in the scant six years since he had entered California's vibrant community of photographers. The subjects listed range from coastal landscapes to documents of mining and agricultural practices to views of the Central Pacific Railroad, with hundreds of views offered in a variety of sizes.

The profound diversity of Muybridge's *oeuvre* poses a challenge to historians who would offer a coherent reading of the artist's career. As Rebecca Solnit writes, "Muybridge's work has long been treated as though it were made by a succession of different artists" (179). For in addition to the subjects listed above, all of which could be subsumed under the broad theme of the Far West, Muybridge also sought out private commissions for portraits, records of people's homes, and photographic copies of legal documents, and undertook a variety of jobs for the United States Government. Moreover, a year before the Bradley and Rulofson catalog was issued, he began his experiments with capturing motion, producing a suite of experimental views of running horses belonging to the railroad magnate and former governor Leland Stanford.

While he is the subject of several substantial biographies and numerous studies that focus on specific periods or aspects of his work, Muybridge did not receive a comprehensive retrospective exhibition until this year, perhaps because of the difficulty of fusing the different strains of his work. An added obstacle to the careful analysis of his *oeuvre* is the attention garnered by his colorful biography—Muybridge is notorious for getting away with the murder of his wife's lover and for eccentric behavior that may have resulted from a head injury received in a stagecoach accident. The Corcoran Gallery of Art's exhibition and catalog *HELIOS: Eadweard Muybridge in a Time of Change* draws our attention away from these incidents and offers a serious and substantial inquiry into the images made across Muybridge's three-decade career. The Corcoran is a logical institution to launch this project, as it was an early investor in Muybridge's work, having purchased a set of illustrations of Animal Locomotion for use by students at the Corcoran College of Art and Design in 1887 (the plates were exhibited at the Corcoran in an exhibition in 1986). The volume offers an excellent introduction for new audiences to appreciate Muybridge's pictures and ponder the changing world in which they were made and viewed.

After a brief introduction by Andy Grundberg which establishes Muybridge's influence on twentieth-century artists, the exhibition's curator Philip Brookman offers his reading of Muybridge's persistent drive to "make something permanent of something temporal" (43) in the most substantial essay of the catalog. As Brookman argues, Muybridge's interest in documenting the transitory was a response to the radical changes in transportation, illumination, communication and even social organization that he witnessed during his lifetime. Brookman offers little new information about Muybridge for scholars of photo-history, but he has tracked down a wealth of primary sources and documented many claims advanced by earlier biographers without substantiation. In addition, he makes excellent use of the work of other scholars of landscape and motion photography.

Brookman's contribution comes from his integration of Muybridge's biography into the broader history of technology, science and art. For example, he devotes time to the two great industrial exhibitions held in London in 1851 and 1862, noting that while there is no evidence that Muybridge attended them, it is exceptionally likely that he did, given the fact that the photographer was also an inventor (his patents include not only technologies related to making and projecting photographs, but also machines for doing laundry and printing). Moreover, Muybridge, who spent most of the Civil War years in London and most likely took up photography during this time, would have learned a great deal about the art and technology of photography through the exhibits at the 1868 exhibition. Brookman's essay also offers his own readings of images and a comparison between his work and those of other artists, particularly painters. While some of the comparisons are routine (the *de rigueur* juxtaposition of Muybridge's "dynamic" Yosemite with the "classic" images of Carleton Watkins, for example) others are more unexpected, such as the connection made between Muybridge's treatment of waterfalls and those in paintings by Frederic Edwin Church, something that may have occurred to Brookman while standing in front of the Corcoran's magnificent Church painting *Niagara*. The success of these descriptions is enhanced by the decision to illustrate both figures and plates in full color allowing the rich tonalities of Muybridge's so-called "black and white" pictures to come across.

The wealth of illustrations recommends this volume to all students of the albumen era. Departing from the convention of exhibition catalogs of putting most plates at the end of the book, Brookman divides the images into four suites that are interspersed between the essays. Arranged roughly according to chronology, they bring together pictures from different series grouped under an evocative title that invites the reader to connect seemingly disparate pictures.

For example, Muybridge's 360-degree *Panorama of San Francisco from California Street Hill* is included in a section titled "Animals in motion," which also comprises shots of domestic interiors and some of the earliest motion studies. This juxtaposition demands meditation on different kinds of movement—the body's mechanical movement, the simulated motion of a panoramic view, and perhaps even the navigation of social space among California's elite class.

The other essays are by scholars who have written about different aspects of Muybridge's work in other contexts. Rebecca Solnit revisits themes from her 2003 book on the first half of Muybridge's career, *River of Shadows*, in which she argued that Muybridge's work illustrated and facilitated the radical break in perceptions of time and space that produced modernity. Solnit sees thematic and compositional coherence in Muybridge's diverse series; specifically, she finds him drawn to the dynamic and chaotic, offering a visual parallel to the social instability of his era. Her observation that Muybridge tended to keep human figures at a spatial and emotional distance ("the special ability of the camera to capture the distinctness of each person is not relevant to Muybridge" [182]) is particularly evocative, as it points both to the photographer's own romantic subjectivity and to alienation as a key aspect of industrial modernity. Corey Keller uses her knowledge of popular science in the Victorian era to situate Muybridge in the context of an emerging visual culture of modernity dedicated to spectacular presentations of "the real" (217). In addition to supporting the exhibition's emphasis on the coherence of Muybridge's career, this essay seeks to recontextualize a man whose eccentricities have often led him to be seen as an outsider. Her essay demonstrates that both the subjects Muybridge photographed and the means he used to exhibit and promote them demonstrate his understanding of the tastes and habits of his viewers, including both the power brokers who sponsored his most ambitious works

and the urban audiences who sought out his stereographs and flocked to his illustrated lectures for entertainment. In the last essay, Marta Braun, the scholar of chronophotography, exposes the underlying logic of Muybridge's motion studies. Through a reconstruction of the order in which the 781 plates of *Animal Locomotion* were shot, she demonstrates that this work continues the interest in aesthetics and theatricality of his early career. While Muybridge's work on this project was sponsored by the University of Pennsylvania and overseen by faculty from the medical school, his plates reveal extra-scientific concerns, in particular the reification of racial, class and gender difference through references to popular and artistic imagery. Using Muybridge's notebooks and analyzing his evolving technique allows her to expose the careful editing and, at times, the insertion of narrative content, which gives the motion studies underlying rhetorical significance and enhances their appeal.

The catalog is written in an engaging and accessible manner, which should appeal to a broad audience but might, at times, seem too generalized or overblown for scholarly readers. Complex ideas such as modernity, the spectacle, or the Victorian fusion of art and science are referenced without being carefully defined and there is a tendency to discuss nineteenth-century audiences as monolithic or, at best, split into elites and non-elites. However, there is an excellent and extensive bibliography provided to invite readers intrigued by the issues raised by these authors to investigate further.

While the catalog carefully traces a variety of factors that inform Muybridge's work, including the demands of his patrons and the impact of technology on modern perceptions of time and space during his lifetime, it is ultimately a portrait of an artist. Brookman sees his work as an expression of an inner drive to create a "mythic identity" (43). Solnit calls Muybridge "radically original" (187). And the luxurious quality of the illustrations—all in excellent condition with none of the foxing, fading or abrasions which one usually sees on stereocards and printed books from over a century ago—emphasize the moments of exposure and printing over the social circulation of the pictures. Yet, while it is clear that Muybridge put together a portion of his work with notions of the picturesque or a familiarity with Greek sculpture in mind, the designation "artist," with its associations of an individual struggling for self-expression, cannot be convincing, as it is a given that a great deal of Muybridge's work was made to meet the standards of his clientele. Indeed, the variety in Muybridge's photographic subjects is best explained by the range of people and institutions that paid for the pictures.

Molly Nesbit's concept of the photographic "author" might be a better match.[1] Coined to help explain the agency of another wide-ranging photographer, Eugene Atget, "author" appropriately describes the photographer's rights to his work as it moves through the economy, as document, tool, artistic study or free-standing work of art. As Nesbit demonstrates, although Atget's work was made to meet the needs of his clients, he was able to insert his own presence in the work in ways which did not interfere with those needs, for example, through point of view, framing, composition, and by including his own body in the image. Similarly, Muybridge fulfilled his clients' and customers' needs for pictures of specific subjects while developing a distinctive set of formal strategies and compositional devices.

Nesbit was writing in the wake of a critique of photographic criticism that severed nineteenth-century documentary images from their original contexts and positioned them as precursors to modernist photography, something that can be traced back to the first appearance of photographs at MOMA in 1939.[2] This critique did not end the practice of exhibiting such work in art museums, of course. Indeed, the appeal

of such work appears to have grown—the past few years have brought us major retrospectives of Timothy O'Sullivan and Carleton Watkins as well as this Muybridge show, and at museums as prestigious as the Smithsonian and the Getty.[3] Each has sought to reconstruct an individual photographer's visual sensibilities without falling into pure formalism. Perhaps because Muybridge's perplexingly broad range of practice takes the authors in so many rich directions, the Corcoran's catalog may be the best at balancing an investigation of the photographer's distinctive vision with an investigation of more widespread transformations impacting the visual culture of his time as dual explanations of the form and success of his work.

Notes

1 See Molly Nesbit, *Atget's Seven Albums* (New Haven: Yale University Press, 1992).

2 See, for example, Rosalind Krauss, "Photography's Discursive Spaces: Landscape/View," *Art Journal* 42, no. 4 (Winter 1982): 311–19. And Douglas Crimp, "The Museum's Old/The Library's New Subject," *Parachute* (Spring 1981): 32–37. For an excellent recent example of this kind of scholarship, see Robin Kelsey, *Archive Style: Photographs and Illustrations for U.S. Surveys, 1850–1890* (Berkeley: University of California Press, 2007).

3 Weston J. Naef, *Carleton Watkins in Yosemite* (Los Angeles: J. Paul Getty Museum, 2008); Toby Jurovics et al., *Framing the West: The Survey Photographs of Timothy O'Sullivan* (New Haven: Yale University Press for the Library of Congress and the Smithsonian American Art Museum, 2010).

Elizabeth Hutchinson teaches the history of North American visual culture at Barnard College and Columbia University. She is the author of *The Indian Craze: Primitivism, Modernism, and Transculturation in American Art, 1890–1915* (Duke, 1999), and *Muybridge's Pacific Coast*, forthcoming from the University of California Press.

**Photography
& Culture**

Volume 4—Issue 1
March 2011
pp. 111–116
DOI:
10.2752/175145211X12899905861870

Reprints available directly from
the publishers

Book Review

Japanese Photobooks of the 1960s and '70s

Ryūichi Kaneko and Ivan Vartanian, New York: Aperture, 2009

Reviewed by Lisa Sutcliffe

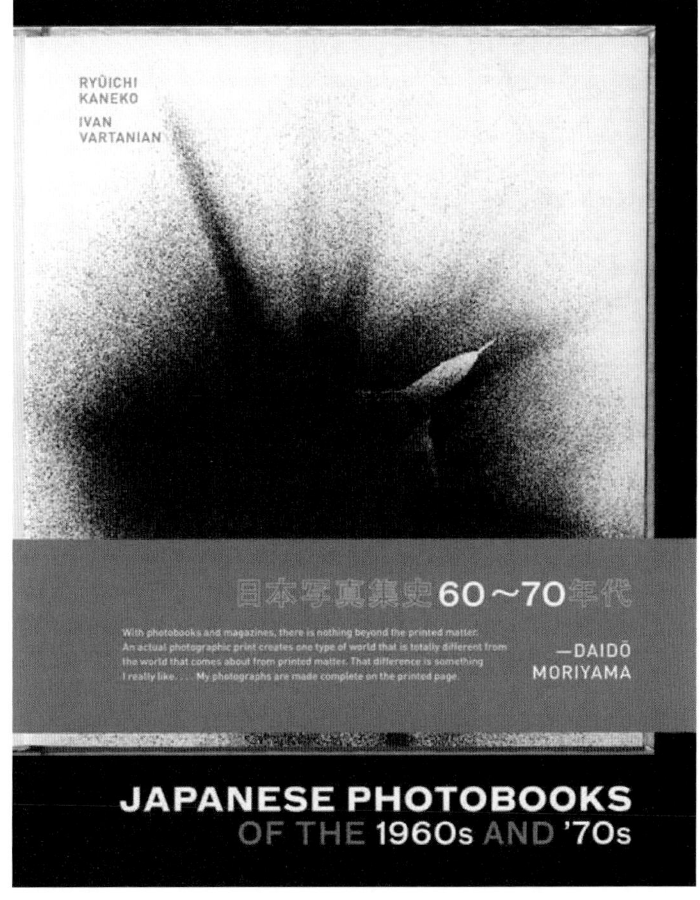

Fig I *Japanese Photobooks of the 1960s and '70s.* Aperture, 2009.

Interest in postwar Japanese photography has grown in the West since 1974, when the exhibition *New Japanese Photography* debuted at the Museum of Modern Art, New York. Numerous subsequent exhibitions and publications have focused on the development of the Japanese avant-garde after World War Two, including *Japan: A Self-Portrait*, presented in 1979 at the International Center of Photography, and the SFMOMA exhibitions *Daido Moriyama: Stray Dog* (1999), *Shōmei Tōmatsu: Skin of the Nation* (2003), and *The Provoke Era: Postwar Japanese Photography* (2009). Yet as Shoji Yamagishi explains in the exhibition catalog for *New Japanese Photography*, it is difficult for museum presentations to fully capture the richness and complexity of photobooks, an essential form in Japanese photographic practice:

> Japanese photographers usually complete a project in book form, joining in series a number of photographs related by a common subject, theme, or idea. The full value or impact of such work cannot be understood if individual pictures are isolated from the series for exhibition on the walls of a museum. To do this deprives the photographs of their intended relationship to those which preceded or followed them in series. In addition, the photographs were originally made to be reproduced in print form, in books and magazines, and not to be displayed as part of an exhibition.[1]

Ryūichi Kaneko and Ivan Vartanian's *Japanese Photobooks of the 1960s and '70s* opens with an italicized restatement of this vital argument: "*Japanese photography is best understood via the photobook.*" Their project focuses exclusively on these books, examining nearly fifty volumes from a broad range of genres, including commercial and fine art photography, highly collectible volumes, and more obscure books. Through their selections, Kaneko and Vartanian expand upon popular assumptions about Japanese photography, moving beyond the well-known, gritty, black-and-white pictures characteristic of the postwar avant-garde to suggest the richness and variety of the broader history.

Announcing an interest in examining the book as art object from the outset—a scan of a page from Shōmei Tōmatsu's *Nippon (Japan)* (1967) graces the cover—*Japanese Photobooks* illustrates the importance the form has held for Japanese photographers. As Kaneko explains in the introduction, the photobook relies on relationships between images to create a more complex form of expression than the single picture. Vartanian argues that through "cropping, sequencing, organization of material into chapters or sections, choice of printing techniques, and the introduction of text elements" these books define the medium in Japan in the 1960s and '70s. The selection featured in this volume makes these qualities and artists' desire to challenge traditional book formats manifest to a Western audience.

The featured publications are drawn from Kaneko's personal library. A premier scholar on Japanese photobooks, he began collecting in the 1960s. Like other photographers at the time, he was deeply influenced by William Klein's *New York* (1957), which he purchased as a college student in 1967. Kaneko charts the history and development of his interest in photographic publications, including the price of each volume, and anecdotes such as the story behind the surprise delivery of Robert Frank's *The Lines of My Hand* by the book's publisher (it was cheaper to deliver it personally than to ship it). This narrative provides a refreshing and personal context for the books, reinforcing the fact that many of them were not mass produced for a general readership but were instead intended for a self-selecting audience, a group that was deeply engaged with photography when there was no gallery or museum culture for it in Japan.

The photobook phenomenon is not unique to Japan. Over the past ten years the rise in the attention devoted to its history suggests that the form is experiencing an international renaissance. Notable recent compilations that have examined and documented the history of the photobook include *The Book of 101 Books* by Andrew Roth,

and *The Photobook: A History* by Martin Parr
and Gerry Badger. As Kaneko and Vartanian
demonstrate, the fact that postwar Japanese
photography was built largely on the platform
of the photobook makes it ideally suited to this
type of examination. Although Andrew Roth
includes just four Japanese works in his list of 101
books, Parr and Badger dedicate a chapter to
the subject in Volume 1 of *The Photobook*. In 2007,
Antoine de Beaupré of Libraire 213 published
*Japon, 1968–1982, Japanese Photography: 31
Books*, a volume that includes a critical selection
of books, magazines, and pamphlets by Japanese
photographers, including rare examples of the
publications of Workshop, a school founded
by Tōmatsu and his contemporaries in 1974.
In 2001, Christopher Schifferli produced *The
Japanese Box*, a custom box of reprinted rare and
out-of-print *Provoke* era publications, including
the three issues of the journal *Provoke*, Daidō
Moriyama's *Farewell Photography,* and Nobuyoshi
Araki's *Sentimental Journey*. This growing interest
in the history of Japanese publications has been
accompanied by a rise in collecting, and *Japanese
Photobooks* serves as a reference to collectors as
well as historians.

Like Parr and Badger's volume, *Japanese
Photobooks* offers the reader an opportunity to
browse books that have become rare, out-of-
print collector's items. Although one cannot
handle the actual books, nor get a true sense
of scale or tonalities, one can examine the
design and image sequencing, through generous
reproductions of page spreads for each book.
In addition, the authors include pertinent
publication information about each volume,
including photographer, date, designers, number
of pages, and price, emphasizing the book's status
as both a commercial product and a design
object. (One might only wish that the authors
had noted the date when Kaneko added these
books to his library to clarify the developing
social history.) Kaneko and Vartanian's work is
set apart, however, by the selection of books

it features. Well-known volumes such as Eikoh
Hosoe's *Barakei (Ordeal by Roses),* a collaboration
between Hosoe and the controversial writer
Yukio Mishima, and Tōmatsu's *Hiroshima*, as well as
the frequently examined issues of *Provoke*, have
been omitted. As Vartanian explains, the project
consciously seeks to balance the rough, blurred,
and out-of-focus *Provoke* aesthetic that Western
audiences typically associate with all Japanese
photobooks by contrasting it with lesser-known
works that reveal the complexities and nuances
within the field. With this selection they suggest
a new history, which may distort rather than
balance the field, and which ultimately underlines
the masterful innovation and complexity of the
avant-garde publications in comparison to the
commercial work.

The books follow a poetic, thematic order
beginning with Hiroshi Hamaya's *Snowland*
(1956). This documentary essay presents
a foil for the following books which often
seek to reject or manipulate straightforward
narrative. Earlier social documentary work by
photographers such as Ken Domon leads into
work by Tōmatsu, Kawada, and other members
of VIVO who produced personal, or symbolic
documentary work. Publications from the
Provoke era photographers which follow are
dark, jarring, and confrontational. Moriyama's
Japanese Theater (1968), a mysterious and
masterful work (Figure 2), stands in stark contrast
to books of portraits of the model Nadia by
commercial fashion photographer Hajime
Sawatari, and a re-introduction of prewar work
by Teiko Shiotani that reflects both pastoral and
pictorialist sensibilities. By including this pre-war
work, Kaneko and Vartanian highlight the range
of photographic expression including work that
we now understand was sidelined by the more
avant-garde publications which sought to erase
the functionality of the photograph and create a
new visual language. As the history progresses,
full bleed spreads give way to standardized
white borders—what Vartanian describes as the

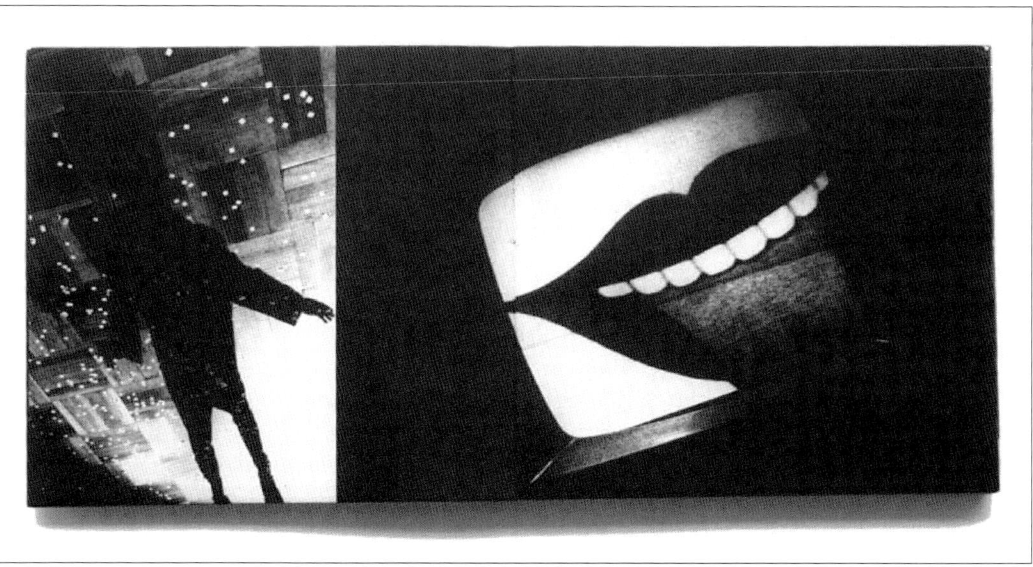

Fig 2 From *Japanese Theater* (1968) by Daido Moriyama from *Japanese Photobooks of the 1960s and '70s* (Aperture, 2009). Moriyama's *Japanese Theater* (1968), a mysterious and masterful work, stands in stark contrast to books of portraits of the model Nadia by commercial fashion photographer Hajime Sawatari, and a re-introduction of prewar work by Teiko Shiotani that reflects both pastoral and pictorialist sensibilities.

Westernizing influence of John Szarkowski—or prioritizing symbolism over the more interactive book design on the previous pages. Indeed, the layout of the last book, Masahisa Fukase's *Ravens* (1986), reflects the influence of Walker Evans's *American Photographs* (1938) or Robert Frank's *The Americans* (1956)—and features one photograph bordered by white, facing a blank page, followed by another.

Kaneko and Vartanian's selection of books is refreshing and sometimes surprising. For example, publications of landscapes and commercial nudes follow fragmentary explorations of graphic urban development. By combining commercial, amateur, pictorialist, and avant-garde books the project pays tribute to the democracy of the medium and the richness of its depth and variations. Certain common themes become apparent: the aftermath of Hiroshima and Nagasaki, Japan's economic boom and subsequent collapse, the changing urban experience, sexual tension between men and women, and the personal impulse to forge a national identity after a time of crisis. Despite their desire for diversity, it is interesting to note that nearly all of the books were made by men (Miyako Ishiuchi, is an exception). The male perspective dominated Japanese photography at this time (note the number of nudes), and draws into question the ability of women to publish during this period. The inclusion of the magazines in which some of this work was first published (*Asahi Camera* and *Camera Mainichi* are notable examples), or some demonstration of how the photographs were changed when they were republished in book format, would have been interesting additions as well. Comparison of spreads from the earlier and later books, or books made for different audiences would likely also make for some compelling discoveries. The 1960s and '70s were certainly a fertile time for photography in Japan, and the book format continues to be one of the best ways to explore its history.

Note

1   John Szarkowski and Shoji Yamagishi, *New Japanese Photography* (New York: Museum of Modern Art, 1974), p. 11.

Lisa Sutcliffe is Assistant Curator of Photography at the San Francisco Museum of Modern Art. Most recently she curated "The Provoke Era: Postwar Japanese Photography" and "Photography Now: China, Japan, Korea" which surveyed SFMOMA's collection of photography from Asia on the occasion of its seventy-fifth anniversary.

Photography & Culture

Volume 4—Issue 1
March 2011
pp. 117–120
DOI:
10.2752/175145211X12899905861717

Reprints available directly from the publishers

Photocopying permitted by licence only

Book Review

In Sight of America: Photography and the Development of U.S. Immigration Policy

Anna Pegler-Gordon

Berkeley: University of California Press, 2009

Reviewed by Mark Rice

In her 2009 article, "Citizenship, Diaspora and the Bonds of Affect: The Passport Photograph," published in the pages of this journal, Lily Cho writes, "photography and citizenship are intimately bound by the work of recognition and misrecognition."[1] Situating her analysis within recent scholarship on the complex relationship between humanity and citizenship,[2] Cho notes that the development of the passport within the bureaucracy of the state was one aspect of a wider rupture between the natural rights of all humans and the rights of citizens as defined within particular legal frameworks.

The policing of the border between citizen and foreigner, between those who "belong" and those who do not, is also at the heart of Anna Pegler-Gordon's provocative book, *In Sight of America: Photography and the Development of U.S. Immigration Policy*. More specifically, *In Sight of America* traces the role of photography in the development of federal immigration policies in the United States, spanning the years between 1875, when the Page Act "barred the entry of prostitutes, coolies, and criminals" (2), and 1924, when the National Origins Act required "non-quota immigrants ... to submit photographs to meet the new law's visa requirements" (18).

Where Cho notes the importance of race in the development of the idea of citizenship in nineteenth-century France, Pegler-Gordon demonstrates that race was equally critical in the development of immigration policy in the United States. Her study is guided by two overlapping questions: "How does the history of immigration policy change when we look through the prism of visual culture?" (7), and "How does the history of photography change when we consider immigrants and immigration identity documentation?" (11). By taking on both of these topics, she sets an ambitious goal for herself and, for the most part, she succeeds.

However, *In Sight of America* does a better job at answering the first question than the second.

Pegler-Gordon reveals how the implementation of photography in US immigration policies developed in a piecemeal fashion before its eventual consolidation as a regular part of immigration control. She also notes that efforts to use photography to help police national borders were occurring on both sides of the Atlantic concurrently: "The development of immigration policy as a racialized system of visual regulation was both particular to the United States and part of broader international changes in immigration policy, identity documentation, and bureaucratization" (8). Cho says that "the idea of the passport photograph" can be traced back to France in 1854. In 1916, "passport photographs became a standard requirement for British passports."[3] The US similarly established a passport requirement during World War One, but rescinded it in 1921. By that point, however, the tide had turned decisively in favor of the use of photographic identification to help distinguish foreigners from citizens. Pegler-Gordon notes that "in 1924 U.S. officials moved forward with regulations requiring photographic identification on citizenship certificates" a plan that was established as law in 1929 (227).

In Sight of America is well written, deeply researched, and elegantly structured. There are six chapters arranged in pairs, with all six framed by an introduction and a conclusion. The first two chapters detail the uses of photography in the documentation of Chinese immigrants. The middle two examine what we might call the spectacle of immigration at Ellis Island. The final two reveal how policies developed in other contexts were refined to control immigration from Mexico. Pegler-Gordon writes, "the development and implementation of new practices to regulate migration did not just circulate between Ellis Island and El Paso. They also moved along a different, less explored circuit: from Angel Island to the Mexican-U.S. border,

from Chinese exclusion to general immigration policies" (176).

For this reader, the strongest chapters concern the uses of photography to document Chinese immigrants. Pegler-Gordon develops a nuanced argument about the slippery nature of photographic identification and uses strong images to ground her analysis. Beginning in the 1870s, as Americans grew increasingly nervous about the large numbers of Chinese immigrants, the US Immigration Bureau implemented a policy of documenting all Chinese residents in the US. Such documentation did not occur all at once, but after the 1882 Chinese Exclusion Act, the documentation requirements were expanded to include more and more people. "By 1909," she writes, "almost all people of Chinese descent in the U.S. were required to possess photographic documentation" (24).

Photography was used in two distinct ways in the documentation of Chinese immigrants. One was that US immigration officials developed policies that required Chinese immigrants to carry photographic identification with them at all times. These photographs were presented as proof of the holder's legitimate residency in the US. Supporters of this policy "argued that photographs were necessary on Chinese documents because all Chinese looked alike" (25). Thus, only the close scrutiny of photographs could allow for immigration officials to distinguish between legal and illegal Chinese immigrants.

Pegler-Gordon turns her attention next to the ways in which Chinese residents, as well as would-be immigrants, subverted the uses of photographic documentation. "Paper sons," the name given to "Chinese immigrants who fabricated familial identities to enter the United States in spite of (and in opposition to) exclusion practices" (13) made frequent use of the slipperiness of identities based on photographic documents. "Although exclusionists and immigration officials believed that documents would authenticate real identity claims," she explains, "Chinese used documents to fabricate new identities and relationships, and although photographs were introduced to control the flow of fraudulent documents, fraudulent photographs themselves became part of this market" (69).

After carefully showing the importance of photography in regulating Chinese immigration, the next two chapters—those examining immigration practices at Ellis Island—come as something of a surprise. Many readers will undoubtedly expect to find that the photographic documentation of immigrants at Ellis Island was a routine part of the immigration process, their understanding of Ellis Island having been shaped in some measure by the photographs of Lewis Hine. However, such wasn't the case. As a result, Pegler-Gordon has to shift gears a bit, discussing the ways in which immigrants were visually examined for disease, were made visible to visitors at Ellis Island, and were the subjects of photographers whose work was not part of the official immigration process.

The main actor in this section of the book is not Hine, but Augustus Sherman, an immigration official who left a small archive of photographs of immigrants at Ellis Island. This is not to say that Pegler-Gordon ignores Hine, but she is more interested in carefully studying Sherman's photography—perhaps because he has not received nearly as much attention by historians. Although his photographs were not an official part of his job, Pegler-Gordon argues that his images "reflect[ed] the Immigration Bureau's understanding of immigrants." She goes on: "They were used by immigration officials, popular magazines, and other publications to shape understandings and influence opinion about immigrants" (129). Pegler-Gordon situates Sherman's photography within existing conventions of anthropometric photography but sees a great deal of complexity in his chosen subjects, settings, and poses, finally concluding that "Sherman's honorific ethnographic nostalgia

functions, in an attenuated way, like Renato Rosaldo's imperialist nostalgia" (149).

The final two chapters discuss the gradual "hardening" of the border between the US and Mexico. What previously had been an "almost imaginary line" became "a place of increased regulation and surveillance" (174). Pegler-Gordon shows that prior to 1917 efforts to guard the border were not aimed at Mexican immigrants but, rather, at Chinese and European immigrants seeking alternate ways into the US. With World War One, however, and then with the National Origins Act of 1924, the regulation of immigration became increasingly standardized, which transformed the US–Mexico border into a site of more heavily regulated passage. With each step, photography played a more and more central role.

My one criticism of *In Sight of America* is that I was expecting that my understanding of the history of photography would change more dramatically than it did as a result of reading the book. Unfortunately, I wasn't as convinced by her readings of photography as I was at her analysis of the uses of photography within the development of US immigration policy. Indeed, *In Sight of America* is an important addition to the history of US immigration policy, and her close readings of individual photographs are more effective in their efforts to link such photographs to the history of immigration than to the history of photography.

Although this is pure speculation, Pegler-Gordon may have desired to more fully intervene in the history of photography than she does, but had a dissertation committee that put limits on such an effort. (The book originated as a 2001 dissertation in American Culture from the University of Michigan.) As I have written elsewhere, "most historians are trained to privilege written texts over visual images," so that "they tend to be more comfortable deconstructing essays, government reports, and speeches than the images that frequently accompany those documents."[4] Books such as *In*

Sight of America can help serve as a corrective to this logocentrism.

I suspect that Pegler-Gordon has a lot more to say about the topics she covers in *In Sight of America,* and a lot more to say about the political functions of photography in the US. Having been freed from the demands of a dissertation committee, and having amply demonstrated her skills as a historian, she can now take even more challenging approaches to such research, helping to move the history of photography more and more toward the center of the study of US history.

Notes

1 Lily Cho, "Citizenship, Diaspora and the Bonds of Affect: The Passport Photograph." *Photography and Culture* 2(3), 2009: 277.

2 In particular, Cho draws from Giorgio Agamben, *Means Without Ends: Notes on Politics* (Minneapolis: University of Minnesota Press, 2000), Ariella Azoulay, *The Civil Contract of Photography* (New York: Zone Books, 2008), and Mark B. Salter, *Rights of Passage: The Passport in International Relations* (Boulder: Lynne Reiner, 2003).

3 Cho, 278.

4 Mark Rice, "His Name Was Don Francisco Muro: Reconstructing an Image of American Imperialism." *American Quarterly* 62(1), 2010: 51.

Mark Rice is Chair of American Studies at St. John Fisher College in Rochester, NY. He is the author of *Through the Lens of the City: NEA Photography Surveys of the 1970s* (University Press of Mississippi, 2005), and is currently working on a book about the photography of Dean Conant Worcester.

Photography
& Culture

Volume 4—Issue 1
March 2011
pp. 121–122
DOI:
10.2752/175145211X12899905861951

Books Received

Badiou, A. and S. Žižek. *Philosophy in the Present.* ed. by Peter Englemann (trans. Peter Thomas and Alberto Toscano), Polity, 2010.

Friedlander, Marti, *Leonard Bell.* Aukland University Press, 2009.

Hanley, Erin. *Photography and Africa.* London: Reaktion, 2010.

Maitland, Alexander (ed.). *Wilfred Thesiger in Africa.* London: Harper Collins, 2010.

Meng, Tsai, Stephanie Tung, Bas Vroege, Louise O. Fresco, and Menno van der Veen. *WATW.* Rotterdam: Post Editions, 2010.

Morton, Christopher and Philip N. Grover (eds.). *Wilfred Thesiger in Africa.* London: Harper Collins, 2010.

Muir, Peter. *Shimon Attie's Writing on the Wall.* Farnham: Ashgate, 2010.

Padget, Martin. *Photographers of the Western Isles.* Edinburgh: John Donald, 2010.

Scott, Hanna, and Anne Shelton (eds.). *Sightseeing.* Rim Books, 2010. In association with the exhibition *Sightseeing* at The New Dowse in October 2010 and Peninsula Arts, University of Plymouth, New Zealand.

Stultiens, Andrea, Kaddu Wasswa John, and Arthur C. Kisitu. *The Kaddu Wasswa Archive.* Rotterdam: Post Editions, 2010.

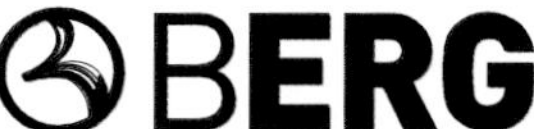

PHOTOGRAPHY & CULTURE
Notes for Contributors

Call for Papers

The editors welcome submissions to Photography & Culture that explore the social and cultural aspects of photography, for example in Art History, Anthropology, Cultural and Media Studies, History and Practice of Science, Contemporary Art and Documentary Practice, Sociology and Popular Culture. The only requirement is that aspects of both photography and its practices form the core of the submission.

Manuscript Submissions

Submissions aimed at being major articles should be approximately 3,000–10,000 words in length and must include a brief (two- or three-sentence) biography of the author(s), an abstract (up to about 200 words) and up to five keywords. Shorter papers ("Notes") should range between 500 and 2,500 words in length. Interviews should not exceed 15 pages (about 4,000 words) and do not require an author biography. Exhibition and book reviews are normally 500–2,000 words in length. It is requested that plain language be aspired to, with the use of jargon or specialized terminology kept to the absolute minimum. (Where specialized terms are unavoidable, please supply a glossary.) All submissions considered for publication will be subject to peer review.

Electronic submissions (preferred, certainly in the first instance) should be sent to photographyandculture@ bergpublishers.com. Microsoft Word is the preferred word-processing program, where possible. Scanned illustrations will suffice, though originals may possibly be requested in certain circumstances if the submission is successful. (Originals will be returned.) Please scan to letter or A4 size at 300 dpi for photographs/halftone, or 600 dpi for maps or illustrations containing text. Illustrations embedded in Word documents cannot be used. Similarly, graphics downloaded from webpages are not of sufficient quality for print reproduction.

A disk as well as a hardcopy of any finally accepted contributions may occasionally be requested. (Please mark clearly on the disk what word-processing program has been used. Berg accepts most programs with the exception of Clarisworks.) Manuscripts or disks should be submitted to the current *Photography & Culture* postal address: Photography & Culture, PO Box 11, Moreton-in-Marsh GL56 0ZF, UK.

Submissions will be acknowledged by the managing editors, and those accepted for further consideration will be entered into the review process. Electronic manuscripts and scanned illustrations will not be returned. Submission to the journal will be taken to imply that the article is not being considered elsewhere for publication, and that if accepted for publication it will not be published elsewhere, in the same form, in any language, without the consent of the editors and publisher. It is a condition of acceptance by the editors of a submission for publication that the publishers, Berg, automatically acquire the copyright of the published article throughout the world. *Photography & Culture* does not pay authors for their submissions nor does it provide retyping, drawing, or mounting of illustrations.

Style

The journal's text will use US spelling and mechanics. *The Chicago Manual of Style* (15th Edition) is our style guideline, and *Webster's Dictionary* is our arbiter of spelling. While it would be preferred if contributors used US English, submissions in British English will be acceptable (though such submissions will be transliterated into US spelling and mechanics). We encourage the use of major subheadings and, where appropriate, second-level subheadings. Manuscripts (whether electronic or hardcopy) submitted for consideration as articles must contain: a title page with the full title of the article, the author name(s), address and affiliation where relevant (do not place the author name(s) on any other page of the manuscript), a two- or three-sentence biography for each author, and a 200-word abstract. Up to five keywords are requested to aid in any future library searches. Please present the keywords after the abstract.

Electronic manuscripts can be either single- or double-spaced. If hardcopy manuscripts are involved, then they must be typed double-spaced (including quotations, notes, and references cited), one side only, with at least one-inch margins on standard paper using a typeface no smaller than 12-point. Authors should retain a copy for their records.

It would be preferred that submissions be presented with paragraph breaks involving a line space (double line space if presenting a double-spaced text, of course) between paragraphs and without first-line indentation, as in this set of guidelines.

Notes and References

References to *notes* are to be by means of consecutive numbers inserted in-text throughout the paper and are to be written up at the end of the text. (Do not use any footnoting or end-noting programs that your software may offer as this text becomes irretrievably lost at the typesetting stage.)

For *references*, the "Harvard system" is to be used in-text, thus:

> Centuries ago in Europe, country people were terrified of the walking dead, of "revenants" (Smith 1989). They developed all kinds of protective procedures (Jones 1957; Morris 1972, 1984), and though these may seem bizarre to us now they were deemed absolutely necessary at the time.

The cited references should be presented at the end of the paper, after any notes, in this manner:

References

Dewdney, S. 1962. *Indian Rock Paintings of the Great Lakes*. Toronto: University of Toronto Press.

Dowson, T. 1992. *Rock Engravings of Southern Africa*. Johannesburg: Witwatersrand University Press.

Fagg, B. 1957. Rock Gongs and Slides. *Man* 57: 30–2.

Goldhahn, J. 2002. Roaring Rocks: An Audio-Visual Perspective on Hunter-Gatherer Engravings in Northern Sweden and Scandinavia. *Norwegian Archaeological Review* 35(1): 29–61.

Hedges, K. 1990. Petroglyphs in Menifee Valley. *Rock Art Papers* 7: 75–82.

Lawson, G., Scarre, C., Cross, I. and Hills, C. 1998. Mounds, Megaliths, Music and Mind: Some Thoughts on the Acoustical Properties and Purposes of Archaeological Spaces. *Archaeological Review from Cambridge* 15(1): 11–34.

Palmer, D. and Pettitt, P. 2001. In Search of our Musical Roots. *Focus* 105: 80–4.

Rajnovich, G. 1994. *Reading Rock Art: Interpreting the Indian Rock Paintings of the Canadian Shield*. Toronto: Natural Heritage/Natural History Inc.

Reznikoff, I. 1995. On the Sound Dimension of Prehistoric Painted Caves and Rocks, in E. Taratsi (ed.), *Musical Signification*. Berlin: Mouton de Gruyter.

Rowland, I. and Howe, T.N. (eds.) 1999. *Vitruvius: Ten Books on Architecture*. Cambridge: Cambridge University Press.

Offprints

On publication, first-named authors will be sent a PDF eprint (with nonprinting watermark) of the final, published version of their article for personal use, and will be able to order a free copy of the issue in which their article appears.

Film Genres Series ⬡BERG

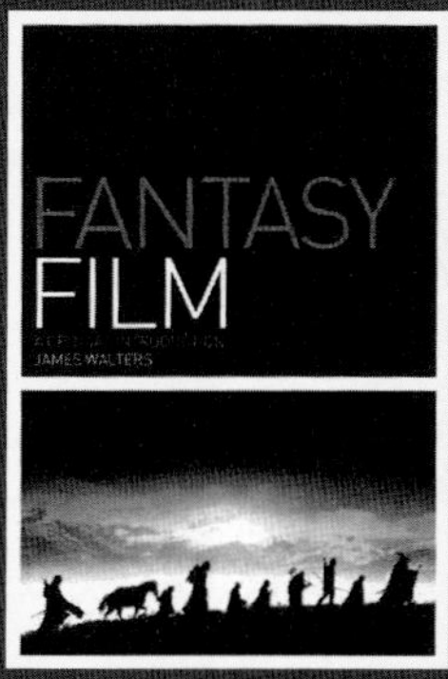

Fantasy Film uses key concepts in film studies — such as authorship, representation, history, genre, coherence and point of view — to interrogate the fantasy genre and establish its parameters.

Moving from Fritz Lang's dark thrillers to Vincente Minnelli's vibrant musicals, from George Méliès' 1904 *Voyage à travers l'impossible* to Peter Jackson's *The Lord of the Rings* trilogy, the creative dexterity and excitement of film fantasy is evoked and explored. The book will be invaluable to students or fans of the fantasy genre.

May 2011
PB 978 1 84788 308 7   £17.99 / $29.95
HB 978 1 84788 309 4   £55.00 / $99.95

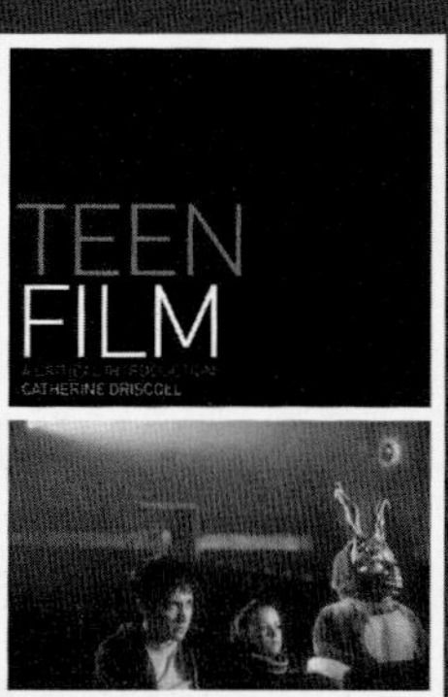

Arguing that teen film is always a story about becoming a citizen and a subject, *Teen Film* presents a new history of the genre, surveys the existing body of scholarship, and introduces key critical tools for discussing teen film.

Surveying a wide range of films including *The Wild One*, *Heathers*, *Donnie Darko* and *Buffy the Vampire Slayer*, the book's central focus is on what kind of adolescence teen film represents, and on teen film's capacity to produce new and influential images of adolescence.

June 2011
PB 978 1 84788 686 6   £17.99 / $29.95
HB 978 1 84788 687 3   £55.00 / $99.95

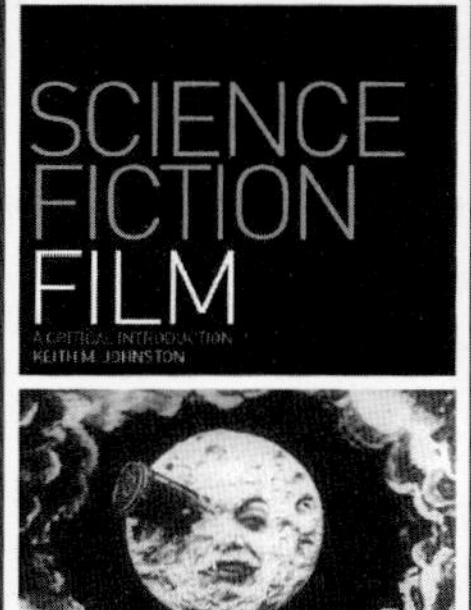

Science Fiction Film goes beyond a textual exploration of these films to place them within a larger network of influences that includes studio politics and promotional discourses.

The book also challenges the perceived limits of the genre — it includes a wide range of films, from canonical SF, such as *Le voyage dans la lune*, *Star Wars* and *Blade Runner*, to films that stretch and reshape the definition of the genre. This expansion of generic focus offers an innovative approach for students and fans of science fiction alike.

October 2011
PB 978 1 84788 476 3   £17.99 / $29.95
HB 978 1 84788 477 0   £55.00 / $99.95

Order online at www.bergpublishers.com

Visual Sense: A Cultural Reader
Edited by
Elizabeth Edwards and Kaushik Bhaumik

Vision is more than looking or seeing. It is integral to all human action. Visual Sense introduces students to the analysis of a wide range of ways of experiencing sight across time and across cultures: from Renaissance Italy, Aztec Mexico and early Christian Europe, to Tibet, West Africa, Aboriginal Australia and South America, amongst others. It is arranged around broad themes of visual experience, ranging from navigating the sacred and ordering knowledge about the world to thinking creatively, socially and beyond vision into cyberspace and daydream. This unique approach allows cross-cultural and thematic connections to be made. A Guide to Further Reading allows students to expand their learning independently, and section introductions place the readings in context.

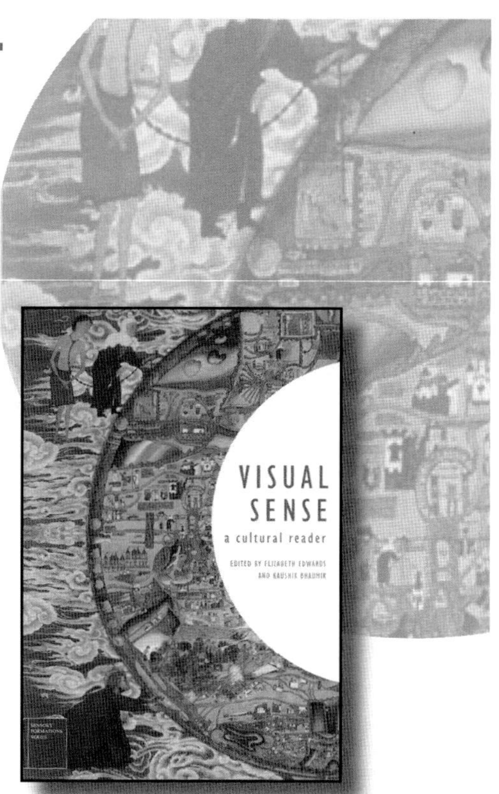

Nov 08 • 496 pp • 15 bw illus • 234 x 156 mm
HB 978 1 84520 740 3 **£60.00 / $119.95**
PB 978 1 84520 741 0 **£19.99 / $34.95**

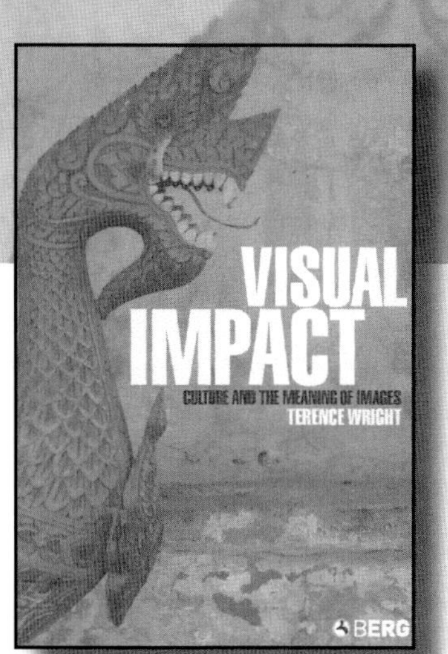

Visual Impact
Culture and the Meaning of Images
Terence Wright

From the office to domestic interiors to shops, images surround us in modern life. Pictures and images provide a cognitive context through which people can explore and understand their world. The internet has increased this visual onslaught exponentially. Is there a systematic order to this seemingly endless array of pictures and depictions?

Drawing on a wide range of examples – from painting and drawing to film, photography and the Web – Visual Impact analyzes the theory and practice of visual representation, and examines how cultural values and traditions shape particular visual styles.

Visual Impact *sets image making in an historical and global context, and uses it as a window for exploring the human condition at a deeper level. Anyone interested in the cultural role of art, film, the internet and interactive media will find this book an exciting and stimulating read.*

Dec 08 • 192 pp
20 bw illus • 234 x 156 mm
PB 978 1 85973 473 5 **£19.99 / $39.95**
HB 978 1 85973 468 1 **£55.00 / $109.95**

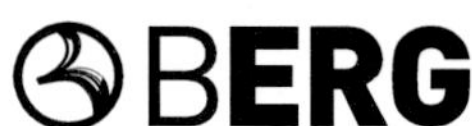

Order now at www.bergpublishers.com